Pickles

and Pretzels

PICKLES AND PRETZELS

Pennsylvania's World of Food

VIRGINIA K. BARTLETT

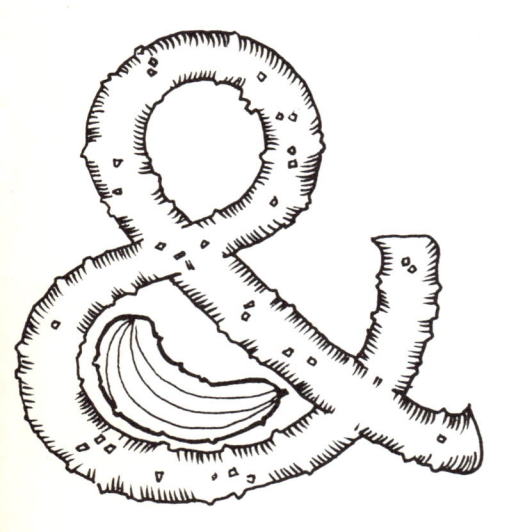

University of Pittsburgh Press

Published by the University of Pittsburgh Press, Pittsburgh, Pa. 15260
Copyright © 1980, University of Pittsburgh Press
All rights reserved
Feffer and Simons, Inc., London
Manufactured in the United States of America

Library of Congress Cataloging in Publication Data

Bartlett, Virginia.
  Pickles and pretzels.

  Includes index.
  1. Cookery—United States—Pennsylvania.
I. Title.
TX715.B3424   641.5'9748   79-3996
ISBN 0-8229-3400-0
ISBN 0-8229-5308-0 pbk.

Publication of this volume
was supported by
a grant from the
Howard Heinz Endowment

For my mother,

Idabelle Kostulski,

with love

and gratitude

Contents

Preface xi

To Market, To Market 3
Collector's Items 12
Maple Sugar 21
At Home with William Penn 29
Chocoholics, Unite 39
Eat Yourself Full 47
A Pennsylvania Paradox 56
The Ladies from Philadelphia 62
Magic Mushrooms 77
Life in a Bologna Factory 85
Springs Comes in the Fall 91
Trains 99
As We Sow 107
Apples of My Eye 115
Grapes of Diverse Sorts 121
Come to the Fair 129
A Pretty Pickle 137

Early American Travelers 145
The Mysterious Middle East 153
Cloistered in Ephrata 162
Toiling in the Nutrition Wasteland 170
American Cuisine 183
The Food Is Simply Wild 189
A Story with a Twist 197
Here Let Us Feast 203
The Cup That Cheers 212
Dollhouses 221
An Herbal Tea Party 228
Glorious Gadgets 233
Kitchens: Restored and Reconstructed 241
There's No Place Like Homestead 253
Festivals for Many Folks 261

Notes 271
Subject Index 279
Recipe Index 285

Preface

To me, Pennsylvania is a miniature America. All the diversity of the United States is here—the melting pot that refuses to melt. Pennsylvania cooks can draw on the heritage of colonial and frontier kitchens; use the bounty of the state's rich farmlands; enjoy the sophistication of urban restaurants and specialty food shops or the simplicity of country cooking; appreciate the unique contribution of the Pennsylvania Dutch; add a new dimension to their culinary repertoire with ethnic recipes from friends and neighbors; tour the facilities and utilize the resources of major food manufacturers; visit fairs and festivals celebrating the foods of almost every country represented in the United States. When you talk about food, no state is more American than Pennsylvania.

Many of the chapters in this book were originally broadcast over WQED-FM, Pittsburgh, in somewhat different form. Others have appeared in *Pittsburgh Magazine*. I am grateful to Metropolitan Pittsburgh Public Broadcasting, Inc. for permission to publish them here.

I would like to thank Mary Ann Sinnhuber for typing major sections of the manuscript. My husband, Irving H. Bartlett, not only ate his way uncomplainingly through various stages of all the recipes but also offered encouragement and approval when it was most needed.

I only wish I could thank Jack Sommers, my very good friend and colleague, who started the whole thing.

Pickles

and Pretzels

To Market, To Market

One of the pleasantest and most delightful excursions anyone can make in the summer and autumn is to visit a farmers' market. On Pittsburgh's North Side, for instance, you will find twenty or more trucks lined up in a large, open field, with the bounty of the month spilling out on tables and into crates and baskets. The prospect is immensely pleasing to the eye. There are baskets heaped with bright green peppers alongside bushels of brilliant red tomatoes and heaps of crisp lettuce—escarole, Boston, iceberg, Bibb, chicory, romaine, ruby-edged crinkly leaves, varieties you never knew existed. There are barrels of new potatoes, tiny pearly white onions, and huge red Bermudas; strings of fresh garlic; and bunches of new beets and turnips and carrots, still wearing their feathery tops. In the fall there are bushel baskets of apples—yellow Delicious, red MacIntosh, bright green, tart, cooking apples—and pumpkins, all sizes and shapes; baskets of green tomatoes, rescued just before the first frost; piles of broccoli and cauliflower; and yellow, orange, and green squash. Wherever I travel, I try to visit a local market; the Mexican section of the Tucson supermarket can be just as rewarding as the bazaar in Karachi.

To Market, To Market

Pennsylvania has its own wondrous variety of shopping possibilities for market freaks. The granddaddy of them all is the Central Market in Lancaster, the oldest continuously operating public market in the United States. The land was deeded to the city in 1730 for this specific purpose, and farmers sold their goods outside until 1889 when the present gaudy Romanesque building was constructed.

The first-time visitor to the market may find the brilliant colors and delicious smells overwhelming. On my first visit, I felt as if I had been physically struck and had to stop to recover. After a moment, it's easier to sort out the huge bouquets of summer flowers, the baskets of eggs, the yards of sausages, and you can begin to stroll slowly through this unbelievable abundance. That is when a second strong impression overtakes you. Everything is so *clean.* That's a pallid word to describe the sparkling, shining beauty of these vegetables and fruits. Each potato is scrubbed until it glistens; scallions are snowy white and dark green; piles of fresh spinach, leaves still wet, show no trace of gritty sand.

Sometimes a whole family runs a stand, the little girls in trim white net caps, the mother plump and smiling, the father in overalls and a dark, wide-brimmed hat, usually friendly and helpful, but occasionally dour, as if he would rather be plowing. The whole range of Mennonite experience can be seen in the variety of bonnets and pinafores, straw hats and gentlemen's chin whiskers. You may be served by a modishly dressed lady in high heels and polyester yet wearing a neat net cap, while just next door, the stall will be staffed with children who seem to belong to the nineteenth century.

Some farmers are artists. Oak-leaf lettuce is arranged in a basket like a bouquet, with three radish "rosebuds" strategically placed. Scalloped patty-pan squash, no bigger than half-dollars, are scattered with studied carelessness from

To Market, To Market

an overturned basket, highlighted with the tiniest of bright green pickling cucumbers and small hot peppers of still another shade of green. A vase of calla lilies stands next to a bouquet of fresh dill. Another stand features apples—early reds, Baldwins, Yorks, Greenings, and crab apples. In the proper seasons, there are great heaps of gooseberries, quarts of blueberries, blackberries, raspberries, strawberries; huge watermelons; canteloupes with their tops sliced off to show the mellow ripeness within. Move along past the bunches of beets, in graduated sizes, fat green peas fairly bursting from their shells, mounds of green snap beans and yellow wax beans that crackle when you break them. There are crisp cabbages of every possible size, green peppers still dewy from their scrubbing, baskets of snowy mushrooms, stacks of brilliant rhubarb. There are piles of sweet corn, and nobody minds if you pull back the husks first. You'll probably get some help from a solemn young straw-hatted boy who carefully exposes the fat yellow kernels for your inspection.

Move on to the sausages, the chickens, the cheeses, the scrapple. There is tongue souse, pigs' feet souse, a feast of pickled meats. Sample the egg cheese, made with buttermilk and eggs, or the Pennsylvania Dutch version of cottage cheese called *schmierkäse.* Try to keep from buying the Lancaster County swiss cheese, the head cheese, or the ball cheese that ages, they say, from the inside out. Admire the neatly compartmented chicken in the glass case: first the whole chickens resting on their bed of ice, then legs, breasts, wings, backs, necks, then a thick row of chicken livers. Halves and quarters come next, with a separate section for barbecued chicken you can eat on the spot if you wish. There is an unbelievable variety of sausages: beer bologna, braunschweiger, Lebanon bologna (mild or spicy), summer sausage, and coriander or sage bulk sausage. A portly butcher answers your questions about

To Market, To Market

his hams, sides of bacon, trays of pork, veal, and beef. The sign above his counter reads, "Country-dressed meats."

Take a rest from the good things to eat and enjoy the cornhusk dolls and miniature apple people made by local craftsmen. The stalls are full of handmade calico sunbonnets, stuffed animals, and cuddly rag dolls. A bouquet of dried flowers is larger and less costly than a city florist's, and living green plants come in all sizes, prices, and varieties. Take a deep breath in front of the herb and spice booth, with its jars of peppermint, sassafras, cinnamon, and thyme, its bottles of cloves, packets of dried mushrooms, boxes with unfamiliar, exotic names like mugwort, vervain, yellow dock, comfrey, and eyebright. *Don't* take a deep breath (unless you need to clear your sinuses) at the fresh horseradish stand, where customers wait in a long line for the pungent root to be grated.

Walk on to the baked goods, the yeasty smell rising to greet you as you try to choose from among the cinnamon sticky buns, the lemon sponge, the *fastnachts,* huge sugar cookies, shoofly pie, cherry and peach and apple tarts, black walnut cake, strawberry pie, apple dumplings, pinwheel cookies, marble cake, gingerbread boys and girls, loaves of white and wheat bread, or the pumpkin nut, applesauce, and date loaves. Above the counter the sign says, "Baked this A.M." Delicatessen counters offer sweet-potato pudding; rice pudding with raisins; blueberry, cherry, and coconut custards; tapioca pudding; jars of preserved peaches, spiced apple butter; dozens of different pickle relishes; chowchow and slaw; pepper cabbage and bacon dressing. Food for the renowned Pennsylvania Dutch sweet tooth is in evidence everywhere, but especially among the bins of hard candies, chewy taffy, and homemade fudge—black walnut, chocolate mint, peanut butter, maple pecan, and divinity.

To Market, To Market

I have never yet left this market without an armload of produce and baked goods, despite my solemn vows to the contrary. It is impossible not to buy. The only problem is *what* not to buy.

There are other markets in Lancaster—the Park City, the Southern, and the West End markets—and more throughout central Pennsylvania, including York, Harrisburg, and Columbia. At Bird-in-Hand, for instance, there is a thrice-weekly market, a miniature of the Lancaster establishment that is no less interesting or beautiful. There are stands selling funnel cakes and homemade ice cream, others with heaps of homemade noodles and noodle squares to slide under your chicken potpie mixture, and pretzels in dozens of sizes and shapes. You'll find a counter specializing in colored eggs, hard-boiled, peeled, and soaked in beet juice and other natural dyes to produce garish but strangely beautiful objects that will surprise your city friends when they turn up on a cold meat platter. There are both brown and white eggs, with a sign over the stall that says, "Our eggs are so cheap, it's hardly worthwhile troubling the chickens."

I was driving along a highway near Lebanon one day and passed what I thought was just another large supermarket. But parked in the adjoining lot were a dozen or more black Amish buggies, and I swung in alongside, just to see what was happening. It was indeed a supermarket, Martin's Farm Market, but it sold items unknown to the A&P. There were substantial numbers of plain people buying the ten-pound bags of bulk pearl tapioca, huge plastic sacks of cornstarch, raw sugar, oatmeal, cocoa, and clear gel. A large meat counter sold handsome cuts of meat, including beef hearts and ox tails, while just across the aisle were three-pound sacks of pretzels and potato chips. All the standard staple items were stocked, along with a superb fresh produce section, a baked goods area where my nose told me that baking was done

To Market, To Market

on the premises, and a cheerful, crowded snack bar. On the way out, you could buy magazines and Mennonite literature.

Not far away, in Intercourse, is Zimmerman's, a combination hardware, dry-goods, and grocery store, the next best thing to an old-time general store. You can buy anything from the straw hats worn by the old-order Amish men to kerosene lamps, calico or dark blue serge or cotton by the yard, plain cotton stockings or fancy nylons. There are always black buggies parked in front, the horses dozing while their owners stock the week's supplies. One time when I stopped in, a young mother in black bonnet and shawl was trying to keep her three barefoot daughters in the checkout line. They looked like a nineteenth-century painting in their cotton shifts of lavender, green, and pink, covered with black pinafores held in place with large safety pins. Their long hair was pulled back into demure buns. The proprietor, Abner Zimmerman, spoke to them in "Dutch," handed them each a lollipop, and was rewarded with shy smiles. Their mother bought fifty dollars worth of groceries, including canned spaghetti, sugar-coated cereal, and four boxes of Duncan Hines cake mix. Somehow I had been expecting heartier, more nourishing farm fare, perhaps bulk yeast and a barrel of flour. I watched, disappointed, as she packed the groceries and the girls into a tattered buggy and drove off.

Lancaster County isn't the only area of the state where the Pennsylvania Dutch live and shop. There is a large community near New Wilmington, up in the northwest corner of Pennsylvania. And south of Somerset, in Springs and in Grantsville, Maryland, I have often seen more buggies than cars on the side roads. On Route 669, less than a mile north of Route 40 in Grantsville, is Yoder's Country Store and Meat Packing Plant, where Pillsbury's Best sits alongside the stone-ground wheat and rye flour. The best hams and bacon I

To Market, To Market

have ever eaten come from Yoder's, and the loose sage sausage is unexcelled. There are nice surprises, too, like the wire basket that sometimes holds a selection of hand-packed herb teas, or the shelf of raw Virginia peanuts in plastic bags, right behind the rows of home-baked pumpkin cakes, date loaves, and applesauce bread. If you arrive around breakfast or lunch time, park your shopping cart and sit at the counter for a plate of buckwheat cakes with Pennsylvania maple syrup and country ham or sausage. Or have the Dutch platter of meats and home fries, with a piece of apple or cherry pie. The Yoder Meat Packing Plant is spotless, and the counters of the store receive a seemingly endless supply of beautiful pork, lamb, and beef cuts. You can rent a freezer locker and fill it with a side of beef or a whole pig if you've a mind to. There are charts available telling you exactly what you get, and if that's not enough, one of the Yoder brothers will patiently answer all your questions.

This is the way shopping used to be, friendly and personal, and apparently many Americans like it. In 1977 new farmers' markets were organized in such widely separate locations as Honolulu and New York City. In Pennsylvania, twenty-eight new public market buildings have appeared since 1975. A recent public farm marketing survey of Pennsylvania showed ninety-six locations in forty-six counties where farmers turned up at least once a week to offer their products to the public. Agricultural experts like to point out that this marketing method has the potential for providing important additional income for small farmers. I'm all for that, but I strongly suspect that the most important benefit is for you and me. Whenever I visit a farmers' market, my spirits rise. It's the only kind of shopping that makes me smile, not only because of the good sights and smells, but also in anticipation of the fine fresh meals to come.

When peaches are plentiful in the farmers' markets, usually in September in Pennsylvania, I buy a large quantity for freezing. When I stagger home with my load, our household routine never varies. My husband is always sure I have bought too many; my response is to buy even more the following week. Yet we never have enough. When March rolls around and I dig the last box from the depths of the freezer, we are both dismayed; I vow to put up more next year, no matter how he protests, and he vows to encourage, not discourage me. The secret of these peaches is the orange juice which serves as their liquid. There is no need for sugar nor additional ascorbic acid. The fruit stays brilliantly yellow, and in the winter, it's like eating liquid sunshine. I ask you to try this way of freezing them, and I will predict you'll never do it any other way.

PEACHES IN ORANGE JUICE

Prepare enough frozen orange juice according to the directions on the can to completely cover the amount of sliced peaches you are freezing. One small can, diluted, should cover three pints.

Peel and slice the fresh peaches, cutting away any brown or soft spots. If they are very ripe, the skins will slip off easily. Otherwise you should dip them quickly in boiling water; the skins will then be easy to remove with a sharp knife.

Fill freezer containers about ⅔ full with peach slices; pour orange juice to cover them within 1 inch of the top. Crumple small pieces of freezer paper or aluminum foil and press these on top of the fruit to make sure it is completely submerged under the juice (otherwise it will turn brown). Wipe rims of containers; seal; freeze.

Before serving, thaw almost completely. The peaches taste better when they are the slightest bit crunchy and the juice is still icy cold. Superior over ice cream, cereal, or just plain.

To Market, To Market

When the first spring peas appear in the markets, buy a large quantity and enjoy them often, because they will never taste quite so good again until next year. This recipe for cooking peas has an odd history. My father called them Polish peas because his mother, my Polish grandmother, always cooked them this way. I have asked every Polish person I have ever met about them, including several chefs in Poland, and no one has heard of them. Snow peas are cooked in this manner, but once you eat ordinary garden peas this way, I will be surprised if you ever shell them again. Perhaps my grandmother invented them.

POLISH PEAS

Wash any amount of fresh peas in the pod you think your family will eat. I usually count on ⅓ pound per person. *Do not shell.* Drop them in boiling water, enough to almost cover them. Let water return to a simmer and cook only until the pods are tender. The time will vary according to the age of the peas; about ten minutes is a good time to test young peas. Drain and serve. To eat them, pick up one pod, hold it between your teeth and literally slide the peas out into your mouth, discarding the pod. They are messy to eat, as some water remains in the pod, so be prepared for leakage. It is a good idea to provide an extra dish for discarded pods.

Collector's Items

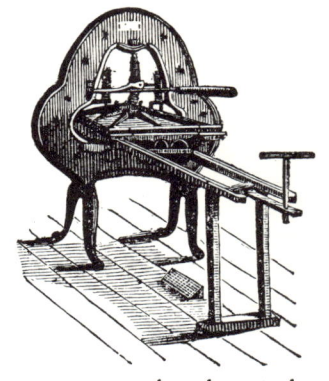

No matter how many cookbooks a woman may possess, she almost always writes one of her own. In most cases it's an untidy accumulation of recipes and household hints clipped from newspapers, handwritten index cards, notations about Mrs. Wilson's white cake or Aunt Louise's chocolate pudding. I, too, have such a collection, a looseleaf notebook spotted with brownie batter, bread dough, and other assorted organic material. But I suspect it tells more about me and the way I keep house than any formal biography ever would. There is a recipe for gingersnaps which dates back to my graduate school days. My Polish grandmother's pound cake recipe is there and my mother's bread recipe, along with mysterious notations from long-forgotten sources. Mary's green beans, for instance. Who in the world is Mary? And Aunt Thelma's shortbread. I don't have an Aunt Thelma, nor does my husband. How did her recipe end up in my notebook?

    I have an awesome array of printed cookbooks, but without my own tattered volume, I would be lost. It is the sum total of my experience in the kitchen. Perhaps this is why I am so entranced by manuscript cookbooks that have grown out of other women's experience. There is a whole life in them, and I like to pretend that I can reconstruct that life by turning the dog-eared pages.

Collector's Items

I have one such book dating from 1833 which belonged to the Boggs family. They lived in Allegheny, just across the river from Pittsburgh, and the plain composition book with its marbleized covers apparently began as an account book for the family store. There are entries for large purchases of flour and sugar and notations of customer accounts. Mr. Boggs must have conducted an informal loan agency and post office as well, for there are numerous entries for postage and for substantial loans. At 25 percent interest, Mr. Boggs was doing all right (see figure 1).

Like most household books of an earlier day, this one contains both recipes and home remedies for ailments ranging from snakebite to dropsy to the bite of a mad dog. There are two recipes for cement on the same page as directions for sweet apple pudding. There are instructions for making soap as well as for lavender cologne water, and advice for raising young ducks. "Ducks, when just hatched, are always inclined to fever, from their pinion wings coming out too soon. This acts on them as teething does on children."

Date	Drawn	Security	Sum paid	Sum due	When due	Profit	[illegible]	Sum to be paid
1834								
May 23	Oliver Spencer	Judge Burnet	3926.09	4000	24 Aug, 1834	73.11		
June 11	C. Whipple	Capilly	973.09	1000	17 Sept	26.11		
July 15	Eliz. ᵗʰWertz	Jerome Wertz	150	190	15 Oct 1835	23.31	15 July 1835	173.31
July 16	W T Thorp	Cyrus Ward	200	250	16 Oct 1835	31.00	16 July 1835	231
July 25	J C Robinot	Wm Thomlinson						
		James Layry						
		Adam Sillan	1000	1250	25 " "	155.40	25 " "	1155.40

Figure 1. From Mr. Boggs's Account Book

Collector's Items

There is one page headed "Valuable Recipe" and tells us "Mr. A. Bronson of Meadville, Pa. says from fifteen years experience he finds that an Indian meal poultice covered over with young hyson tea softened in hot water and laid over burns as hot as can be borne will relieve pain in five minutes." Since packs of cold tea are still *de rigueur* for relieving the pain of sunburn, Mr. Bronson apparently knew what he was talking about. Occasionally the cure sounds worse than the disease, as in the counsel for curing deafness. "Take a large onion, bore ten holes two-thirds through with a double tin gimlet; fill the holes with rattle-snake grease; roast the onion upon a fire shovel, until the grease begins to run through the onion. Then squeeze out the oil and juice; and preserve them together. Drop one, two, or three drops into the ear at once."

Mrs. Boggs, if indeed it was she who took over the account book and made it her household reference book in order to use up the blank pages, clipped poems from the newspaper, including a humorous one called "My Aunt" which must have reminded her of a relative. "On the Loss of a Child in Infancy" begins:

> *Our beautous child we laid amid the silence*
> *of the dead,*
> *We heaped the earth and spread the turf above*
> *the Cherub head.*

How many children did she have, I wonder, and how many did she lose in this frontier town of the 1830s? I know there was a farm, because one section lists purchases for it.

Collector's Items

1834	Farm	
Augt 25	12 bus. timothy seed & bag Taylor for plowing seeding same	4.75
April 4 1836	Mrs. Biddle to Farm for 60 lbs bacon @ 8 cts for 15 lbs corn meal 2 lbs butter 1 lb coffee	4.80 .15 .25 .16
7th	load wood 1 bush potatoes	.50 .25

On October 14, 1839, someone noted the purchase of a cow, Stately, and two calves, Hawkeye and Emily. Stately calved on January 5, 1841, and again on April 9, 1842.

Later on, tucked between recipes for Indian cake and a brown dye made from black oak bark, there are two clippings about the Civil War. One refers to the illegal activities in South America of the Southern battleship *Sumter*. The other is a poem "To My Brother," sentimental verses calling on the brother to think of the writer in times of trouble. I wonder about this. Is Mrs. Bogg's brother fighting in the war? Does she worry about him and want to help him?

The final pages are in another handwriting. Her daughter's perhaps? But in the same eclectic tradition, there are recipes for Buckeye cake, Jackson sponge cake, and a carefully written treatise on agriculture and electricity, with diagrams of fields and buried wires.

I have another manuscript cookbook from Pittsburgh, begun by Sallie Seely in 1868. This one is more like mine, with recipes pasted in every which way, many of them handwritten and by a wide variety of hands. I can imagine Sallie visiting Mrs. Chamberlain, enjoying her pudding, and asking her to

Collector's Items

jot down the directions for her. At the bottom of one scribbled recipe is the notation, "Please save this recipe for me until I get home." There are several written in pencil on the back and inside of an envelope, still stamped and dated "Philadelphia, January 4, 1883" and addressed to C. B. Seely, East End, Pittsburgh. Grandmother McCook's Pickle Lily is there, along with several variations of gingerbread and fruit cakes, plus puddings by the dozen. As I turn the pages, I come upon a pressed fern leaf, and a few pages beyond, there is a drawing of a mother with a child on her lap. Several pages are wildly scribbled with meaningless pencil marks, and I can visualize Sallie Seely finding her precious cookbook on the verge of mutilation by a small child who only wanted some paper to draw on. There is a recipe for currant jelly on the back of a slip of paper that says "carpet tacks," perhaps a reminder to buy some. A recipe for white sauce is on the reverse side of a list of names. Who, do you suppose, were Ella, Frank, and Georgie?

Although everyone interested in cooking knows that the first American cookbook was published by Amelia Simmons in 1796, there is ample evidence that American colonial ladies were keeping their own recipes and notes for their families long before that. Mary Plumsted's Cookery Book, titled and written in her own hand, is dated 1776, and after the reader stops smiling over the quaint spelling, it is possible to learn a great deal about the life of an eighteenth-century American housewife from the information she chose to record. Since a woman's job was to provide her family with food the year round, there are many recipes for preparing and preserving domestic as well as wild animals, poultry and game. Mary Plumsted wrote out directions "To Choler a Flank of Beef or Pig"; "To Make a Venison Pasty"; "To Make a Goose and Turkey Pye"; "How To Do Tongues and Udders"; "To Make a Ragou of Pigs Ears and Feet"; "Gravey for a Broyld Stake"; "To Do a Calf's Head"; "To Frigasey Chicken or Rabits." There were plenty of sweets, including jumbles, almond cheesecakes, yam pudding, "red mamaled of quinces, eyecing for a Great Cake." To preserve angelica, "take your angelicae fresh out of the garden," she wrote, "and cut it about 2 fingers long." A recipe for marrow pudding begins, "Take 14 eggs," and she writes of "Sirup of Lemon for to moisten a sick bodies mouth or for a Coff." One of my favorites is "A Dish to Help Out Supper For a Side Dish. Take spinnage stewed greens and put in your dish and half a dozen silver spoons with a poached egg in every spoon and fry sasge between every spoon with a slice of toasted bread under every spoon with a little melted butter thrown over it."[1]

About 1800, Mrs. Sarah Yeates of Lancaster began keeping her household book, a wondrous collection of useful information. Mrs. Yeates came from England rather than Germany, as did so many of her Lancaster neighbors, but her syntax was pure Pennsylvania Dutch. In a recipe for French Flummery she suggests, "Lay round it baked pears. It both looks nice and eats fine." Many of her recipes are very sophisticated, such as the one for dulmas, the stuffed cabbage leaves we now find so common in Syrian and Greek restaurants but which surely must have been an exotic item on Lancaster tables. Her book is typical of others, however, in its motley assortment of rules for everything from liquid shoe-blacking and directions for knitted stockings to a method for taking claret stains out of a carpet and how to dye cloth scarlet, yellow, and "a cheap blue, but will not stand much washing." She has a special section devoted to "Observations" on the making of puddings, cakes, and the like, some of it still sound advice for today's cook. "When butter is used, take care to beat it to a fine cream before you put in your sugar, as afterwards if you were to take ever so many pains it would not

Collector's Items

answer as well." If you want to roast a pig with the skin on, "let your pig be newly killed, draw him, flea him and wipe him very dry with a cloth." She includes Lady Charlotta Finch's Receipt for Deafness from Governor John Penn, and a few pages later there are directions "to take white and yellow spots out of purple leather gloves." There are distinctly American recipes, such as the one for "An Excellent Maple Sap Wine," as well as ice cream. And at the very start of the book, she notes that beef should be killed and soap should be made at the increase of the moon.[2]

A book begun in 1790 in Waterford, New York, made its way to Pittsburgh and continued to be kept by other family members. It is filled with good recipes spelled in wondrous ways. There is Plumb Pudding, Cocer-nut Puffs, Chease Cakes, and Pumcan Chips. "To make Souer Kraut," the author writes, "take your cabbage and cut it very fine, than take a bag that fits in the cask or vessel you mean to pack it in—and between every two or three doubbel handfulls—sprincal some salt—but not too much—between every lair a few hole pepper—and so on till full—then cover your bag over the top—and lay two slips of board and on them two good large stone—half hour is suficient to stew it—take small tin cup of water, two or three slises of pickel pork and a small lump butter—and salted pickel beans—have a bag like above—put them on to boil well up—than throw them in a pale of water to freshen."[3]

Despite the persistence of our nutritional experts, I would hate to think that our gastronomic future lies in vitamin tablets and compressed, high energy food bars. And I don't think I am being excessively fanciful to suggest that men and women one hundred years hence might very well carry their personal recipe records with them in spaceships, with special notations on the effect of altitude and gravity on grandmother's fruit cake recipe.

Collector's Items

Rice pudding seems to have gone out of style in America, but eighteenth- and nineteenth-century cookbooks always had several variations of this old standby. A good rice pudding can be served to guests as well as friends without any apologies. The following recipe is from the Waterford, New York, manuscript cookbook mentioned in this chapter, and I have adapted it to modern methods and appetites.

RICE PUDDING

Boil half a pound of rice in milk until it is quite tender   beat it well with a wooden spoon to mash the grains   add three quarters of a pound of sugar and the same of melted butter   half a nutmeg   Six eggs a gill of wine some grated lemon peel   put a paste in the dish and bake it   for a change it may be boiled and eaten with butter sugar and wine.

SHERRY RICE PUDDING

¼	cup raw rice (not instant)	½	cup butter or margarine, melted
¾	cup milk, or you may use half milk, half cream for a richer flavor	2	eggs, beaten
		3	tablespoons sherry
½	cup sugar	3	tablespoons raisins
1	teaspoon nutmeg	1	tablespoon grated lemon peel

Cook the rice, covered, in the milk over low heat until tender. Do not boil. This should take about 30 minutes, but watch it closely as it scorches easily. The milk should be completely absorbed. Stir in sugar and nutmeg. Cool to lukewarm. Soak raisins in sherry while rice mixture cools. Add melted butter, eggs, sherry, raisins, and lemon peel. Pour into small souffle dish or other baking dish. Bake at 325° for 30 to 40 minutes or until firm and lightly browned. Serve warm or at room temperature. Pass soft whipped cream or Whiskey Sauce (see page 220).

Collector's Items

I like this recipe of Sallie Seely's because it is so personal. I found it tucked between the pages of her recipe book on a piece of lined paper. On the back is a pencil drawing of a mother and child. Here is her recipe exactly as it is written, followed by a modern recipe for a crisp, chewy cookie.

COCOANUT JUMBLES
One pound of Cocoanut, grated; Three fourths of a pound of Sugar; Three Eggs; large ironspoonful of Flour. Drop on Buttered pans—

Dear Mrs. Seely,

    This is all I can find which is at all like what you were making and may not be what you want but I thought I would send Lulu over with it. Yours in Haste

                                                              Minnie

COCONUT JUMBLES

3	eggs, well beaten	½	teaspoon salt
1½	cups sugar	1⅓	cups all-purpose flour
1	teaspoon vanilla	1½	cups grated coconut

Beat the eggs with the sugar until thick and creamy; add vanilla, salt, and flour. Stir in coconut. Drop by the teaspoonful on very well greased cookie sheets. Bake at 350° for 8 to 10 minutes or until the edges are light brown. Remove from sheet at once and cool on a rack. If cookies harden before you can remove them, put back in the oven briefly to soften again. These jumbles freeze very well.

Maple Sugar

All those among you who believe that the best maple syrup comes from Vermont, please write one hundred times, "Pennsylvania also produces fine maple syrup." As a transplanted New Englander, I confess to having been quite chauvinistic about all things maple until I happened upon a can of syrup labeled "Made in Meyersdale, PA." It passed all taste tests with high marks, and after all, why not? Maple trees abound in Pennsylvania, and the process is essentially the same no matter where your maple grows. Indeed, the routine has changed very little since the first Indian gashed open a maple tree with his ax.

There are all kinds of legends about the discovery of maple sugar. The aforementioned Indian may have been enjoying target practice or aiming at his squaw, leaving his tomahawk in the tree where it landed. Next morning when he saw the sap running down the tree, he must have tasted it and shouted the Indian equivalent of "Eureka!" Other stories would have us believe that a frugal squaw used what she thought was water from the tree to cook the evening's meat. Wandering off, to locate a lost child, perhaps, she let the meat cook longer than usual and returned to find it covered with a sticky sweet sauce which was not unpleasing.

Maple Sugar

Whatever its origins, maple sap provided Indians and early settlers alike with a very precious commodity. Sugar, like salt, was hard to obtain on the frontier, and here, like a miracle, was a reliable source of sweetening. Syrup boiled down became sugar, which could be stored easily for long periods and which tasted delicious. Very early travelers' accounts take note of the presence of the unusual sweetening, and all spoke of it in glowing terms. As early as 1703, a Frenchman wrote, "The mapple-tree yields a Sap, which has a much pleasanter taste than the best Limonade or Cherry-water, and makes the wholesomest drink in the World. . . . Of this Sap they make Sugar and Syrup, which is so valuable, that there cannot be a better remedy for fortifying the Stomach."[1]

An Irish traveler in 1792 was surprised to find sugar in a public house and thought it looked like cheese. "I observed to him that I had seen many a farm in my country who had three-score of milk Cows, but never knew them to make a cheese of that size at that season of the year. He said that it took more than that number of his cows:—that he had milked above an hundred to make that cheese. This I could not divine, as I knew he had only four milk Cows, which I saw that morning, until he began to slice it down, when, to my great surprise, I found it to be a loaf of maple sugar made in the form, and of the colour of a cheese; which proved what he had said to be true, as he had pierced that number of trees to make it."[2]

To the hardy settler who pushed his way over the mountains, maple sugar must have seemed an extra gift in this already abundant land. The trees were there, the sap merely waiting to be collected at the proper time. Equipment was simple, the process easy, as Benjamin Rush wrote in 1792. "No more knowledge is necessary for making this sugar than is required to make soap,

Maple Sugar

cyder, sour crout, etc., and yet one or all of these are made in most of the farm houses of the United States. The kettles and other utensils of a farmer's kitchen will serve most of the purposes of making sugar, and the time required for the labor (if it deserves that name) is at a season when it is impossible for the farmer to employ himself in any species of agriculture."[3] I suspect Rush had never stood over a huge kettle of boiling sap waiting for the proper moment to sugar off, or he wouldn't have been quite so casual in his description of the ease of the project. Yet it probably was easier than many tasks required of the frontiersman, and the final results, sugar and syrup, must have made an extraordinary difference in the often monotonous pioneer diet.

    We think of maple syrup as an expensive luxury these days, so a trip to an old-fashioned maple festival in western Pennsylvania can be a useful exercise, if only to observe the amount of hard work actually involved. These rapidly proliferating festivals are also great fun, with plenty of non-maple-related activity for the carnival minded. The oldest of the festivals is in Meyersdale, begun in 1947, complete with demonstrations of sugar making, a simulated sugar camp, a maple king and queen, exhibits, parades, and plenty of maple sugar in every form known to mankind. Each maple tree in town has a bucket hanging from it, and though they are tin now and their spouts, or spiles, are plastic instead of wood, the result is the same. At the sugar camp you can observe the almost clear maple sap boiling away in huge vats until it changes color and texture and can be drawn from a spigot at the other end for pressure canning. It takes between forty and fifty gallons of sap to make one gallon of syrup, a ratio that helps keep the price high. And natural food folk might like to know that nothing is added to the sap—it changes into an amber-colored, thick, smooth syrup all by itself during the boiling process.

Maple Sugar

In the old days, a simple two-inch gash was cut into the tree trunk, but nowadays a hole is made with a brace and bit. Then a spile is inserted, a little trough that conducts the sap from the tree to a collecting receptacle, a sugar bucket called a keeler. Early frontiersmen collected buckets of sap by hand, sometimes using shoulder yokes, or, later, transferring it to barrels on horse-drawn sleds. It was taken to storage tanks which emptied into boiling vats, or in small operations, was hand-dipped from the barrels into large iron or brass kettles. Joel B. Miller, a farmer from Grantsville, Maryland, made an improvement in 1868, when he invented a large flat iron boiling pan to replace the kettle. It is said that he hauled 600 barrels of sugar water from his sugar camp on Cornucopia Farm and boiled it down in his new-fangled invention faster than it had ever been done before.[4]

Sugar was more important to the settlers than syrup, and that meant long boiling—the longer the cooking, the harder the final product. The whole family was pressed into service, as Jean Maust Mann tells us in her reminiscences about sugar time in southern Pennsylvania. Sugar making could last from daylight one morning until daylight the next, if there was a good run, and even the small children could help, watching the boiling pans while their parents did farm chores. Potatoes wrapped in clay could be baked in the hot coals of the sugar furnace for supper, and eggs were often boiled in a cloth sack suspended in the syrup. "And there were cupfuls of delicious half-boiled sugar water," she writes, "truly fare fit for a king."[5]

In the absence of a thermometer, there were several so-called surefire tests for readiness. Cora Maust from Springs, Pennsylvania, used to drop syrup into a tin of cold water. If it snapped or crackled, it was ready to pour for hard molded cakes. For brick sugar, much larger cakes, she added a

Maple Sugar

second spoonful to the same tin. If it crackled again, it was ready to pour. Three crackles with three spoonsful meant it was ready for crumb sugar, poured into a wooden trough and stirred until sugar formed.

At the Meyersdale festival I watched the old-time method of making that crumb sugar, syrup at the right stage being poured into a cucumber wood trough more than one hundred years old. Three ladies took turns stirring the syrup with long-handled wooden paddles, working to get the moisture out of it. I took a turn, too, and it is hard work—twenty or thirty minutes of constant stirring, the mixture getting thicker and heavier by the minute. The dark amber turns creamy, then a light beige as the sugar begins to crumble and the last moisture disappears. Makers of this particular batch had plenty of helpful—and not so helpful—advice.

"The syrup burned didn't it?" suggested one gentleman observer.

"It did not!" was the indignant response.

"Sure looks burned to me," another commented.

Paddlers worked in thin-lipped silence. When the sugar seemed slow to come, the worker asked her critic, "Do you really think we burned it?"

"Is the Pope Catholic?" he replied.

Thus challenged, they worked harder, and the lovely stuff turned a beautiful beige and crumbled on cue, amid admiring cries and "Didn't I tell you?" looks from the laborers.

Next to the sugaring-off booth you could purchase a spoza, a dab of hot syrup on snow or cracked ice, which doesn't solidify but remains sweet and soft and incredibly delicious. The exhibit building houses dozens of products—elaborate molds of sugar shaped like hearts, fans, leaves, or abstract forms. There are boxes of divinity, pots of maple cream, pies, cakes, cookies, syrups in

Maple Sugar

jugs, cans, bottles, jars, and cruets. And if the free samples haven't done you in, head for the town's recreation building, where the Lion's Club serves up some ten thousand pounds of sausage to go with several tons of pancakes and three hundred gallons of maple syrup.

What makes the local folks say "This was a good year"? Cold nights and warm, sunny days, it seems. Trees in Pennsylvania are usually tapped in February while the snow is still on the ground and night temperatures fall into the teens. Then the sun brings out the sap, which continues to run until buds appear and the sap takes on a bitter flavor. In 1724 a French observer wrote: "For the trees to give their water in abundance there should be at the base of the trunk a certain amount of snow, which keeps the water fresh. It should freeze during the night and the day should be clear, without wind and without clouds; because then the sun has more strength, which dilates the pores of the trees, and which the wind closes—so much so that it stops the running."[6]

Maple trees have been transplanted to foreign climes over the centuries, but they have never done very well except here where they belong. You can still observe this early American industry throughout Somerset County. There are sugar camps scattered over a wide area, and most of them welcome visitors. In a good year, the county will produce 50,000 gallons of syrup and 25,000 pounds of sugar. So eat your heart out, Vermont. But whether it comes from New England or Pennsylvania, that unmistakable taste has what naturalist John Burroughs described as "a wild delicacy of flavor no other sweet can match. What you smell in freshly-cut maple-wood," he wrote, "or taste in the blossom of the tree, is in it. It is then, indeed, the distilled essence of the tree."[7]

Maple Sugar

☙ Try baking these apples along with your roast. Take them out of the oven while you are enjoying the main course and they will be just warm enough for dessert. Or bake extras and have them cold for breakfast.

MAPLE BAKED APPLES

Allow one apple for each serving, preferably Rome Beauties or other large baking apples. Take out the cores and make a substantial hollow in the center. Peel each apple about ⅓ of the way down from the top. Fill the center with a mixture of raisins and/or prunes and chopped walnuts, pecans, or filberts. Place apples close together in a shallow baking pan (a bread pan works well if you have only two or three apples). Pour 2 tablespoons of maple syrup over the top of each apple and dot with butter. Pour about 1 inch of boiling water into the bottom of the pan. Bake at 350° for 35 to 40 minutes, depending upon the size of the apple, or until a fork inserted in the side shows it is done. Remove from water; serve warm with cream, additional syrup, or plain.

Maple Sugar

Ordinarily I do not like recipes that use evaporated or condensed milk, since I prefer fresh milk. This flan, however, is so good and so simple that I make an exception. The recipe was given to me more than twenty years ago by my friend Helen Thompson, and the only change I have made in it is to substitute maple sugar for regular sugar. When you invert the mold, the maple sugar runs down over the flan and makes a delicious sauce without any more effort on your part.

MAPLE SUGAR FLAN

- 7 eggs, lightly beaten
- 2 cups milk (I use skim, but whole milk may be used)
- ½ can (7 oz.) condensed milk
- 2 teaspoons vanilla
- grated orange or lemon rind (approximately 1 teaspoon)
- ½ cup maple sugar

Combine all ingredients except maple sugar. In a 1 or 1½ quart metal mold heat the maple sugar directly over very low heat, stirring constantly, as the sugar scorches easily. When the sugar has melted, tilt the mold so that the liquid sugar coats the sides and bottom evenly. Don't leave a puddle in the bottom. Remove from heat and sprinkle a few drops of cold water inside to harden the sugar. Drain water and pour in egg mixture. Place in a shallow pan with about 1 inch of hot water and bake at 300° for 1½ to 2 hours, or until a knife inserted in the middle comes out clean. Cool and refrigerate; unmold before serving. Note: if you do not have a decorative metal mold, use a 1 pound coffee can or a 1 quart metal mixing bowl. Almost any pan will do if it has straight sides.

At Home with William Penn

Pennsylvanians may be surprised to learn that their state was almost called New Wales. That's what William Penn wanted to call the land he received as a grant from King Charles II in 1681, but the king thought it was a terrible idea. He felt the Penn name ought to be in it somehow, so William obligingly called the province after his father, Admiral Sir William Penn, and added *sylvania* to it because on his first visit he was impressed by the thick forests which grew here. When he came to the new world, he chose a site on the Delaware River, northeast of what is now Philadelphia, on which to build his new home. A beautiful manor house was begun, but illness, financial worries, and problems with Pennsylvania's charter plagued him, and he finally returned to England, leaving James Harrison to oversee the construction and planning of the estate. He wrote to Harrison regularly, with instructions for the garden, the house, and the grounds, and we are fortunate that he did, for these letters, along with some artifacts and some pieces of building materials enabled archeologists and historians to reconstruct the house now on the site of the original Pennsbury.

I had wanted to visit Penn's home to see the kitchens and bake house

At Home with William Penn

ever since I had discovered the little book called *Penn Family Recipes,* the cookbook of Penn's first wife, Gulielma.[1] The day I chose was a fiercely cold but brilliantly sunny and clear February day, hardly the most appropriate time to sightsee in the Pennsylvania countryside. But it turned out to be exactly the right day, as I was the only visitor to the estate. It belonged to me alone, and despite the icy puddles and the muddy, thawing roadways, it was easy to imagine what it might have been like some two hundred years ago.

The road from the main highway is well-marked but eerie, winding through flat, barren fields with views of New Jersey factories on the horizon. Suddenly you are there, driving through the large gate, up the long, tree-lined driveway to the visitors' center. In summer it must be lovely, with fields and gardens as far as the eye can see. There are picnic tables and a small car-park, but little else in the way of amenities. In winter, the tables look forlorn, displaced. The herb garden has only faint outlines of the bounty to come. The dirt road—ankle deep in mud and slush on my visit—leads past all the outbuildings necessary to maintain an estate of this size, now some forty acres, but once much bigger. The manor house itself is large and imposing, facing the Delaware River. Penn had to come by barge from Philadelphia, a trip he apparently enjoyed, as he wrote that "of all dead things, I love most my barge." He also loved the land and the soil, and he wanted his children to love them as well. He wrote to Gulielma during his first visit, "Let my children be husbandmen and housewives," and asked for "a few fruit trees of the Lord Sunderland's gardener's raising out of his rare collection."

It is interesting to speculate about Gulielma's recipe book. She never lived to see America, but the editor of her cookbook suspects that it survived because William Penn, Jr., wanted a copy of it to bring to America in 1702.

At Home with William Penn

It is interesting to speculate too about the younger Penn, tucking his mother's recipes into his trunk. Did he want the comfort and pleasure of good home cooking in the strange new land? What were his favorites—stewed larks with broth, currants and wheaten bread? Or perhaps fried veal in a fritter batter with crisp parsley? There are directions for seed cake and parsnip pudding and French bread made with meal, ale yeast, and beer. There are dozens of recipes for warming drinks—apple beer, cider, and cowslip wine. Did he give the recipes to the cook? Or find a wife and present the book to her, then moan because the almond cakes didn't taste the way mother used to make them?

The elder Penn had returned to Pennsylvania in 1699 and moved to Pennsbury in 1700 with his new wife, Hannah, and a baby, John, born in America, as well as his grown daughter, Letitia. The Penns entertained a good deal, and the handsome house with its fine furnishings (fine for an unworldly Quaker, that is) must have been a showplace. The kitchen as reconstructed is not as large as one might expect for a man of Penn's standing, but I was told that the room, with its somewhat shallow fireplace and plenty of nooks and lofts for storage was essentially a holding area. Most of the important cooking was done across the path in the bake and brewing house; then the food was brought to the main house to be warmed before serving.

When I appeared at the door of the manor house, the young man who was on guide duty for the afternoon was not exactly brimming with enthusiasm at the prospect of showing it to a single visitor. "Do you want to see everything?" he asked, hoping against hope that I didn't.

"No," I said kindly, "I'm really most interested in the kitchen and dining room."

At Home with William Penn

This relieved him, and he cheerfully rattled off his spiel about the various sideboards and tables and chairs, leading me into the kitchen. Later his natural enthusiasm got the better of him and he showed me everything—even some things I didn't want to see. From him I learned that William and his family left Pennsbury after a little less than two years because of financial difficulties, and the house slowly sank into ruins. His son Thomas once came to America to inspect the estate, and as the young guide put it, "sent a letter home to his Mom saying they would have to put a lot of money into it if they wanted to save it." Clearly Mom—Hannah Penn, that is—didn't have a lot of money, and the buildings disintegrated. The land reclaimed itself. Not until 1939 was work started on the restoration, and a meticulous reconstruction of the original Pennsbury now stands on the site of the ruins. The house is beautifully furnished with seventeenth-century antiques, the finest collection in Pennsylvania, but only two of the pieces are known to have actually belonged to Penn.

Outbuildings were required to maintain the estate properly: an ice house, a tiny brick and frame structure with a deep pit for the ice, an enormous saw still hanging at the ready; the plantation office, with a sturdy table and chair, built-in shelves and bookcases, a hinged desk with a strongbox for valuable estate papers; a sheep barn where stock is still housed in the summer; a stable for the horses then, and now. In the spring and summer, it is still a working farm, with hens and some cattle, a vineyard, and the herb garden in full bloom.

For me, one of the most interesting buildings was the bake and brew house. The first section housed the laundry, with stoves and cast-iron kettles large enough to wash a whole pig if need be. The brewery occupied a

At Home with William Penn

double room with a built-in bin for storing grain and another large vat in which the grain was soaked for twenty-four hours or more. It was then spread to dry on the floor of the loft overhead until it sprouted, then dried again in large brick ovens built into the wall. Extracting the malt, mashing it, adding the hops and yeast, then brewing it was an arduous process, but since the resulting beer was an accepted part of the daily diet, it was as important a process as the baking of bread, which was done in the room adjoining.

Before wood stoves were brought into the house, all breads and sweets were baked in a brick oven. A good roaring fire would raise the oven temperature to about 350° in three hours. Then the coals and ashes were raked through a trap door in the oven floor, and it was ready for business. A baker had to be an expert at timing. Heavy dough items, such as pies and apple dumplings, were baked first while the oven was hottest. Then came the quantities of bread needed to feed servants and family and guests at Pennsbury. If there was too much for one baking, the whole process had to be done again, right from the beginning.

Pennsbury was undoubtedly large enough to allow the family to be self-sufficient. Penn brought some fruit and nut trees to the estate from Maryland and had others sent out from England. Many of Gulielma's recipes from England would have been well-suited to the abundant eastern Pennsylvania produce. There are recipes for making new cheese and then cheese cake with butter, currants, rose water, sugar, nutmegs, cream, and the yolks of twenty eggs. There is a gooseberry preserve and one of damson plum, and cakes made of caraway, oats, and almonds. The gingerbread recipe is poetic, ending, "If thee hast any orange or lemon peel, slice some very thin into the treacle [molasses] 3 or 4 days before thou makest the gingerbread."[2]

At Home with William Penn

Even though Gulielma never saw Pennsbury, she was very much a part of the life of William Penn in Pennsylvania as well as in England. During their courtship and early marriage, he was in jail and the Tower of London more often than he was at home, imprisoned for his unorthodox religious views. She was totally in accord with Penn's wish to found a new government based on the principles of tolerance and freedom of conscience. Her estate contributed materially to his travels in America. Surviving letters from her, few as they are, reveal her as a woman of intelligence and strength. She bore eight children, but only two lived beyond their parents, and Gulielma herself died before she was fifty. Although she never left England, it would not be incorrect to say she made a substantial contribution to the founding of Pennsylvania.

One wonders if William, living in Pennsbury with his second wife, ever walked about the estate, enjoying the splendors of the river view, inspecting the bounty of his fields and gardens, arriving with good appetite at the manor house in time for a tasty supper—perhaps a partridge pie, a fricassee of chicken, a mug of cider, and a plum tart—all made from Gulielma's recipes.

At Home with William Penn

Gulielma Penn's recipes are very sketchy, written in a kind of personal shorthand. The "buttered Lofe" which I have chosen makes a somewhat coarse shortcake, delicious when eaten warm and spread with jam or cinnamon and sugar, or split and toasted the next day. First you can enjoy reading Gulielma's recipe; then try mine or experiment with a version of your own.[3]

>   Too make a buttered Lofe
> Take a good Dele of wheat flouer,
> as many yeolks of egs as you thinke fitt
> a Litell yeist
> butter
> suger
> cloves
> mace
> a Littell salte
> work all these together
> breke it into small peces and that will make it short,
> then bake it well and Cut in the midell
> and buter it with sweet buter and suger
> then Lay the 2 halfes together
> and keep it warme by thee till you eat it

At Home with William Penn

GULIELMA'S LOAF
2　cups all-purpose flour
2　teaspoons baking powder
½　cup sugar
¼　teaspoon salt
¼　teaspoon mace
½　teaspoon cinnamon
½　cup butter or margarine
3　eggs, lightly beaten
(¼　cup sugar)
(1　tablespoon cinnamon)

Sift dry ingredients together; work in butter with pastry blender or your hands; add beaten eggs. Pat into a lightly greased pie tin or layer cake pan; bake at 400° about 25 minutes or until lightly browned. Split open and spread with butter; sprinkle with a mixture of cinnamon and sugar if desired.

At Home with William Penn

Gulielma Penn's recipe for a "Fregasy" of chicken is very similar to the modern method. She added what she called "Littell biskets" which were more like egg drops than dumplings. I have taken a few liberties, especially when she suggests the cook "putt . . . other things." First, here is her original recipe, then my adaptation. [4]

> Too Make a Fregasy of Chicken
> Take your Chicken flea [flay] them and
> Cutt them in peces
> and boyle them gently in butter
> with a bunch of sweet herbs.
> after they have bin a prittey while in,
> putt sum good broath to them,
> and when allmost enough, a gill of white wine
> then take the yeolks of 4 or 5 eggs,
> and sum parsley
> ½ a nutmeg grated
> and sum juce of Lemon
> but if you have not that 2 or 3 spunfulls of vinegar
> beate them well together,
> and when the other is enough, put this to it
> sturing it up and downe together a Litell while
> you may putt mushrons to it, and slised Lemon,
> this is 4 Littell biskets
> putt a bitt or 2 of butter too the eggs and other things
> when you mix them together

GULIELMA'S CHICKEN AND DUMPLINGS

1	stewing chicken, cut up	1	teaspoon summer savory
½	cup all-purpose flour	3	tablespoons butter or margarine
salt and pepper		2	quarts chicken broth, seasoned
1	teaspoon marjoram		

Mix flour and spices and put in a paper bag. Shake chicken pieces until thoroughly coated. Melt butter in large skillet and brown chicken pieces on all sides. Bring broth to a boil, put in chicken pieces, cover and simmer until done, between 25 and 45 minutes depending on age and toughness of fowl. Remove chicken pieces to warm platter while you make dumplings.

DUMPLINGS

3	egg yolks	2	tablespoons lemon juice
¾	cup fine bread crumbs	1	tablespoon soft butter
2	tablespoons chopped parsley	salt and pepper to taste	
2	tablespoons chopped mushrooms		

Mix all ingredients to form a stiff dough. Mold into balls about the size of a small walnut. Drop in boiling chicken broth and cover; simmer 10 minutes without moving the lid. *Don't peek* or the dumplings will be heavy. Remove from broth and add to chicken platter. Serve in shallow soup plates, spooning some of the broth over chicken and dumplings. You may make a thicker gravy if you prefer, but the clear broth is very light and tasty. Serves 4.

Chocoholics, Unite

On really bad days, my fantasy is to imagine myself reclining upon a pink chintz chaise longue, wearing a negligee and a feather boa and high-heeled backless mules, reading a good mystery novel, and dipping my hand regularly into a box of expensive chocolates. Meanwhile, downstairs, my fantasy cook is preparing a marvelous dinner of anything at all as long as the dessert is chocolate.

I am not exactly what Craig Claiborne would call a chocoholic, but I have to watch myself: the smell and taste of that heavenly substance is, to me, what temptation is all about. I, of course, am not alone in my allegiance to chocolate. Columbus found the natives growing it and brought a few beans back to Isabella, and later Cortez found Montezuma consuming fifty cups of chocolate a day from golden goblets with tortoiseshell spoons. The Spaniards didn't think much of it until someone thought of adding sugar to it and heating it up. Whereupon the Spanish nobility took it to their hearts—and stomachs—and hips. One by one other countries discovered the secret of cultivation and preparation, resulting in the *mousse au chocolat* of France, the Italian *gelato al cioccolato,* the Austrian Sacher torte, dark Dutch chocolate, creamy Swiss milk chocolate, Cadbury bars in England. And in America, the Hershey bar.

Chocoholics, Unite

In the eighteenth and nineteenth centuries, new processing techniques were developed which made chocolate products less expensive and more palatable. In 1876, a Swiss candymaker named Daniel Peter added milk, then developed a formula for making a solid cake suitable for eating. We never stop at a local drugstore and ask for a Peter's bar, however. That distinction belongs to the man who made the chocolate bar synonymous with his name—Milton Hershey.

Hershey grew up in Derry Township in the heart of Pennsylvania Dutch country and became involved in the candy business first as an apprentice, then later with an unsuccessful business of his own. His story makes him the Horatio Alger of the chocolate world, with its combination of pluck and grit, of determination in the face of numerous setbacks. He developed his own formula for a chocolate bar, built a factory in his hometown, which he named Hershey, and concentrated on the single product, the Hershey bar. It was a good move, and sales reached $5 million by 1911, only six years after the factory was completed.

The story of Milton Hershey is so wholesome and filled with goodness that I find myself looking for flaws, just to prove the man was human. He founded the Milton Hershey school for orphan boys; he built a town, with tidy houses, green lawns, an inn, a bank, a store, a trolley line, an amusement park, a zoo, and a golf course. Then came a football field, a dance pavilion, an outdoor theater, a community building, and the huge, old-fashioned, rambling, Hershey Hotel. During the depression his building campaign employed hundreds of workers who might otherwise have been jobless. And on his eightieth birthday, six thousand of his employees gave him a birthday party which sounds like a commercial for America. It took the sports

Chocoholics, Unite

arena to hold the three-foot-high birthday cake, the four bands and orchestras, the dozens of blue and white uniformed Milton Hershey School boys, the hundreds of roses and cards from well-wishers. His birthday gift was a diamond ring, shaped like the Hershey trademark, a child emerging from a cacao pod. It was a triumphant day for the old gentleman, but short-lived. He proved to be human after all, for he promptly had a stroke and hovered near death for several months, then miraculously recovered to live another eight years.

It is impossible to visit Hershey without hearing about the founder. His good works are everywhere. Hershey is the ultimate company town; it even smells like chocolate. When you check into the Hershey Hotel or motor lodge, you get a Hershey bar along with your room key. The dessert menus in these establishments don't just list chocolate cake or chocolate ice cream, they say *Hershey* chocolate cake. The street lights on the main street—Chocolate Avenue, of course, intersecting Cocoa Avenue—are five-foot-wide reproductions of chocolate kisses, some foil-wrapped, others naked chocolate. The side streets are named for places where cocoa beans are grown: Aruba, Bahia, Caracas. The town drugstore carries drugs and cosmetics and acres of souvenirs—T-shirts and mugs and ashtrays carrying the Hershey trademark—along with pounds and pounds of Hershey candies. They even stock some chocolates from other companies, too, but I didn't see a Nestle label anywhere.

When the number of visitors to Hershey reached one million a year, Chocolate World was created to divert the tourist from the plant's daily operations. Chocolate World, located near the sports arena and the amusement park, is a Disney-like trip by automated car through the wonderful world of

41

Chocoholics, Unite

chocolate. I visited on a rainy and cold October day when I naively assumed I would be the only tourist. The place was jammed; bus loads of tour takers, long lines of small children eagerly expecting free samples which never materialized. We were funneled through a well-organized system of ramps onto a moving turntable and physically helped into the little rail cars. As soon as I was seated, a hostess checked me to make sure no parts were hanging out, the safety bar was lowered, introductory music came seductively to my ear from a speaker in the head rest, and we were off to the land of chocolate.

For all my cynicism, I was impressed by the experience. It's a little corny—but not too much. The car moves through jungles and plantations where automated models of workers harvest the cocoa pods, and the lush voice of the narrator talks about rainfall, sunlight, and soil conditions. The little model men open the pods, the women and children scoop out the beans, the fermentation process begins while the beans rest in baskets under the leaves. We move on to a huge ship being loaded with beans, and suddenly we are in the farmlands of Pennsylvania, where we learn that Hershey chocolate is good in part because it is made with milk from superior cows, some fifty thousand of them. The car then moves into a short tunnel simulating the roasting process. We become, in effect, a roasted cocoa bean, and we can feel the warmth of the oven. Just in time, we emerge to watch the cooling process, the forming of the cocoa butter. There are machines rolling the chocolate to powder; then we see the conching process, so-called because the original machines were shaped like shells. Conching means rubbing the chocolate with heavy rollers, and the duration of the conching determines the refinement of the chocolate. Things get a little hazy after that, as the car moves through a bewildering array of machines, moving parts, conveyor

Chocoholics, Unite

belts. Hershey bars whirl by and are wrapped and packed before our very eyes. Hershey kisses drop like hailstones, are twisted in foil, and disappear. We pass a test kitchen, a simulated quality control panel with whirring computer tapes and flashing lights. It is all razzle-dazzle, with music to match. The climax is a burst of flashing pictures which assault us on all sides, hundreds of happy faces eating chocolate, as we move back to the beginning of the turntable and are helped off our own conveyor belt.

The ramp guides us through an effective display of old photographs, past an indoor tropical garden with, we are told, 99 varieties of trees and 1,350 flowering plants and shrubs. And finally we reach the gift shop, with about 99 varieties of souvenirs and dozens of kinds of Hershey candy for your buying pleasure, just in time, as the need for a chocolate fix has become unbearable.

I stood bemused, watching the long line of purchasers at the counters. They were buying ordinary Hershey bars, peanut butter cups, kisses, and the like. And waiting in line. I left and went to the Hershey drugstore to buy mine. No waiting. It never occurred to me that I probably shouldn't be eating one at all. But how could you be in Hershey and not have a chocolate bar? It would somehow be un-American, wouldn't it? As to temptation, let Eve have her apple. Make mine chocolate.

Chocoholics, Unite

This dessert is for true chocoholics. Very rich and chocolaty, it is not so sweet as to be cloying. It takes a little time to produce, but the effect on your guests will be worth it.

DOUBLE CHOCOLATE PIE

CRUST
- 1 cup crisp chocolate cookie crumbs, finely ground
- 1½ cup walnuts, finely ground
- 2 tablespoons sugar
- 3 tablespoons melted butter

Mix cookie crumbs and walnuts together with sugar; mix in melted butter. Pat mixture into a 9 or 10 inch pie plate, patting and squeezing it up to the edge. Make sure the bottom is well covered, without holes. Bake at 350° for 10 to 12 minutes. Cook on a cake rack.

FILLING
- 8 oz. (8 squares) semisweet chocolate
- ½ cup strong coffee (½ cup water plus 1 tablespoon instant coffee will do)
- 1 teaspoon vanilla
- 2 egg whites
- ½ cup sugar
- ½ cup heavy cream, whipped
- (additional whipped cream for garnish)

Melt the chocolate over hot water in a double boiler. Stir in coffee and vanilla. Beat egg whites until they make soft peaks. Add sugar gradually and continue beating until they form stiff peaks. Beat heavy cream until it is thick and soft but

Chocoholics, Unite

not stiff. Carefully fold whipped cream into beaten egg whites. Stir in two or three tablespoons of the chocolate mixture to lighten it, then carefully fold remaining chocolate into egg-white mixture. Fold only until no white is visible (excess folding will make the filling heavy). Pour into pie shell, smooth with spatula, and refrigerate until serving time, at least 4 hours. Garnish with more whipped cream if desired.

Chocoholics, Unite

I have been making these brownies for more years than I care to admit, and the recipe has been modified so that it is now virtually a one-bowl operation until the batter is poured into the baking pans. Some day I'll find a way to mix everything in the baking pan and really get the system down to one pan. I always double this recipe and freeze one batch. They freeze very well, thaw quickly, and are just the right thing to have on hand for unexpected guests.

THE WORLD'S BEST BROWNIES

- 2 oz. (2 squares) unsweetened chocolate
- ½ cup margarine or vegetable shortening
- 1 cup sugar
- 1 teaspoon vanilla
- 2 eggs, unbeaten
- ½ cup all-purpose flour
- dash of salt
- ½ cup or more coarsely chopped walnuts or pecans

Melt chocolate and margarine or shortening together over hot water. Remove from heat and add remaining ingredients in order. Pour into a well-greased pan 9 inches square or approximately 8 × 11 inches, and bake at 350° for 25 to 30 minutes. Do not overbake. Cut into squares while still warm and let cool in pan. They should be somewhat moist and chewy.

Eat Yourself Full

Watch the signs along any main road out of Lancaster, Pennsylvania, and you will think that seven sweets and seven sours are served in all restaurants and that all Pennsylvania Dutch wear funny hats and bonnets, dress in somber black, and constantly say "Eat yourself full." In reality, it is as difficult to find good Pennsylvania Dutch food as it is to find any other kind of good food—French, Chinese, or "real" Southern cooking. My own personal criterion is a restaurant's menu. If it is cluttered with *distelfinks,* hex signs, and cute sayings, I order a hamburger. If it reports in a straightforward manner that potato filling, chicken potpie, country ham, and Dutch fries are available, I relax and enjoy myself. I am oversimplifying, of course, and there are always exceptions. But as the tourist business booms, good honest food becomes increasingly hard to find.

Hundreds of thousands of words have been written about the Pennsylvania Dutch, one of the few remaining, uniquely American folk cultures. A special mystique surrounds their food, although it is rarely more than good, plain, American farm food with German overtones. But add that to the interesting folk art, the quaint costumes of the "plain people," the magnificent

Eat Yourself Full

farms, the deep religious convictions of many communities, and the insistence upon isolation from the materialistic world and we can begin to understand the fascination these people have for us. Americans romanticize life on the farm, especially if they have never lived on one. The advertising agencies long ago discovered the magic of adjectives like "wholesome," "natural," "farm-fresh," "homemade." Since we have become so aware of additives and preservatives, a culture that honors the natural bounty of the earth has a special appeal.

When the German immigrants arrived in Pennsylvania, they followed the Biblical injunctions to till the soil and multiply. Increasingly skillful as farmers, they tilled the fine soil they found and produced excellent crops. They also produced quantities of children to help on the farm. Hard work means large appetites, and the women of the region exercised *their* skills, combining familiar and new products, to create sausages, hams, apple butter, bread, cakes, pies, jams, and pickles of excellent quality. Waste was abhorred, so scrapple was born, and head cheese and hog maw. Apples were preserved by drying, as was sweet corn. Money may well have been scarce, but farms were virtually self-sufficient, and good wholesome food was rarely lacking.

One unusual ingredient in Pennsylvania Dutch cooking has always interested me. Many recipes, including a number of sweet yeast doughs and chicken potpie, call for the addition of saffron. It adds a distinctive flavor and a luscious shade of deep gold to the food, but at today's prices, saffron seems a curious luxury for these frugal folk. Apparently saffron was grown and used in the sections of Germany these settlers came from, and after arriving in America, families continued to grow the crocus (saffron is obtained by drying the stigma of the flower) for their own use, with no concern for

Eat Yourself Full

price. It is now an established ingredient, so if you would attempt some of these recipes, save your pennies. Saffron is probably the most expensive spice on the market.

If you are willing to go off the main roads in your search for good Pennsylvania Dutch food, there are two special places where you will be guaranteed an unusual meal.

Drive northeast from Harrisburg or Lancaster, and just off Interstate 78 in Shartlesville you will find the unprepossessing Haag's Hotel. It's the kind of place your mother probably wouldn't want you to go into alone, an old-fashioned wooden building, complete with peeling paint, rickety porch, and rocking chairs. To get to the dining room, you walk through the bar, a seedy-looking operation, where a few rubber-booted farmers are probably drinking beer. But persevere, because just beyond is a plain but sparkling clean little dining room with another very large one opening off it.

On my first visit, I was the only diner. It was late for lunch and early for dinner, and I was concerned that I might not get anything at all. But the friendly waitress assured me that they served lunch *or* dinner every day, all day. And what a dinner! The menu offers three choices: roast chicken; fried ham and chicken; roast beef, ham, and chicken. This is the nucleus of the family-style meal, consisting of twenty or more dishes.

In rapid succession I was served substantial portions of sweet potatoes, pickled beets, huge dill pickles, stewed apricots, tapioca pudding, lima beans, and apple butter. There was a large dish of crisp celery, the water still sparkling on the leaves. A dish of chunky applesauce appeared, followed by cottage cheese, canned peas, a sweet vegetable relish, and the best pickle slaw I have ever eaten. The platter of chicken was enough for three large men, legs

Eat Yourself Full

and wings and second joints and a big hunk of white meat, all moist and tender. Three big slices of fried country ham arrived next, with a bowl of creamy gravy for the meat and the potato filling, one of the great Pennsylvania Dutch contributions to civilization, made with mashed potatoes, eggs, milk, and cubes of bread, baked as a stuffing is baked. There were moist and slippery homemade noodles, cooked in rich chicken stock, a superb accompaniment for both the ham and chicken. And there was a large bowl of that great American invention, dried corn, cooked in milk.

Dish followed dish, and I was exorted to eat all I wanted. When I was full to bursting, the dishes looked almost untouched. I was savoring one of the large sugar cookies and toying with the tapioca pudding when the waitress asked what I would like for dessert. I thought I was already eating dessert, but I concealed my ignorance and considered lemon sponge, shoofly pie, and cherry tart before I settled on apple pie. "With ice cream," she said, and it was not a question. I nodded and thoroughly enjoyed the pie, unexpectedly made with applesauce in a crumb cake crust, topped with a scoop of vanilla ice cream. With vast amounts of good coffee, my bill for the feast was $5.25.

The menu guarantees at least twenty dishes from a long list of possibilities which vary according to the season and, I suppose the mood of the cook. On another day I might have had rhubarb sauce, chicken potpie, mustard beans, cucumber salad, or pumpkin custard. I asked the waitress if anyone ever managed seconds, and she said, "Oh, my yes. It's not at all unusual to refill the chicken and ham platters."

West of Lancaster in the little town of Mount Joy you will find Groff's Farm, where another unusually good eating experience awaits. The farm-

Eat Yourself Full

house and grounds are as unreal as a painting. The old stone house, built in 1756, has been lovingly restored and is set among vineyards, vegetable gardens, handsome barns, and a small pond. Inside, deep-set windows are draped in light green brocade against white walls and gray green woodwork. Tables are set with bright blue cloths, pewter, and heavy white china. Betty Groff, a trim, outgoing lady, greets guests personally, and you feel you've been invited to a private party.

Dinner begins with a square of chocolate cake and a dish of cracker pudding, sweet and creamy with coconut. Serving sweets before and during dinner was once a way of dealing with large appetites and restless children. Then came a superb soup, a rich beef stock thick with crisply cooked vegetables. Meat choices are ham and chicken, beef and chicken, or a combination of all three, which was our choice. We were served a large platter of good rare roast beef, another of country ham slices, and a substantial platter of chicken Stoltzfus, large chunks of chicken in a rich cream sauce, served on pastry squares. Accompanying the meal was a fine corn and onion relish, sweet dill pickles, green beans cooked with ham, fresh beets, and boiled potatoes shiny with butter. There was homemade bread, coffee, and dessert, the only disappointment, since the choices were mundane parfaits, a chocolate sundae, or pumpkin chiffon pie.

Betty Groff moves from table to table talking with the guests. She told us both of her sons are chefs, graduates of the Culinary Institute of America where they were told you can't run a restaurant the way their parents do. She laughs as she says this because it is clearly working extraordinarily well. "Only if people are prompt for their sittings," she is quick to add. "The food is ready at five and at seven, and if they are late, the food, especially the

Eat Yourself Full

vegetables, really suffers." Abe Groff has gradually given up farming to devote himself to the restaurant, where he cuts and supervises the cooking of the meats. He is also a viticulturist, working closely with scientists at Penn State to improve his stock. Guests are invited down cellar for a sample of his wine, and it tasted very good indeed. No liquor is served with meals.

After dinner Betty Groff usually brings out her cornet and asks one of her children to play the piano for a sing-a-long. The night we visited, she said this wasn't possible, since all the children were away. One of the guests, a lady in her sixties, called out that she would be glad to substitute, and the two of them conferred happily over the sheet music. The pianist's son turned to the other guests and said, "I'll bet this is the first time she was ever accompanied by a real Las Vegas piano player." And it was an extraordinary evening. The two ladies bounced through "Tea for Two," "Don't Fence Me In," and a number of others, the ricky-ticky piano style a perfect foil for Betty Groff's horn. A rousing version of "God Bless America" completed the musical portion of the evening, and we asked if we might visit the kitchen. Betty led us into a tidy work area where a plump, flushed lady and a gentleman with marvelous chin whiskers smiled shyly as we offered congratulations on a fine meal. An eight-burner gas stove made the kitchen excessively hot, but no one seemed to mind. There is a huge butcher block, stainless steel sinks, and a large hanging rack festooned with pots and pans. But Betty Groff maintains that neither the kitchen nor the staff is "professional": the cooks have learned on the job. And that undoubtedly adds the homey touch which helps to make the farm so successful.

Both the Haag Hotel and Groff's Farm provide simple Pennsylvania Dutch food and plenty of it. They emphasize good, fresh ingredients, cooked

Eat Yourself Full

with care, and offer little in the way of frills. There is an absence of sauces, other than natural gravy, an abundance of fresh vegetables, and an ample selection of dishes for the traditional Pennsylvania Dutch sweet tooth. There is, after all, no magic about Pennsylvania Dutch cooking, but as Betty Groff would be the first to tell you, when you start with the best and keep it simple, it's hard to go wrong.

Eat Yourself Full

Even if your Pennsylvania Dutch meal doesn't include seven sours, it won't be complete without a taste of pickle. This recipe for chowchow or relish or whatever you prefer to call it is magical. You can halve it or double it; increase the amounts of special vegetable favorites and omit others; change the vegetables to suit your own taste. It's almost impossible to spoil it. But you will find it more pleasureable to make if you have a food processor or an electric food grinder. The chopping chores can ruin an otherwise splendid adventure in relish-making.

CHOWCHOW

- 1 quart small cucumbers
- 1 quart small zucchini
- 1 quart corn, cut from the cob
- 1 pint string beans
- 1 pint celery
- 1 pint white onions
- 1 pint red and green peppers (sweet)
- 2 cups sugar
- 1 tablespoon dry mustard
- 1 quart white vinegar

Chop vegetables coarsely; cook each separately in very little water until barely tender; drain and mix together. In a separate pan mix sugar, mustard, and vinegar and bring to the boiling point. Fill clean canning jars (with two-piece lids) with cooked vegetables to 1 inch of the top. Fill with vinegar mixture; seal; process in boiling water to cover, on a rack, for 10 minutes. Check seal according to manufacturer's instructions; cool and store.

Eat Yourself Full

One of the best ways to eat mashed potatoes is in potato filling, a blend of vegetables and spices which can bake along with the meat or turkey. If by some remote chance you have leftover filling, refrigerate it and next day shape it into small patties and fry them in butter.

POTATO FILLING

2 cups mashed potatoes, unseasoned	½ cup chopped onion
1½ cups milk	4 slices stale bread, cubed
3 eggs	½ teaspoon salt
¼ cup chopped parsley	¼ teaspoon marjoram
3 tablespoons butter or margarine	¼ teaspoon thyme
2 stalks celery, chopped	pepper to taste

Mix together the potatoes, milk, slightly beaten eggs, and parsley. In a skillet, melt the butter and sauté celery, onion, and bread cubes until the bread is light brown. Sprinkle with salt, marjoram, thyme, and pepper. Add to potato mixture and turn into greased 1 quart casserole. Bake at 375° for 1 hour or until browned on top. Serves 4.

A Pennsylvania Paradox

The Farm Show Building in Harrisburg was packed, not only with people, but also with an astonishing array of food, quilts, and handicrafts. This was the Mennonite Central Committee Relief Sale, and people had come from all over Pennsylvania to eat and buy in a good cause. The Central Committee, or MCC as it is called, is the cooperative relief and service agency of the North American Mennonite and Brethren in Christ churches. Their relief sales are held throughout the United States and Canada to raise money for their many projects around the world. Combined efforts in 1977 raised more than a million dollars.

My first impression of the sale was a sudden awareness of a bewildering paradox. Everywhere within sight and smell there were luscious homemade goodies, high in calories and cholesterol. Yet one of the missions of the Mennonite church in its search for long-range solutions to the world food crisis is to suggest a drastic revision in lifestyle, particularly in personal food habits.

As I moved past the rows of tables, I saw huge sugar cookies displayed, decorated with bunnies, clock faces, flowers, sayings like God Is Love and Jesus Loves You. There were people cookies dressed in overalls, in frilly hats, in ruffled dresses. Trays of thick apple dumplings were displayed next to

A Pennsylvania Paradox

tables of angel cakes, lemon sponge, pumpkin bread with Happy Easter spelled out in pink icing. Homemade fudge in flavors of chocolate mint, peanut butter, black walnut, maple, and chocolate almond were near the booth selling huge slices of fresh strawberry pie, topped with whipped cream, in a thick crunchy crust. Decorated mince pies were sold next to the booth featuring hot sausage and mashed potato dinners. The long line waiting for buckwheat cakes and maple syrup snaked around a table of cakes in elaborate flower basket or bunny shapes, decorated to order. Then at the bookstall, I saw copies of Doris Longacre's *More-with-Less Cookbook,* and I was struck again by this display of traditional Pennsylvania Dutch abundance in juxtaposition to the stated goal of self-denial.[1]

The cookbook, whose profits go to the MCC, is packed with sound, nutritional information about our overindulgence in protein, sugar, animal fat; the inconvenience of convenience foods when it comes to health; ways to change our mind-sets about certain foods; and some very practical advice for building a simpler, healthier diet. Underlying all of the information is a deep conviction that this is the right thing to do. It is a difficult proposition to argue with.

It is also a difficult proposition to put into practice. We have been exhorted since childhood to "eat your carrots, you naughty girl. Think of all the starving children who would love to have them." Suggestions to ship said carrots abroad to the children were met with stony silence. But the problem stays with us. If I cut back on carrots, how can I be sure that the surplus will ever get to the starving children?

Longacre replies that there is certainly no guarantee, but adds that we always tend to underestimate the power one person has to make changes.

A Pennsylvania Paradox

Still, her motivation for these self-denials is moral rather than practical. It is irresponsible, she says firmly, to overindulge, to waste, to be profligate with our resources even in the midst of plenty. "In our complex world," she writes, "it is hard to visualize how the struggles of a few families to save food will help. Channels to the needy are long and circuitous. Yet deconsumption is an obvious first step. The very complexity which frustrates easy answers also means that our decisions in the global family are inter-related. 'Life is like a huge spider web so that if you touch it anywhere you set the whole thing trembling,' says Frederick Buccher in *The Hungry One*."[2]

Longacre is a pleasant, mild-mannered person. She states her ideas very matter-of-factly, as if it must already be clear to everyone that our luxury food habits result, among other things, in the exploitation of less developed countries when we accept food imports from them—vegetables from Mexico, Africa, the Philippines, South America. Or that any thinking person would understand that reusable containers in standard sizes are one answer to waste. We discussed the European style of shopping with one's own basket. "We should charge for paper bags," she suggested. "If you forgot your basket, you could buy a bag, and the chances are, you wouldn't forget it so often."

I asked her about her own family's reaction to this way of life, and she smiled. "The children understand that we are different," she said, "that we eat in a different way from other people. Their snacks are fresh fruit, homemade granola, nuts, wheat bread, carrot sticks. I'm amused when they come home from spending the night with a friend, complaining bitterly about the terrible food they had to eat—sugary cereal and such." She smiled, pleased. "They think I'm the best cook around." She admitted it had not been easy

A Pennsylvania Paradox

for them to resist peer pressure, "and I still can't get them off dry cereal entirely. You know, there's a lot of sugar, even in the plain varieties."

I asked her about the paradox of her crusade and the Pennsylvania tradition of superabundance. She admitted that she has been concerned about this herself. "Yet, the eat-yourself-full tradition grew up because farm families worked very, very hard at physical labor. There were big families, everyone was active. The kids walked to school, sometimes very long distances. Men worked in the fields, women did everything to keep the house going, from gardening to soap making, spinning, canning, weaving. Besides, many rooms weren't heated, and more calories were needed to stay healthy. That is certainly no longer true. In my memory, it never was. In my family and my husband's, there was never more than one meat served at mealtimes. Perhaps a relish or two, but I can never remember seven sweets and seven sours. On a day-to-day basis, our people ate very simply, although at festivals and celebrations, there was a good excuse for a more elaborte menu." She feels that the tourist restaurants give a distorted view of Pennsylvania Dutch food by providing too much. "I understand their problem," she said, "but the amount of waste in the course of a day must be appalling."

I have believed for years that the portions of food in most American restaurants are indecently large, yet we prefer to fight our way through it all rather than live with the guilt which results when we don't heed those childhood admonitions to clean up our plates. Perhaps one small step toward solving the world food crisis might be to pressure restaurant owners and associations to serve smaller portions, with seconds available to those who insist. Even if you don't agree with the Mennonites' moral concern for economy, you might give it a try on behalf of your waistline and cardiovascular system.

A Pennsylvania Paradox

☙ When it comes to leftovers, most of us have very little imagination. Yet the idea of wasting good food is unattractive and impractical. Some years ago I began keeping a soup kettle in the refrigerator. It doesn't sit on the back of the stove the way grandma's did because I am too conscious of bacteria to take chances. Every night after dinner, into the kettle goes any water left from cooking vegetables, and juices from canned vegetables, bits of meat juices, and so on. At the end of the week, I clean out the vegetable crisper. The tired lettuce leaves, limp celery and carrots—anything that is full of vitamins but past the first freshness of youth goes into another pot with an onion, a bay leaf, and some water, and simmers for about a half an hour. Strained, this vegetable juice joins the other liquids in the soup kettle and behold—instant stock!

Season the stock as you wish, perhaps adding a bouillon cube or two if the week's pickings were thin. Just a few minutes before serving, you may add slivers of fresh celery, slices of carrot or potato, macaroni, noodles or rice, even grated cheese at the last moment, or croutons made from stale bread you have cleverly saved.

Homemade soup went out of style when good canned soups came in. It's time we revived the custom, especially when it's delicious, nutritious, and practically free.

A Pennsylvania Paradox

❧ *These crunchy, good-tasting cookies have the extra bonus of being very nutritious. They freeze well and are good travelers, should you need to ship a box to family or friends far from home.*

HEALTHY COOKIES

1 cup all-purpose flour	1 tablespoon grated orange peel
½ teaspoon baking soda	4 tablespoons orange juice
½ teaspoon salt	1 cup raw oatmeal (quick-cooking but not instant)
½ cup wheat germ	½ cup raisins
½ cup shortening	½ cup coarsely chopped nuts (walnuts, peanuts, pecans, etc.)
1 cup dark brown sugar, firmly packed	
1 egg	

Sift flour, baking soda, and salt together. Add wheat germ and set aside. Cream shortening and sugar until light and fluffy; add egg and blend well. Beat in orange peel and juice, then add flour mixture and beat until just combined. Stir in oatmeal, raisins, and nuts. Drop by teaspoonfuls onto greased cookie sheets, at least 2 inches apart, as they spread. Bake at 350° for 15 to 18 minutes or until golden brown. Cool on wire rack. Makes about 3 dozen cookies.

The Ladies from Philadelphia

There must be something special about Philadelphia, for it seems to have spawned a number of ladies who liked to cook, and wrote about it. Not only did a substantial number of cookbooks with a Philadelphia imprint appear during the nineteenth century, that city has also been the center of publishing for ladies' magazines. The *Ladies' Home Journal* was headquartered there until early 1970; *Graham's* was a long-lived literary and women's monthly; *Petersen's Ladies' National Monthly* bore a Philadelphia mailing label; and the most famous of all, *Godey's Lady's Book,* called Philadelphia home from its beginning in 1830 until its demise in 1898.

For years I thought of *Godey's* as a series of charming fashion plates. The dainty, doll-like models have been reproduced *ad nauseam* on fabric, place mats, and lamp shades, yet still manage to retain their charm. I can still remember the first time I actually looked at the magazine itself. It was while I was in college, attending a school in a pleasant, Victorian, Ohio town. An art teacher, in a discussion of architecture, referred to *Godey's* as an important influence. I went to the library, and after some time spent admiring the fash-

The Ladies from Philadelphia

ion plates, I looked at the drawings of gingerbread houses. They looked exactly like the houses in Delaware, Ohio.

As I pursued my project I looked further into the magazine and discovered its editor, Sarah Josepha Hale, who for forty years led the American housewife through the mysteries of kitchen and dining room, with side trips into the parlor. She believed strongly in what she called the "women's sphere," allotting to women the responsibility for the moral and spiritual well-being of the family. Their refining influence, Mrs. Hale believed, improved the home, led to happier marriages, and produced superior children. While she rejected the feminist ideas of the day, Mrs. Hale nonetheless was far ahead of her time, filling the pages of her popular magazine with columns of information on diet, sensible dress, and time- and energy-saving devices. She praised the first mechanical washing machine and printed detailed drawings of apple corers and superior cooking pots. In 1854, for example, she ran a series of articles on various kinds of custards and egg dishes, offered guidelines on hiring and keeping servants, information on the importance of fresh air and exercise, and advice for the home nurse. Before she retired, she had raised the money for Bunker Hill Monument, persuaded Lincoln to proclaim the first official Thanksgiving Day, encouraged the founding of both the first women's medical school and Vassar College, founded the first society to aid the wives and widows of American seamen; and published a multitude of novels, books of poetry, Victorian gift "annuals," and numerous cookbooks and volumes of household hints.

Her recipes, although mired in somewhat archaic language, are generally simple and straightforward. She gives classic directions for soups and sauces, and her rules for making pickles are very sensible and sound quite modern indeed for 1852, cautioning as they do against the boiling of vinegar in metal

The Ladies from Philadelphia

vessels and warning that all vegetables should be completely submerged in the pickling brine. Her recipe for a rich chicken stock in which to boil fowl calls for veal, bacon and butter, herbs, carrots, and onions—far better than water for boiling various kinds of poultry, she writes, and it can be used several times. Her suggestions for dinner parties sound more like the twentieth century than the overstuffed nineteenth.

> Large dinner parties, as 14 or 16 in number, are rarely so satisfactory to the entertainer or the guests as small parties of 6 or 8. . . . To ensure a well-dressed dinner, provide enough, and beware of the common practice of having too much. The table had better appear rather bare than crowded with dishes not wanted. . . . This practice of overloading tables is not only extravagant but troublesome. The smaller the dinner, when sufficient, the better will be the chance of its being well cooked. . . . In giving dinners, avoid ostentation, which will not only be very expensive, but will make your guests uncomfortable.[1]

Mrs. Hale's influence, through her books and most particularly through the pages of *Godey's,* is impossible to measure. Her feminist contemporaries thought her too Victorian, but surely the majority of women and their husbands found great comfort in her philosophy, expressed eloquently in the preface to *Mrs. Hale's New Cook Book.*

> Cookery is an Art belonging to women's department of knowledge: its importance can hardly be overestimated, because it acts directly on human health, comfort, and improvement.
>
> When studied, as it ought always to be, for the sake of the duties involved, it is an Art that confers great honor on those who understand its principles, and make it the medium of social and domestic happiness.

The Ladies from Philadelphia

> The TABLE, if wisely ordered, with economy, skill, and taste, is the central attraction of Home; the Lady who presides there, with kindness, carefulness and dignity, receives homage from the Master of the House, when he places at her disposal the wealth for which he toils. The husband earns, his wife dispenses; are not her duties as important as his?[2]

Mrs. Hale retired at the age of ninety in 1877. A few years later, Sarah Tyson Rorer, also of Philadelphia, opened a cooking school; during her lifetime she wrote a total of fifty-four cookbooks and pamphlets, causing literary historian Frank Luther Mott to call her "the nation's instructress in cookery."[3]

Mrs. Rorer was a determined and outspoken lady who believed firmly that most of the world's ills, at least the physical ones, could be improved by a better diet. Like Mrs. Hale, she campaigned to improve kitchen efficiency, but also like Mrs. Hale, she hoped that the resulting free time would be put to use improving the mind and body through reading and exercise. She taught courses in her own school, at missions and homes for "fallen" women, at the Woman's Medical College Mrs. Hale had helped found, on lecture platforms, and at food expositions and world's fairs. She had a good platform presence and was in much demand as a lecturer at events such as the Pennsylvania Chautauqua. She was the Julia Child of the late nineteenth century and would surely have had her own television series if she were working today.

Mrs. Rorer preached her doctrine of simplicity and economy in her books as well as on the platform. In the preface to her *New Cook Book,* published in 1898, she wrote:

> There are still a few women who do elaborate cooking to please the palate and appetite, and the general habits of people. They are still in the palate

> stage of existence. Strive to reach a higher plane of thought—eat to live. Why should any woman be asked to stand for hours over a hot fire mixing compounds to make people ill? Is this cookery? Is the headache that follows a food debauchery more pleasant or pardonable or less injurious than that which follows drink? Results of intemperance are identical. Simple living and high thinking have the approval of learned men and women, but, like all temperance questions, depend so much upon habit, education and palate that progress must be slow; but there is no better stimulant to the enthusiastic worker than slow progression—the constant but regular improvement.[4]

Strange and strong words for the end of the nineteenth century, when a fully laden table was considered a sign of affluence, taste, and hospitality. But perhaps this very extravagance and its unhealthy aftereffects made Mrs. Rorer's public more willing to listen.

> A "perfect diet" consists of common food materials blended to suit the age, sex, occupation and climate in which the individual lives. They must not only be well proportioned, but well selected and taken in proper quantities, or they are worse than waste, as their presence clogs the delicate digestive organs, throwing them out of order. There is more danger from over-eating than from under-eating. When persons reach middle life or a little beyond there is less vigor, hence, less necessity for a large quantity of food. People who disobey this rule either accumulate fat and become unwieldly, or wear out the secretory organs, and have such diseases as gout, rheumatism, Bright's disease, and many kindred complaints. . . .
>
> Men as a class eat too much meat, and are prone to kidney and liver troubles; women eat too much starch mixed with sugar and cooked butter, as in cakes, preserves and puddings, and are prone to corpulency and constipation.[5]

The Ladies from Philadelphia

In her biography of Mrs. Rorer, Emma S. Weigley tells us that Mrs. Rorer became domestic science editor of the *Ladies' Home Journal* in 1897. Her first articles for the magazine set forth her principles of food preparation, answered readers' questions, and gave detailed cooking lessons. Individual articles ranged over such diverse topics as "Actual Living on Small Incomes," "The Training of a Waitress," "Why I Am Opposed to Pies," "Best Diet for Bloodless Girls," and "How I Lived One Summer Without Fire and Ice." She wrote articles on the servantless home as well as on how to train and treat servants if you had them. She had advice for women living alone and must have been one of the first to recognize that there were women who worked and kept house as well.[6]

By 1914 there were 152,000 copies of *Mrs. Rorer's Philadelphia Cookbook* in print, an impressive number in any age. Her writing combined all the elements important to the housewife—basic chemistry and nutrition; directions for broiling, basting, roasting and such; and some very good recipes. In the *New Cook Book,* there was even a section of Jewish recipes, including mazoth balls and Passover raisin wine. This was followed by chapters on Mexican, Creole, and Hawaiian foods, displaying the exotic side of this earnest lady.

In her professional capacity, she traveled abroad, visiting cooking schools wherever she went. She had much praise for the French, but found German cooking abysmal. Emma Weigley quotes one of her "Table Talk" columns from a culinary magazine: "A good French dinner one must have now and then to keep body and soul together in Germany. It is said that suicides are very prevalent among Germans, and one believes this after even one month's stay in Germany on real German food."[7]

The Ladies from Philadelphia

Along with Mrs. Hale and Mrs. Rorer, there were a number of other less renowned ladies who wrote about food, many of them anonymously, signing themselves "A Philadelphia Housewife" or "A Good Cook." Perhaps the most influential, and certainly the most popular, was Eliza Leslie, known as Miss Leslie to her thousands of devoted fans.

Elizabeth, as she was christened, was born in Philadelphia in 1787, but her father's business took the family to London until she was twelve years old. When they returned to Philadelphia, they were, as the phrase goes, in reduced circumstances, and after her father's death, Eliza and her mother opened a boardinghouse where, it is almost certain, she began to learn the very practical side of American cookery which later made her famous. She attended a Philadelphia cooking school conducted by one Mrs. Elizabeth Goodfellow. She graduated with honors, apparently with reams of notes, and was constantly being called on by, as she put it, her five hundred friends, for recipes and kitchen advice. Her brother suggested she write a book instead, and in 1828, *Seventy-five Receipts for Pastry, Cakes and Sweetmeats* by A Lady of Philadelphia was published. This was one of the earliest cookbooks by an American author, and it went through several editions.

The publication of *Seventy-Five Receipts* opened all kinds of literary doors for Miss Leslie, and she turned to writing fiction and juvenile stories as well. She was a regular contributor to all the leading magazines, including *Godey's Lady's Book,* and although she had many followers of her literary work, her domestic science books were the source of her greatest income. They included such titles as *Domestic French Cookery,* a translation; the *House Book; Directions for Cookery;* and her most complete book, finished in 1857, just a year before her death, *Miss Leslie's New Cookery Book*.

The Ladies from Philadelphia

Modern readers are frequently struck by the apparently endless abundance of early America. Miss Leslie's recipes are apt to begin, "Take a pair of fat fowls," or, "Take half a dozen of the finest lobsters." For venison soup she requires four pounds of venison and a pound of ham. Clear gravy soup requires three pounds each of beef and veal, plus half a pound of ham; black cake calls for two pounds of currants, twelve eggs, and a pound of the best fresh butter. For chocolate custard the cook needs half a pound of the best chocolate, eight eggs, and a quart of cream.

In the 1830s much of the daily cooking was still done on the hearth. Although Miss Leslie discusses Dutch ovens and how to roast a pig on a spit, many of her recipes focus on the difficulties of this kind of cooking. Her directions for baking bread, for instance, apply to the kind of oven without flues that was frequently built into the side of the fireplace: "If it is a brick oven, it should be heated by faggots or small light wood, allowed to remain in till burnt down into coals. When the bread is ready, clean out the coals, and sweep and wipe the floor of the oven clean. Introduce nothing wet into the oven, as it may crack the bricks when they are hot. Try the heat of the bottom by throwing in some flour; and if it scorches and burns black, do not venture to put in the bread until the oven has had time to become cooler."[8] With this kind of problem to contend with, small wonder that housewives had repeated failures with cakes, bread, and other baked foods. It was more likely to be miraculous if a pie or cake turned out exactly the same twice in a row.

Added to the eccentricities of open-hearth cooking was the total lack of interest of most cookbook writers in measurements. "Butter the size of an egg" was a common phrase, or "a wine glass full of brandy." Miss Leslie could be casual too, with directions for "3 spoonfuls of wine," or a "handful of almonds." But she was much more precise than anyone had been prior to her publications, and most of her recipes are based on the closest thing to standard measurements it is possible to find in the early nineteenth century. If the cook followed her instructions, success was certainly more assured than if the traditional handful of this and pinch of that were thrown in the pot. In *Directions for Cookery* she writes, "Unless you are provided with proper and convenient utensils and materials, this difficulty of preparing cakes will be great, and in most instances a failure; involving disappointment, waste of time and useless expense. Accuracy in proportioning the ingredients is indispensable; and therefore scales and weights, and a set of tin measures (at least from a quart down to a jill) are of the utmost importance."[9] In other volumes, she prefaces the recipes with tables of equivalencies, some of which seem imprecise by today's standards but must have been lifesavers to her readers. "Four wine glasses," she writes, "will fill a half-pint or common tumbler or a large coffee cup. . . . about 25 drops of any thin liquid will fill a common sized tea-spoon."

The French influence in the upper classes was very strong at the time Miss Leslie was writing. Cooking in the French style was certain to impress one's neighbors. Miss Leslie was aware of the pitfalls, however, and in 1837 she suggested that "the safest way to avoid a failure in an omelette soufflé . . . is to hire a French cook to come to your kitchen with his own utensils and make and bake it himself."[10]

Her books did offer truly American ideas for native foods, however. Indian pound cake was made with corn meal, butter, eggs, and applejack, and she suggested a filling of cranberries for a boiled Boston pudding. There are directions for pumpkin chips and preserved green crab apples, for buckwheat

The Ladies from Philadelphia

cakes, Indian batter cakes, Johnny cake, Indian flappers, hoe cakes, Boston cream cake, Connecticut loaf cake, and Yankee tea cakes. She has a recipe for rye and Indian meal yeast bread, and she describes how to make yeast from pumpkins. The recipe for fox grape shrub directs the cook to "gather the grapes when they are full grown but before they have begun to purple." Boil them in water until the skins burst, press out the juice and add sugar, then boil some more. When the liquid is cold, add a jill of brandy, and bottle in jars.

Indian Hasty Pudding sounds very American.

> Put two quarts of milk into a clean pot or sauce pan. Set it over the fire, adding a level teaspoonful of salt and, when it comes to a boil, stir in a lump of fresh butter about the size of a goose egg. Then add (a handful at a time) sufficient Indian meal [corn meal] to make it very thick, stirring it all the while with a mush stick. Keep it boiling well and continue to throw in Indian meal until it is so thick that the stick stands upright in it. Then send it to the table hot and eat it with milk, cream or molasses and butter. What is left may be cut into slices and fried next day or boiled in a bag."[11]

For the last ten years of her life, Miss Leslie lived in the United States Hotel in Philadelphia, where she had become an institution, meeting every celebrity and being sought out as one herself. She was opinionated and sharp-tongued, but generous and affectionate to her friends and relatives, so much so that she spent her declining years in poverty, dependent on the very friends she had helped. Her biography, written by her friend, Sarah Josepha Hale, in her *Biography of Distinguished Women,* is quaint but sincere, an effort to put Miss Leslie's eccentricities in the best possible light.

The Ladies from Philadelphia

Miss Leslie has quick observation, a retentive memory, a sprightly fancy and a persevering mind; she has also the great merit of being free from affectation; her purpose is always to be useful, to correct faults, expose follies, and wage war with what is perverse and contemptible. If, in doing this, she sometimes seems severe on what are called trifles, it should be borne in mind that from these little faults grave misfortunes not infrequently have their origin; and Miss Leslie is such a truehearted American that she earnestly desires to aid her countrywomen in becoming perfect.[12]

The Ladies from Philadelphia

Despite Mrs. Rorer's concern with accuracy and measurements, she tended toward vagueness in some of her recipes, such as the one here for a corn meal loaf. With just a little experimentation, however, it was possible to translate her intentions into a fine, sturdy loaf of real bread. [13]

MRS. RORER'S CORN MEAL LOAF

1	pint of milk	1	pint of water
1	level teaspoonful of salt	1	compressed yeast cake
1	pint of white flour		corn meal

Put the milk and water into a double boiler over the fire. When hot, stir in two-thirds of a measuring cupful of granulated yellow or white corn meal. Stir this until it thickens, then allow it to stand over the fire to keep hot for twenty minutes. Take from the fire, and when lukewarm, add a level teaspoonful of salt, and the yeast cake, dissolved in a quarter cupful of cool water. Beat into this the flour, cover and stand in a warm place (75° Fahr.) for three hours, until it has doubled in bulk, is light and porous. Begin to add slowly sufficient white or whole wheat flour to make a dough that can be turned out on the board and kneaded thoroughly. The dough must become elastic and lose its stickiness. Cut into three loaves; mold, place them in greased square bread pans, cover and stand in the same warm place for one and one-half hours, or again until very light and porous. Brush the top with water, and bake in a moderate oven (300° Fahr.) for three-quarters of an hour.

The Ladies from Philadelphia

UPDATED CORN MEAL LOAF
- 2 cups milk
- 2 cups water
- 1 teaspoon salt
- ⅔ cup corn meal
- 1 package dry yeast
- 1 teaspoon sugar
- ¼ cup lukewarm water
- 3½ cups whole wheat flour
- 1½ cups white flour

Combine milk and water and scald. Stir in salt and corn meal and cook over very low heat, stirring frequently, until thick, about ten minutes. Cool to lukewarm. Dissolve yeast with sugar in ¼ cup lukewarm water and stir in large mixing bowl. Add corn meal mixture, then beat in whole wheat flour. Cover and let rise in warm place until doubled in bulk, about 1½ hours. Punch down and beat in or work in with hands enough of the white flour to make a stiff dough. Turn onto floured board or cloth and knead until smooth and elastic, about 8 minutes. Divide into 2 or 3 loaves, depending upon the size you prefer, and place in medium-sized, greased loaf pans, approximately 8 × 4 × 2½ inches. Cover and let rise in warm place until doubled in bulk, about 45 minutes. Brush tops with water; bake at 325° for 45 minutes or until lightly browned. The loaves should sound hollow when tapped with your knuckles. Cool on wire racks before slicing.

The Ladies from Philadelphia

👁️ *This recipe from Mrs. Hale's* The Ladies' New Book of Cookery *is both simple and delicious. I am giving her version of this apple charlotte along with my somewhat more precise directions. If you don't like the proportions of lemon, for example, experiment until you arrive at the right combination.* [14]

AN APPLE CHARLOTTE
Pare and slice a quantity of apples; cut off the crust of a loaf, and cut slices of bread and butter. Butter the inside of a pie dish, and place bread and butter all round; then put in a layer of apples sprinkled with lemon peel chopped very fine, and a considerable quantity of good brown sugar. Then put on a layer of bread and butter, and another of apples, lemon peel, and sugar, until the dish is full, squeezing over the juice of lemons, so that every part shall be equally flavored. Cover up the dish with the crusts of bread and the peels of apple, to prevent it from browning or burning; bake it an hour and a quarter; then take off the peels and the crust, and turn it out of the dish.

A MODERN APPLE CHARLOTTE

5 to 7 medium-sized tart apples
½ loaf unsliced white bread
3 tablespoons or more butter or margarine

zest of ½ lemon (about 1½ teaspoons), finely chopped
juice of 1 lemon
1 cup brown sugar, firmly packed

Pare and slice the apples, taking care to save the peelings. Try to keep them in fairly large pieces or spirals. Cut crusts from bread loaf and save them as well. Slice bread slightly thicker than you would for sandwiches, and butter each slice. Butter a large pie dish or shallow casserole; place bread slices on bottom, butter side up. Try to arrange this first layer symmetrically, as this is what you will see

The Ladies from Philadelphia

when the charlotte is unmolded. Add a layer of apples; sprinkle with half the lemon peel and ½ cup brown sugar. Make another layer of bread and butter, apples, lemon peel, and sugar. Squeeze or pour the lemon juice over the mixture, making certain all of the apples are covered by the juice. Take the saved apple peelings and crusts and lay them over the charlotte, covering as much area as possible, to prevent burning and browning. Foil may be used instead, but the peelings and crust seem to add extra flavor. Bake at 325° for 1¼ hour. Remove the crusts and peelings or foil; with a spatula, loosen the crusty edges. Invert a large plate over the top of the pie plate and turn the charlotte upside down onto the plate. Serve warm or at room temperature, with cream if desired.

Magic Mushrooms

I put on the hard hat and got into the electric golf cart, and I was transported through vast limestone corridors far underground. I was visiting a mine, but not the traditional kind. This was where mushrooms are mined, in limestone caves in Butler and Armstrong counties, almost 100 million pounds a year. It is eerie to ride silently through these dimly lit caverns and then suddenly veer off into a totally dark room, watching the car's headlight illuminate the stacks and rows of mushroom babies. Mushrooms like darkness, and the growers are happy to oblige, for they are repaid by the rapid and prolific growth of these succulent delicacies.

I don't know exactly what I expected to see when I set out to visit the Moonlight Mushroom Farm in Worthington, Pennsylvania—perhaps a few elderly men mucking about in the back yard—but surely not what I found. The building above ground is modern and efficient and doesn't prepare you at all for the trip underground to a world where the temperature is always 60° and some six hundred people spend their full working day in the dark. A wall map shows the crazy scale of the entire farm. A small square in the middle of the page represents the aboveground operation, while several square feet are devoted to charting the one hundred miles of corridors and five hundred acres of growing rooms.

Magic Mushrooms

Wild mushrooms, I'm told, are the most delicious and delicate in the world, but frankly they scare me to death. I would no more pick a mushroom in the woods than I would swallow a bottle of iodine. There are expert mushroom pickers who have lived to a ripe old age, but I will surely not be among them. It is one of the gourmet pleasures I will forego in favor of longevity. One wonders who did eat the first mushroom, and whether he lived to tell the tale. Commercial mushrooms are entirely safe, I was told, grown under carefully controlled conditions with no possibility that a poisonous field fungus will get in your basket by mistake.

People have been eating mushrooms for hundreds of years, beginning in recorded history with the Egyptians and later the Greeks and the Romans. Ancient peoples often attributed magical powers to them, probably because they can appear so magically overnight, in the woods and fields, or in our own backyards. Although they were, in ancient days, one of the free foods, even then people seemed to understand that mushrooms were something special. Julius Caesar decreed that the ordinary man in the street was unworthy of these delights and limited their sale to the upper classes.

The French developed such an inordinate appetite for the fungi that one seventeenth-century writer called it a disease. In *Food of France,* Waverly Root tells an anecdote about the Count of Guiche during the reign of Henry IV, when elaborate practical jokes were very popular. The count was served a huge dish of mushrooms at a dinner party. After he had greedily eaten them all, the other diners began telling terrible tales of the weird effects of mushroom poisoning. The count woke the next morning to find he had apparently swelled up, since his clothes were all too small. He was convinced by his friends that he was suffering from mushroom poisoning, only to find out later

Magic Mushrooms

that during the night the jokers had taken his clothes apart at the seams and sewed them up again in a smaller size.[1]

During the reign of Louis XIV, some Parisians discovered that mushrooms could be cultivated in caves. The technique spread from France to England and then to America. Residents of Long Island began growing them, mostly in cellars and caves, and florists in Chester County, Pennsylvania, grew them under the benches in their green houses.

Pennsylvania might well be known as the mushroom state, since it grows some 75 percent of the nation's crop, divided between northwestern Pennsylvania and the little community of Kennett Square near Philadelphia. Moonlight Mushroom is one big company, producing 42 percent of the total crop in their limestone caves. Kennett Square has dozens of smaller producers, cultivating their mushrooms in specially designed houses aboveground. In either case, the process is the same.

Unlike the forest mushrooms, the commercial fungi drop their spores or seeds in the sterile atmosphere of the laboratory. Nourished with special food, the resulting spawn is allowed to mature, then injected into the rich compost used as a growing medium. Made of hay, corn cobs, and horse manure—from the racing stables of Kentucky—the compost looks and smells like compost the world over, as I noticed on a fragrant swing through the yard in Worthington. Lest this cause you to strike mushrooms from your list, let me hasten to say that the compost is pasturized before the mushroom spawn is implanted. Then the huge trays of compost and spawn are delivered to their underground homes or the mushroom house, as the case may be, where they remain until the mycelium, a white, threadlike substance which is equivalent to the roots of green plants, spreads throughout the compost. A layer of rich soil is then placed on top, and the trays are left in the quiet darkness with only water to help them grow. The first mushroom can be harvested in about three weeks, and each tray continues to produce for about seven weeks. The Moonlight Mushroom Company harvests about seventeen thousand trays per day and expects each tray to produce about two hundred pounds before the cycle is finished. And mushrooms don't wait for anything; there are no weekends or days off for Christmas. The harvesting process goes on 365 days a year.

Although parts of the business have been mechanized, the harvesting of mushrooms must be done by hand. I saw dozens of trained pickers, all wearing hard hats with miners' lamps flickering to illuminate their work. They have two baskets, one for the mushrooms, one for the root end which is sliced off with a kind of paring knife. The mushrooms are graded as they are picked—good and better. Size has no effect on quality or taste, but relates only to use. Larger ones are more appropriate for stuffing, while the tiny button mushrooms look elegant in more elaborate dishes. The mushroom pickers work a seven-hour day, transported to their picking rooms by large electric cars that look like vehicles from a low-budget science fiction film. They spend the day down under, eating lunch in underground snack bars, and the question most asked of visitors is "What's the weather like?"

Up on top again, I watched the packing operation in a huge bright room filled with moving conveyor belts and baskets of mushrooms being sorted, weighed, packed, and labeled. The life of a mushroom is short at best, so the completed packages are quickly cooled to prolong their days. Then they are carried away in refrigerated trucks.

Tremendous strides in growing techniques have been made in the past twenty years. Old-timers grew mushrooms by instinct, relying on sight and smell. It was a seasonal industry until air-conditioning allowed temperature control to standardize the product for a year-round yield. A mushroom industry grew up in southeastern Pennsylvania, probably because between the farms and the Philadelphia livery stables, growers were close to a source of manure for their compost. And the biggest markets were there: New York, Baltimore, and Philadelphia. Then in 1936, the Yoder brothers began growing in the Butler County limestone caves, and another section of the state became involved.

Although only one variety of mushroom is grown commercially, *Agaricus campestris bisporus,* mycologists keep hoping they may someday find ways to produce some of the delectable wild varieties, such as morels or chanterelles. Meanwhile, scientists work on increasing the yield and look for ways to deal with the so-called diseases which affect the appearance of the mushroom—bumps and brown spots and odd-looking circles.

People who really love mushrooms tend to wax poetic about them. In 1896, Elizabeth Pennell wrote: "Mushrooms you must make yours at any cost. Learn to like them; *will* to like them, or else your sojourn on this earth will be a wretched waste." Her emotions got a little out of hand as she continued:

> Possibility of rapture there is in a white fricassee of mushrooms, which, if you have your own happiness at heart, you cannot afford to despise. Secure then, without delay—for who would play fast and loose with happiness?—a quart of fresh mushrooms. Clean them with hands as tender as if bathing a newborn babe. In three spoonfuls of water, and three of milk, let them boil up three times. See that temptation leads you not to violate the sanctity of this thrice-three. Nutmeg, mace, butter, a pint of rich thick cream

> alone, at this juncture, will appease the saucepan's longings. Shake well; and all the time, mind you. Be careful there is no curdling, or else—damnation. The masterpiece once triumphantly achieved and set upon a table covered with a fair white cloth, great will be the rejoicing in the Earthly Paradise of your dining room.[2]

In Worthington, I was amused by the posters in the underground lunchrooms exorting the viewer to eat mushrooms, but I was told that the employees buy large quantities, apparently unsatiated by their daily proximity. And why not? Mushrooms are low in calories, high in vitamin C, niacin, and riboflavin, and taste good with practically anything, except possibly oatmeal.

Magic Mushrooms

☙ *Often the simplest recipes are the best. If you like mushrooms and spaghetti, try this easy combination without the usual addition of tomato sauce. The amount of mushrooms varies according to the number of people served and how much they like mushrooms. The recipe which follows is for two real mushroom lovers.*

MUSHROOMS AND PASTA
12 oz. fresh mushrooms, washed and sliced
approximately ¼ cup butter or margarine
salt to taste
(oregano)
spaghetti, fettucini, or other pasta
grated Romano or Parmesan cheese

While the pasta is cooking *al dente,* brown the mushrooms in the butter, add salt, and oregano if desired. Drain pasta and pour mushrooms over it. Pass the grated cheese.

Magic Mushrooms

◈ *This frittata, a firm omelet, can be served as the main course for luncheon or a simple dinner, but it also makes a fine accompaniment to a more hearty meal.*

MUSHROOM ZUCCHINI FRITTATA

½ cup sliced fresh mushrooms	4 eggs, well beaten
4 small zucchini, unpeeled	½ teaspoon salt
2 tablespoons olive oil	pepper to taste
2 tablespoons butter	⅓ cup grated Parmesan cheese

Shred the zucchini on a hand grater or with vegetable peeler. Place vegetable in a small dish towel and twist it as hard as you can, extracting as much liquid as possible. (The towel will turn green, but it comes out in the wash.) Heat oil and butter in a 9 or 10 inch skillet with a broiler-proof handle. Sauté the mushrooms briefly, then added shredded squash. Cook until squash is barely tender, about 4 minutes. Pour beaten eggs over vegetables, sprinkle with salt and pepper and stir once to coat mixture. Cook over low heat until eggs are just set. Sprinkle with cheese; place under broiler until brown on top. Remove from heat, let stand two or three minutes, then cut in wedges. The frittata is also good cold. Serves 4 as a main course, 6 as a side dish.

Life in a Bologna Factory

One long ago Christmas in New England I was given a fine spicy loaf of Lebanon bologna. I loved every last bit of it and searched in vain for more. Miraculously, when I moved to Pennsylvania, there it was in every supermarket and butcher shop, in abundance. In my unquestioning ignorance, I had thought it was a Middle Eastern specialty, never dreaming that Lebanon, Pennsylvania, was the source of so much goodness. And when I recently found myself in central Pennsylvania surrounded by bologna factories, I decided to give in and take the tour, just one tourist among many.

The word *bologna* comes, of course, from the town of Bologna, Italy, where the famous sausage is made of veal, pork suet, and bacon. The word has been corrupted to *baloney* in America, and here it usually means a particular kind of semisoft, mildly spiced sausage. Who is there among us who has not existed on baloney and cheese sandwiches in college, taken them in our brown bag lunches, and sometimes in moments of stress, eaten them for dinner. They are an American institution, running only slightly behind tuna fish salad and apple pie.

Recipes for baloney sausage abound in old cookbooks. *Housekeeping in*

Life in a Bologna Factory

Old Virginia, for example, has a recipe calling for ten pounds of beef and four of pork, two-thirds lean, the rest fat. Run this through the grinder—by hand, of course—add seasonings and stuff it into the casing of your choice.[1]

Commercial makers of Lebanon bologna are fond of saying that their recipes are secret, either passed down through the family or brought over from the old country. Their literature uses phrases like "closely guarded," "old, original recipe," "secret blend of special herbs." Indeed, most of the plants look like the old family homestead, with tidy white frame buildings surrounded by trees and flowers. I visited Weaver's, just outside Lebanon, on a lovely golden October day, with few visitors and alas, very little bologna making, either. But the bologna factories are numerous, and I pressed on.

Just down the road in Palmyra is Seltzer's, where the family has been making good sausage since Harvey Seltzer began in 1902. On the back of each Seltzer truck, a smiling Pennsylvania Dutchman, drawn from the likeness of the company founder, looks down on the world, while underneath is the message, "This truck is full of bologna—Seltzer's, that is." That phrase, full of bologna, has cloudy origins. One source credits *Variety,* the show business journal; another suggests that Al Smith first used it in reference to certain practices of the Roosevelt administration. But it is a fine phrase, extremely useful when other, more intellectual phrases simply will not serve.

Richard Gehmann, in *The Sausage Book,* tells us that the Pennsylvania Dutch simply refined Italian sausage until it was more to their taste, perhaps the local way of showing who was boss. His mother, he writes, used to give him bologna sandwiches for his school lunch so thick he could have choked a horse, if he'd had one. On top of the half-inch-thick slices of meat she would add Lancaster County sharp cheese or Amish-made swiss cheese,

Life in a Bologna Factory

covered with mustard. As he grew up, she added onions or those wonderfully colored hard-boiled eggs the Pennsylvania Dutch pickle in beet juice, or homemade pickles from a large stone crock.[2]

I made some major discoveries at Baum's bologna factory, just north of Elizabethtown. I learned, for instance, that I was a victim of all the prejudices that drive meat packers wild. I was properly astonished to discover that the beef which goes into Lebanon bologna is good. It's better than good, it's fantastic. I viewed the sides of beef hanging from giant meat hooks in the refrigerator rooms, then watched the skillful butchers cutting away steaks and roasts and sirloin tips of lovely red beef and groaned inwardly as they all went into the huge meat grinder, along with quantities of spices and seasonings. It's reassuring, somehow, to know that what you had always believed about bologna isn't true—it really isn't made from snips and snails and puppy dogs' tails.

There is a federal meat inspector on the premises all the time, and visitors are required to wear little paper hats to prevent untidy wisps of hair from dropping into the pot. The ground meat is forced into casings by means of a power device which literally blows the meat into the long plastic tubing placed on a special nozzle. Then a loosely woven cotton stockinette is wrapped around the tube of bologna to give it support during the smoking process.

The smokehouses smell delightful, and modern technology hasn't improved much on our grandparents' methods. The tubes of bologna are hung in the rafters of a wooden shack. A fire is built in a deep pit below, fed with hickory and oak logs, covered with a heavy steel plate, and loaded down with wet sawdust. Presto! Instant smoke. The Baum people told me that their

Life in a Bologna Factory

smokehouses date back to 1885, and even the sawdust is specially blended and aged to produce a so-called cold smoke for deeper penetration. Bologna is smoked for six days, then makes a trip to the giant slicing machine in a spotlessly clean packaging room. The machine is magical, slicing huge quantities of the sausage, weighing it, and dividing it into neat little piles. There is something anachronistic but strangely reassuring about watching this great machine at work, then seeing a prim young lady in a Mennonite cap place the slices in plastic cups, feed them into another machine that pressurizes and seals them, paste on a label, and pack them into shipping boxes.

This particular plant ships most of its meat within sixty miles of Elizabethtown. Some goes much further—they send mail order packages to lonely Pennsylvania Dutch folk in foreign parts—but the greatest demand is from local people.

The last stop on the tour is the food shop, where a fine array of free samples is laid out—chunks of Lebanon bologna, of course, plus sweet bologna, somewhat less spicy; hickory sticks, good-keeping, hard little sticks of spicy meat sealed in plastic, perfect for lunches or picnics where refrigeration is a problem; paper-thin slices of dried beef; smoky cheese; thin slivers of home-cured ham, pink and succulent; thick slabs of streaky bacon, and even Canadian-style bacon. It's a hardy soul who can leave without buying. I managed to get out with only a dozen hickory sticks and a package of dried beef, but in Elizabethtown I happened to pass Groff's Meat Market, and I was a goner.

Groff is a good Pennsylvania Dutch name. The sign outside the tiny store suggests that you try their homemade ham spread, pork chops, homemade sweet bologna, smoked tongue, or front and hind beef quarters. They

Life in a Bologna Factory

will cut, wrap, and freeze meat for your freezer. I walked down the four steps below street level to the small shop and found two customers before me. I was happy to peer into the meat case and gaze at the glass-walled refrigerator beyond, filled with hams and bacon and tongue. But one of the three old gentlemen waiting on customers was worried I would get restless. He kept coming over to me with samples, like lollipops for a good child.

"Here," he said, "Try our bologna; it's delicious." It was. He came back. "A little piece of ham?" he invited. I accepted. Once more he came. "Try this cheese," he suggested, "it's smoky." It was.

When my turn came, he wanted to know where I was from. When I said Pittsburgh, he smiled. "I was there once, thirty years ago. Do you still have cobblestone streets?" I assured him that some things never change. I ordered a four-pound slab of bacon. I bought sliced sweet bologna. I asked about ham and bought the smallest—sixteen pounds. I asked him to put the weight on the wrapper so I would cook it properly. "You aren't going to cook this whole?" he said, astonished. I allowed as how I might and sensed disapproval.

"What *should* I do?" I asked.

"Well," he pondered, "you could take out some nice center slices like those." He pointed to thick pink slices of lovely ham in the case. "And you could boil up the butt end with some green beans. That's nice."

I said I would do just that, staggered out to the car with my load, and remembered I was driving a rental car and would have to fly home.

I spent the plane trip from Harrisburg watching my fellow passengers sniff the air curiously and heard one man say, "I thought they didn't have food on this flight. I could swear I smell bologna." I managed to restrain myself from replying, "You are correct, sir, this plane is indeed full of baloney."

Life in a Bologna Factory

Lebanon bologna is like smoked salmon—I wouldn't insult its integrity by combining it with other ingredients. One of my cocktail party standbys is a Lebanon bologna roll-up, simple and satisfying. Spread each slice of bologna with a good mustard, perhaps add some chopped parsley, roll it up and place on a platter, seam side down. The mustard must be hot and spicy to hold its own with the strong flavor of the Lebanon balogna, so if you don't have a favorite, try this recipe. Making your own mustard is very easy and infinitely better than most store-bought varieties. I am giving you a very small amount so you can sample it and perhaps change the seasonings to your personal taste.

MY MUSTARD

¼   cup dry mustard
1   teaspoon sugar
dash of salt
¼   teaspoon dried tarragon
2   teaspoons red wine vinegar
approximately 2 tablespoons water or enough to give desired consistency

Make a paste of dry ingredients and vinegar; slowly add water until desired consistency. Warn your guests this is *very hot*.

Springs Comes in the Fall

If you have visited a county fair recently, you know they aren't making them the way they used to. Motorcycle daredevils and hot-rod racers come close to outnumbering the cows and pigs, and they certainly make more noise as they roar around the arena. The last time I spent a few hours at a county fair, I wished I hadn't. The prize lettuce wilted quietly in an obscure corner; the blue-ribbon peach pie attracted more flies than people. There were dozens of popcorn stands, a depressing sideshow tent, and a tired elephant enduring the indignity of being ridden by hordes of screaming children. Nobody really seemed to be having any fun except some 4-H kids grooming their calves and turning the hose on one another when things got dull.

But down in Springs, Pennsylvania, things are decidedly different. Its annual Folk Festival may be one of the last old-time fairs. You can watch wood-chopping contests and cornhusking; see people spinning, weaving, or making apple butter; study the big display of quilts and other crafts. But best of all, there is Pennsylvania Dutch food, either at a sit-down dinner with platters of sausage and Dutch fries, or at booths selling homemade pies and sugar cookies.

Springs Comes in the Fall

Before you talk about the Folk Festival, you have to talk about the museum, and Alta Schrock. Dr. Schrock is a quietly dynamic lady in her sixties who was the first Mennonite woman ever to receive a Ph.D. She has always lived in and around Springs, except for her years as a biology teacher at Goshen College in Indiana. She was, she says, always concerned about the unique quality of this community on the fringe of Appalachia, afraid that its history and lifestyle would slip way unless someone tried to capture it.

"This community is unusual," she said. "Many of the residents are descended from the same twenty families. They're Mennonite, some old order, some not. And there is such a pool of talent, of old skills, a knowledge of a culture we'll never know again."

Each time she returned to Springs, Dr. Schrock worked on her oral history, interviewing residents over seventy. "I began collecting artifacts, too," she said. "Every time I'd see an old farm tool or a kitchen utensil, I'd ask for it. Pretty soon I had so much stuff I just had to find a place to put it." That was the beginning of the Springs Historical Society and the museum, a wonderfully eclectic collection which illustrates the everyday life of the last hundred years. There are the farmer's hand plow and harrow, his wife's collection of heavy black kettles, her spinning wheel, loom, and flat irons. This is not a sophisticated museum, and perhaps because of this, the impact is even stronger. These utensils belonged to real people, were used, cared for, passed on to the children.

A year later, in 1958, the first festival was held. Pennsylvania Dutch food was a featured attraction from the very beginning. Lura Folk was the first food chairman. Now in her eighties, she is an enthusiastic, energetic woman who remembers that first year very well indeed.

Springs Comes in the Fall

"We didn't know anything," she said. "Alta—Alta Schrock, who started the Springs Museum—said we had to have a festival, and she always seemed to know what she was about, so we had one. But none of us had ever even been to a festival. We were just plain country folks, and we didn't have any money or equipment for cooking. There was just me and two other ladies and one man, and we decided to keep the menu simple, to do it Pennsylvania Dutch style. We didn't want to copy anybody else, so we decided to just have the kind of food everybody seems to like around here." She started to laugh, remembering. "We decided on dried corn, of course, and we told everybody to save their extra corn for us. Well, people kept dumping it out here in back until we had a heap as big as the house, seemed like. Then we had to ask all the neighbors to get their dryers going for us."

Neighbors also gathered apples and got together to make applesauce which was then frozen at Yoders, a local freezer plant and meat-packing establishment. "The high school kids picked surplus apples for apple butter," she said, "and we got that made up at Beachey's Cider Mill. We bought homemade bread from a lady in Grantsville [Maryland] who made it for a living. And there were some Amish people who made their own butter, and we bought from them."

Coleslaw was also on the menu, "the old-timey kind, with cream," and Dutch fried potatoes, along with country sausage. "We bought the hogs and took them up to Yoders, and they made the sausage for us. The neighbors got together again and cut it up into the right lengths for frying."

Mrs. Folk said that the committee argued long and hard over what to have for dessert. "We tried out tapioca pudding, but it just wasn't practical for a big crowd. And besides, the milk and eggs made it too expensive. So

Springs Comes in the Fall

we finally decided on just plain old-fashioned canned peaches, and homemade cookies—sugar and ginger. And the menu has stayed exactly the same all these years."

Mrs. Folk laughed as she told about her own merchandising idea. "I thought we should have a stand that sold slices of homemade bread and apple butter," she said, "and some of the people around here were scandalized. Apple-butter bread at a festival! But we went ahead anyway, and we've done it every year since. It's one of the most popular stands. I just have to laugh every time I see those doctors and lawyers walking around eating a slice of it."

The festival was a success from the very first day, but Mrs. Folk remembers how nervous they all were. "We had no idea if anybody would come," she said. "One lady was supposed to demonstrate quilting, and her family kept trying to get her to hurry up because she'd be late. She told them there was plenty of time, nobody was going to be there early. And when they finally got there, they couldn't find a place to park, there were so many cars." She shook her head, still unbelieving. "We were amazed at ourselves. We kept saying, 'How could we do it?' since we didn't have any experience at all. But we've been doing it ever since."

Folk Festival crowds number in the thousands, now, but the event has somehow sustained the old-time feeling. There have been some concessions to progress—the applesauce isn't homemade anymore—but there is a steam engine to gaze at and hayrides for the children and apple butter bubbling in a huge black cauldron.

Alta Schrock has moved on to other projects now, but all of them are concerned in some fashion with preserving the rich past of the area as well as helping to create economic opportunities for the young people who want to stay around. She founded Penn Alps, located in nearby Grantsville, a crafts cooperative and attractive restaurant which encourage local craftsmen to market their products. She is involved in a drug rehabilitation project and, when I last talked with her, was busily selling bonds for a new furniture manufacturing concern which would provide good jobs for young Appalachian workers. She is active in the Mennonite church and talks of the day when she will settle down and write the story of her father and his family.

Meanwhile she encourages others to write down what they remember about the past. The *Casselman Chronicle* is the official publication of the Springs Historical Society and contains many pleasant reminiscences. Rhoda Miller Maust, for example, wrote about her days in the old Children's Home. "In the bake shop in the basement was the huge oven in which the regular baking was done. A wood fire was built in it in the morning, and the ashes were scraped out and then the baking began. We baked mostly brown bread, tasty and nutritious, with no additives. Pies and cakes were rare and only for special occasions. Potatoes, squash and various other things were baked sometimes."[1]

Dr. Schrock, whose father was a miller, shared her own early memories, remembering the family's two apple orchards and "the smell of the forty-five varieties of apples stored in the apple-shed between the house and the orchard. . . . Mother bringing in a basket of Buff Orpington eggs from the chicken house; the round hanging pie-shelf in the cellar, full of pies mother had baked for the week."[2]

Mrs. Folk told me that Springs was " a good cooking community." At church suppers the food is always good, she said. Her own family especially

Springs Comes in the Fall

loves the Dutch fried potatoes, as well as rice pudding, "just plain cooked rice with an egg beaten in with some milk and sugar. You serve it cold with a little whipped cream. Pies are also popular—grape, egg custard, and shoofly—but she never bakes bread. "My husband carried a bucket to school and later to work, and he always had homemade bread, so he was tired of it. But I can remember when the little store down here got in ten loaves of baker's bread, and they had a terrible time selling it. People weren't used to buying bread."

Mrs. Folk remembers walking home from school as a little girl—it was two miles—in the early spring and smelling the vapor from the maple sugar camp where her mother was boiling and stirring off the syrup. "We had maple sugar parties and taffy pulls," she remembered. "And my mother always made spruce beer and cookies around Easter." She laughed. "My sister brought me some spruce beer this year, thank goodness. Otherwise I'd never get through the Easter season."

Spruce, or schpruce, beer is a nonintoxicating beverage, similar to sharp root beer. Traditionally made by thrifty farmers at the end of the maple sugar season, spruce beer used up the "leavin's" of the syrup or crumbs of maple sugar. In the old days, custom called for throwing a few branches and twigs—usually hemlock, sweet birch, spice bush, or sassafras—into boiling water. The maple sweetening was added and simmered. When the concoction was cool, old-timers added *satz,* a yeast made from hops and cornmeal. Then the beer was put behind the kitchen range to ripen for a few days until it reached the proper degree of sharpness, whereupon it was moved to a cool place for the pleasure of family and *psuch*—visitors.

The Springs Folk Festival is always held on the first Friday and Saturday

Springs Comes in the Fall

in October, rain or shine. "It never rained when I was chairman," Dr. Schrock said with a touch of smugness. The festival is a kind of unofficial homecoming for former Springs residents, and Alta Schrock still laughs remembering the first year when a man came up to her and said, "My name is Folk and I came to see the other Folks. This is supposed to be a Folk Festival, isn't it?"

Springs Comes in the Fall

The ladies who cook for the Springs Folk Festival make wonderful sugar cookies as well as old-fashioned ginger cookies. The recipe I want to share with you is a little different. These are old-fashioned ginger snaps, the kind with the crinkly tops. They are very easy to make, and if you want to bake only a few, the dough keeps well in the refrigerator for several days, or you may freeze it.

GINGERSNAPS

¾	cup shortening	2	teaspoons baking soda
1	cup sugar	1	teaspoon cinnamon
4	tablespoons molasses	1	teaspoon cloves
1	egg	1	teaspoon ginger
2	cups all-purpose flour		granulated sugar

Cream shortening and sugar until light; add molasses and egg and beat well. Sift dry ingredients together and stir in, beating until smooth. Roll in small balls, about 1 inch in diameter; dip into sugar. Place 2 inches apart on greased cookie sheets and bake at 375° for 15 to 18 minutes or until firm. Makes 4 dozen.

Lura Folk told me how she makes Dutch fries: "Have cooked potatoes on hand. Make sure they are cold. Slice them very thin and fry in a heavy iron skillet in lard. Salt and pepper, and at the end, add a little milk." I have experimented with using butter instead of lard, and they taste good but they are different. I have used cream instead of milk, which makes a richer dish, but I'm not sure it's any better.

Trains

If you want to trigger a flood of nostalgic reminiscences in anyone over the age of thirty, start a discussion entitled Memorable Train Rides I Have Taken. Instantly, stories of pathos, humor, and, yes, gluttony, will come pouring forth. You can spend a delightful hour or two recalling those wonderful days when you could board the Super Chief in Chicago and alight in Los Angeles three days later, rested, relaxed, and extremely well fed. Contrast this gracious mode of travel with the cramped and claustrophobic airliners, their plastic toy food and ever present undercurrent of terror.

Fortunately in Pennsylvania we have two antidotes for Train Depression. In Pittsburgh, simply walk into the Grand Concourse of the old Pittsburgh and Lake Erie station on the South Side and you will be instantly transported back into the Edwardian era of marble staircases, potted palms, and shiny brass fittings. In a remarkable partnership of private enterprise, charitable trusts, and the Pittsburgh History and Landmarks Foundation, a miracle has taken place, transforming the once elegant but decaying railroad station into a complex of restaurants, shops, and offices. Completed in 1901 and built in the classical style, it is a transition between the Victorian and Edwardian eras. The outside is relatively simple, but the interior is an elaborate series of

Trains

domes and arches, with great fans of colored glass, gilt, mosaics, marbleized plaster, and brass. The Grand Concourse is now a restaurant specializing in fish, and its owner, Chuck Muer, has retained many of the original fittings—the shiny wooden rows of waiting-room benches, the tall light posts with large globes, the mosaic tile floor, the brass plates on the swinging doors with elaborate P&LE monograms. There is a series of rooms for dining, including one overlooking the Monongahela River, and a white-tiled oyster bar serving fresh shellfish and draft beer. If only we could enjoy all of this opulence, and then walk out to the platform to hop a luxurious train for Chicago or California or Boston.

I remember my first rain ride very well indeed, eating perfectly sectioned grapefruit from a silver dish in the swaying diner. I remember the total joy of being alone in a lower berth, tucking my clothes into the green string hammock that swung beside the window, and waking up dozens of times in the night to raise the window shade and peer into the mysterious darkness as we sped through villages and farmland.

I think we should all have realized that trains would soon disappear when the diners began to deteriorate. But do you remember the sheer pleasure of watching handsome black waiters deftly balancing trays on the way to your table, as the train lurched and swayed on its way? They must have dropped a plate sometimes, but I never saw it happen. The tablecloths were always sparkling white and the coffee pots were shiny and silvery. The plates always had B&O or Atchison, Topeka and Santa Fe decorating the rims, and the Chesapeake had a picture of a little cat as well. The ice cream was served in round silver dishes, and there was almost always a cookie on the plate beneath. The hot dishes were covered with round silver lids, and the waiters

Trains

unveiled them with a flourish. I remember that the diners wrote out their own orders—a tricky business when the roadbed was rough—and waited for the dining-car host, always a white man in a black suit, to come around and okay it before sending a waiter off to the kitchen with it. If the car was crowded, and you had to stand in the corridor and wait for a table, you could peek into the incredibly tiny kitchen where perspiring chefs stirred steaming kettles and talked to each other in a strangely beautiful combination of dialects and accents. Often between mealtime rushes, perhaps on the way to the club car or the observation car, you would pass a cook on the little platform between cars, still in his whites, his chef's cap pushed back on his head, sleeves rolled up, smoking a cigarette. I always wondered what he thought about—the evening meal perhaps. I also wondered if the male chefs on the train ever cooked when they were at home or if their wives did all the work.

During railroading's golden age, dining cars were not expected to make money, and the opportunity to offer the diner the best of everything far outweighed the need to economize. The story goes that Fred Harvey, whose chain of restaurants and catering services for the Santa Fe railroads was unsurpassed, once fired a dining-car manager who was losing a mere $500 a month and replaced him with a man who upped the deficit to $1500 and was promoted to superintendant for his work. By the 1890s, foreigners traveling by train in the United States were astonished to be confronted with menus equal to the finest hotels in Europe—and this while hurtling through a country only recently swarming with red savages.[1]

Most railroad lines had specialties which helped their passenger lists climb. The B&O was famous for terrapin stew and Chesapeake Bay seafood, put aboard live at the beginning of each run. The Santa Fe served broiled

Trains

sage hen, Mexican quail, and a charlotte of peaches with cognac sauce. The famous S. S. Pierce grocery in Boston's Back Bay supplied the New Haven with all of its wine and staple groceries to go with the scrod, Maine lobster, and Cotuit oysters. The Wabash Railroad had a particularly succulent creamy chicken pie, and the Northern Pacific advertised itself as "The Line of the Great Big Baked Potato."

The interior decoration of the dining cars reflected the mature opulence of the gilded age. The Pennsylvania Railroad put a diner on its Jersey City–Chicago run in 1882 that had stained glass windows, "large double silver chandeliers . . . an exquisite silver adorned sideboard of carved mahogany, plate glass and dark velvet plush. . . . curtains that ran on silver rods above the windows are of carmine and golden-olive velvet plush, relieved by rich salmon-covered cloth, stiff in patterns of gold bullion."[2] Theodore Dreiser's first meal on a train seemed to him "the acme of elegance and grandeur. Could life offer more than riding about the world in these mobile palaces?" he asked, and added that, when breakfasting on broiled chicken, he saw "poor looking farm boys in jeans and 'galluses' and wrinkled hats [looking] up at me with interest."[3]

A second way to relieve your railroad nostalgia is to visit the Railroad Museum in Strasburg, Pennsylvania, southeast of Lancaster, and ride on an old steam train. The huge museum houses twenty-six locomotives, including one built in Philadelphia in 1875. Constructed at the Baldwin works, it was used on the Virginia and Truckee Railroad in Nevada during the Carson and Virginia City silver-mining days. There are passenger cars and model trains, a 111-ton locomotive, and plenty of railroad memorabilia.

If you crave the real thing, the Strasburg Railroad Station is just outside

Trains

of town, and the train runs every day from May until October and on selected weekends after that. Just because the run takes only forty-five minutes and some four hundred thousand tourists ride every year, don't get the idea it's not a real railroad. It's regulated by the Interstate Commerce Commission, the Federal Railroad Administration, and the Pennsylvania Public Utilities Commission. It must comply with all safety regulations imposed on other trains, and rates are regulated as well. The nine-mile trip winds through lovely farm country and passes the home of Philip Ferree, Jr., a master builder of the Conestoga wagons once made in Lancaster.

It's not necessary to call up images of famous transcontinental trains to start the memories flowing. Pennsylvania had some fine local railroads—the Pittsburgh and Lake Erie, the Reading, the Baltimore and Ohio, and of course, the Pennsylvania. Less known, perhaps, but still full of enticing possibilities, were the Western Maryland, the Wabash, the West Shore, the Pittsburgh and Western, the Sunbury and Erie, the Lehigh Valley, and the Delaware, Lackawanna and Western.

Just prior to World War II it was still possible to travel by train almost anywhere in America and enjoy it. Movie stars took the 20th Century Limited and luxuriated in the service and the privacy of their drawing rooms. Corporation executives had private cars for their own use, and every presidential candidate included a whistle-stop tour as an essential part of his campaign.

The elegance of train travel was shattered by World War II. Soldiers were packed into cars designed for half their number, and civilians were jammed into even worse accommodations or traveled not at all. Like many other war wives, I followed my soldier husband around, usually on trains that had seen better days. On one memorable trip to Sacramento, I boarded a

Trains

train in Chicago without a reservation and spent three days and four nights in a coach with green plush seats and gas lamps—no electricity. The car had been hauled out of storage to accommodate the thousands of passengers generated by the war, on their way to mysterious destinations. Our car was jammed, sometimes five persons wedged into seats for four. There was no diner, so obliging service men scrambled out at each infrequent stop to forage for provisions, just like the railroading pioneer passengers of the nineteenth century. After three days of gulping stale sandwiches and cold coffee secured in Des Moines and Kansas City and points west, I ate a dubious spam sandwich in Omaha and spent the rest of the journey in the ladies' room. I got off in Sacramento pale, wan, and many pounds lighter. And that's my only war story.

Nowadays Amtrak provides limited services for those determined to travel by train. One look at the machines that dispense stale sandwiches and bitter coffee to passengers, however, is enough to send me into deep depression. I long for red plush seats, efficient waiters and plates of hot food waiting under elegant silver covers. And I shed a figurative tear for the generations of children who will never know what they have missed.

Trains

◈ *Many railroad lines originating on the east coast specialized in fish, but it was also possible to get excellent clam and fish chowders aboard some of the diners. Here is a simple, hearty chowder which is a meal in itself.*

FISH CHOWDER

2 slices bacon, chopped	1 pound fish fillets—cod, haddock, or other firm white fish
1 large onion, chopped	
2 medium potatoes, peeled and sliced	2 cups milk
3 cups water	salt, white pepper
	butter

Fry bacon slowly until crisp. Drain and reserve. Cook onion slowly in bacon grease; do not brown. Push to one side of pan and add potatoes, sliced "skithering" as they say in Maine—thicker at one end than the other so the thin ends will break off and slightly thicken the chowder. Cook potatoes briefly, just enough to get the bacon and onion flavor. Add 1 cup water, bring to a boil, and cook until potatoes are tender, about 10 to 15 minutes.

Meanwhile, cook fish gently in 2 cups water, only until done. It should flake easily. If fish has skin, remove fish, drain, and peel off skin; return fish to water. Pull fish apart so it is in fairly large bite-sized chunks. Add potato-onion mixture; add milk; season to taste. At this point you may heat the chowder (but don't boil it) and serve immediately. I prefer to make mine a day ahead and refrigerate it until serving time, as the flavor seems to improve. Whenever you serve it, add a generous piece of butter to each bowl at the last minute, and sprinkle a few pieces of bacon on top.

Trains

This rich and fragrant seafood combination is just the sort of thing you might have found waiting for you under the silver domed cover of the serving dish on an elegant train before World War II.

SEAFOOD SCALLOP

- 1 cup dry white wine
- 1 cup raw bay scallops, or sea scallops, cut into small pieces
- 3 tablespoons butter or margarine
- 1 cup cooked lobster meat, in bite-sized pieces
- ½ cup sliced fresh mushrooms
- ⅓ cup butter or margarine
- 2 tablespoons flour
- ½ teaspoon salt
- 1½ cups light cream
- ½ cup fine bread crumbs
- ½ cup grated Parmesan cheese
- 2 tablespoons butter or margarine

Heat the white wine and simmer scallops in it 3 to 4 minutes or until barely tender; drain, reserving wine. In a small skillet, melt the 3 tablespoons butter and sauté lobster meat and mushrooms briefly. In a saucepan over low heat, melt ⅓ cup butter; stir in flour and salt and let cook briefly; then stir in light cream and reserved white wine from scallops. Cook, stirring constantly, until thickened. Add scallops, mushrooms, and lobster. Pour into 1½ quart casserole or individual baking dishes. Mix bread crumbs and cheese; sprinkle on top of casserole. Dot with butter. Bake at 325° about 20 minutes, or until heated through and top begins to bubble. Serves 4.

As We Sow

I can't think of anything that raises my natural level of optimism higher than a seed catalogue. I know I'm not alone in this, because I have noticed that many of my friends have visibly brighter spirits just after the first of the year, and their conversation tends to include references to cabbages and roses and mulches. What could be more fun than leafing through the bright pages of the catalogues on a snowy February day, dreaming of the harvest ahead. Never mind that your thumbs are purple and your back is still not quite right since last summer's spading chores. The fantasy is wonderful while it lasts, which can be all the way through May, before the real work begins.

A substantial number of companies have made their fortunes feeding the dreams of prospective gardeners, and the biggest of them all is the W. Atlee Burpee Company, right here in Pennsylvania. Each year more than 4 million seed catalogues go out to growers like you and me, plus many more professional brochures to the industrial trade. The headquarters of the company are in Warminster, just north of Philadelphia, which is also the distribution center for the eastern part of the United States. There are warehouse and packing facilities in Clinton, Iowa, and Riverside, California, and experimental farms in several states, but the first and still the most famous is Fordhook Farm, in

As We Sow

Bucks County. It is also the home of David Burpee, now retired, the son of W. Atlee, who took over the small firm at his father's death when he was just twenty-two and built it into the multimillion dollar corporation it is today.

It is not a family company any more, but Jonathan Burpee, David's son, is manager of customer relations—that's shorthand for complaints—and his own sons spend their summers working in the fields, just as he did and his father before him. I spent a rewarding day talking with Jonathan Burpee and other long-time employees of the firm, watching the packing and mailing operation, and gaining new respect for the magnitude of the operation and the variety of skills required to maintain it. And at the end of the day, I wanted desperately to begin digging in my own garden.

W. Atlee Burpee gave up medicine after two years of medical school, and at eighteen, in 1876, he started a seed business with $1,000 borrowed from his mother. He was interested in poultry, and although he soon concentrated exclusively on seeds, his first catalogue described land and water fowls as well. He was shrewd enough to realize that a catalogue would carry his name and his business well beyond Philadelphia. Burpee's Surehead cabbage was offered in the 1877 catalogue, and more than one hundred years later, it still sells well. There are other popular old-timers that are still in stock: golden self-blanching celery, introduced in 1884; iceberg lettuce and the stringless green pod bean in 1894. Golden Bantam sweet corn was born in 1902, and the famous Fordhook bush lima bean, still one of the most popular items, came in 1907.

W. Atlee started his first experimental farm in Doylestown, Pennsylvania, in 1888, even before the U.S. government had one. In 1906 he acquired another in the Lopac Valley of California, where the long, cool growing sea-

As We Sow

son opened up a new kind of seed-growing operation for peas, lettuce, cabbage, and celery. Fordhook Farm, however, has always been the central experimental farm, as it's here that all the fourteen hundred or more varieties listed in the catalogue are grown under average conditions, usually far from ideal. When David took over in 1915, at his father's death, World War I had interrupted shipments of European seeds. The experimental farms were a lifeline, then, and today European markets are eager for American seeds, a complete reversal of the original trend.

The Burpee story sounds so much like Horatio Alger that one wonders if there could possibly be so much goodness in the world. David Burpee, writing about his own life, said:

> When people ask me how could a young man of only 22 years successfully manage a business like Burpee seeds, I am tempted to repeat what my father once said—"Youth is a handicap that is soon overcome." But actually running the Burpee seed business was not as difficult as it may seem. My father had laid the groundwork, building Burpee seeds on a solid foundation of scrupulous honesty. He always kept his word, and always gave his customers seeds of the highest quality. In his 1913 Catalogue he wrote, "You can buy seeds at lower prices, but you cannot buy seeds that are of equal quality anywhere for less money. We have no second-grade, or so-called cheap seeds, and seek the trade only of planters who want to grow the best it is possible to produce."
>
> What a wise policy that was. For the fact is, you can't tell if a seed is good by looking at it. You buy your seeds entirely on faith. And through the years people all over the world had discovered that Burpee was a name to be trusted, that when you buy your seeds from Burpee, you get your

As We Sow

> money's worth—and more. So all I had to do was follow in my father's footsteps, using the same principles he used to guide the business he had established.[1]

The success of the business attests to the intelligence and skill of the Burpee family. And yet, despite its size and success, there is a kind of family feeling about the place. Jonathan Burpee introduced me to Jerry Cantor, now in charge of the commercial division, but I was told that over his forty-year span he had held a greater variety of jobs than anyone else in the company. Cantor suggested that this was because they kept trying to find the right one, but Jonathan Burpee's obvious admiration of him was heartwarming to observe. "Tell her about your first job," he would say, and Jerry told me how he went to Bucknell on a Burpee fellowship and studied genetics and plant breeding, then took a job with Burpee as a plant breeder. "Tell her about your home garden," he would prod, and Cantor explained that he had about a quarter acre and grew about twenty different varieties. "Just enough for me and the birds," he said.

Cantor has an obvious affection for the Burpee family, and likes to quote Jonathan's father, David. "Your father used to say, 'breeders don't taste.' That's why we think the public can help us. Home-tested vegetables are better than laboratory-grown produce. Our test gardens simulate home conditions, and we are looking for a lot of things—better yield, for example; better adaptation to climatic conditions; more disease-resistant strains. These days people want smaller sizes, the dwarfers are very popular, icebox size." He paused to grin. "That dates me, doesn't it? But smaller families and smaller gardens need smaller varieites, so we developed bush beans and smaller squash."

110

As We Sow

Cantor told me that the public has a great influence on what they do at Burpee. Home gardeners are cautious about using potentially harmful chemicals, so disease resistance must be built into the plant genetically. During periods of inflation, seed sales go up, and the new interest in ecology, while leveling off somewhat, has had a marked influence on the business. "Home gardeners are really quite conservative," Cantor said. "There are some fads, some interest in exotic items, but generally, the home gardener is reluctant to change. If he has grown Burpee Early Boy tomatoes and they were good, he's not about to experiment very much. The public—the people we deal with—are very nice people," he continued. "They let us know what they want, and they tell us when we're doing things right."

Planning for the commercial grower is quite different, Cantor told me, since the shipper wants the antithesis of what the home gardener wants— uniform products that ripen slowly, pack easily, ship well. "We'll probably develop a square eggplant someday," he mused. "Think how easy they would be to pack in crates."

Cantor's desk was littered with packages of mung beans, his shelves lined with books on plant breeding, mulches, English gardens. He is genuinely concerned about plants and takes every opportunity to find out what other people are thinking. "If I asked you what was the one thing you wanted in a vegetable garden you don't have, would you know?" he asked me.

"I certainly do," I replied promptly. "I want a tomato that cutworms aren't going to ruin."

"Ah," he said happily, "now in order to do that, we have to develop a tomato with a tough stem but not a tough fruit. We must build in a defense against the cutworm, secretion perhaps," and he was off and away, answer-

As We Sow

ing me in great detail, earnestly and with enthusiasm, giving me a small lecture on plant breeding, minerals, organic materials, and finally concluding that for the moment, paper collars around the plants are still the best defense against the evil cutworm.

I toured the computerized order department; walked miles in the huge warehouse to watch orders being filled; observed seeds poured mechanically into small packages; looked into the dry room, where some seeds are held at 20 percent humidity; the cold room, where I saw bulbs from Japan, boxes of hybrid cabbage seeds, stacks of crates all needing a lower temperature. I visited the testing room, where the U.S. government sets the rules for seed production and sprouting seeds are stacked in special breeding trays, carefully observed before they are approved for the home gardener. And then I came home to prepare for that ultimate act of faith, planting a tiny seed in the vegetable patch, wondering if there will be a miracle once again and that funny little brown seed will turn into a crisp head of lettuce, a brilliantly red, juicy tomato, or a firm green squash, just for me.

As We Sow

I once had a neighbor ask me if I were planning to start a basil farm, since at the time I had about twenty plants growing in the back yard. Most home gardens seem to manage with only one or two plants, but if you like pasta with pesto sauce, you will want to increase your yield.

There are two schools of thought on making pesto. The purists insist on using a mortar and pestle to crush and grind the basil, garlic, and other ingredients. This is certainly possible, but I prefer the blender or food processor for this particular chore. Automation seems to produce a smooth, thick sauce which I find superior to the totally handmade variety.

PESTO

- 2 cups fresh basil leaves, tightly packed
- ½ cup pine nuts
- 1 large clove garlic, cut into several small pieces
- 1 teaspoon salt
- ½ cup grated Parmesan cheese
- ½ cup olive oil or good quality vegetable oil

Put all ingredients in processor or blender and process at high speed until a thick, smooth sauce is made. You may have to stop, especially in the blender, and wipe down the sides once or twice. Serve a heaping tablespoonful or more over a dish of hot pasta. Fettucini is especially good. Serves 4 to 6.

Note: Pesto freezes very well if you do not add the cheese before freezing. Follow above procedure but omit cheese. Freeze in ice cube trays, and when solid, remove to plastic bags. One cube equals one average serving. Thaw cubes at room temperature, and when completely thawed, beat in desired amount of cheese. The oil may separate out somewhat when thawing but responds quickly to a thorough beating.

As We Sow

Those of us who have gardens never seem to have enough recipes for zucchini. Every time the gardener turns his back, the squash multiply magically. This casserole helps to solve the problem of too many squash, since it can be made with all zucchini, all crooknecks, or pattypans, or any combination of them. It can be doubled or even tripled for larger crowds.

SUMMER SQUASH CASSEROLE

- 5 small summer squash, sliced into ¼ inch rounds (half yellow, half zucchini is very attractive as well as good)
- 1 tablespoon butter
- 1 tablespoon olive oil
- 1 onion, coarsely chopped
- 2 cloves garlic, minced
- 1 teaspoon oregano
- salt, pepper
- 1 large ripe fresh tomato, peeled and chopped, or 1 cup canned Italian plum tomatoes, drained and chopped
- ⅓ cup fine bread crumbs
- ⅓ cup grated Parmesan or Romano cheese
- 2 tablespoons butter or margarine

In a heat-proof casserole or deep pan, heat butter and olive oil; cook onion and garlic until wilted. Sprinkle with oregano, salt and pepper to taste, and add squash. Cook briefly, stirring to distribute onion-garlic mixture; add tomato. Bake uncovered at 400° for 15 minutes. Combine cheese and bread crumbs. Stir half into squash mixture very gently. Return to oven; reduce heat to 350° and cook 15 minutes. Sprinkle with remaining crumb mixture; dot with butter; bake 30 minutes. Serves 4 generously.

Apples of My Eye

If we ever hold a popularity contest for an all-American fruit, the apple simply has to win. Our language abounds with metaphors and similes based on the apple. Upsetting the apple cart, for instance. He's full of applesauce. Her house is in apple-pie order. They're as American as apple pie. Not that we invented them. First records of this fine fruit date back thousands of years to the area around the Caspian Sea. Hebrews, Romans, Celts, and Scandinavians all celebrated the beauty and virtue of the apple. Even King Solomon asked somebody to comfort him with apples. And, of course, there was Eve.

Governor John Endicott planted the first apple tree in America in Plymouth, brought from England, no doubt, as seed. The Indians took to the apple immediately, and often made long trading trips to secure the seed for their own plantings. Richard Townsend, who came to Pennsylvania with William Penn, was told by the Indians of a great apple tree near his Bucks County farm. He investigated, and indeed, there was an apple tree "in an Indian clearing vastly larger than any seen in England, heavily loaded with larger and better apples than he had ever seen before." In 1760, it measured more than four feet across and there was speculation that more than one hundred years earlier, the Indians had procured the seed for it from Dutch colonists in New York. He bought the property on which the tree stood, but not the tree itself, since the Indians stipulated that it be reserved freely for everyone who wanted apples. The Townsend family observed the stipulation until the tree died in 1792.[1]

Apples were an important crop for Pennsylvanians. They were delicious eaten fresh, had excellent keeping qualities, and could be peeled, sliced, and dried for the winter. A familiar sight on the frontier, according to firsthand accounts, was the strings and strings of sliced, dried apples festooning cabin rafters waiting to be cooked in pies, puddings, and main dishes. The Pennsylvania Dutch were especially adept at using *schnitzen,* as well as boiling up the excess crop for apple butter, a welcome healthful treat in mid-winter. Quantities of apples were grown for cider alone.

In 1753 a Pennsylvania farmer recorded: "We have a great variety of Apples for The Table and The Cellar. The Newtown Pippin exceeds everything for fine taste and duration. . . . We have lately introduced a high, red-colored Apple of good Gust, called the Spitzenberg. . . . The House apple and the Vandeveers are most esteemed for Cyder. Some few have the Golden Russeting and the Golden Pippin, but not plenty. Every Body has an Orchard and makes commonly Cyder enough."[2]

Most of the colonial Pennsylvania apple trees came from seeds rather than grafts, limiting the varieties available. But after 1850, farmers and horticulturists began competing with one another to grow new and exotic apple stock. The unfamiliar names of the resulting apples roll off the tongue like an epic poem—Blue Mountain, Fallawater, Paradise Winter Sweet, Westfield-Seek-No-Further, White Winter Pearman, Ridge Pippin, and Romanite. Even

Apples of My Eye

the varieties that survived disease and pests, to say nothing of the public's fickle fancy—York Imperials, Rambos, and Baldwins—are difficult to find today, but no one ever sees Jersey Sweet, Gilliflower, English Winter, Aunt Mary Sweet, Spice, Smokehouse, or Roxbury Russett.

Early in the 1800s Western Pennsylvania settlers used to talk about the eccentric who traveled long distances with stocks of apple seeds, planting them carefully and tending them with love and skill. My own image of the man called Johnny Appleseed must come from a children's book. I see him as a tall, gaunt figure, striding through the countryside with a sack of seed, broadcasting it randomly. In each spot, a small apple tree magically grew. Although he did indeed become a legendary figure with an aura of mystery about him, he knew what he was about, planting his seeds carefully, surrounding them with brush for protection, often returning to look after their development, creating, in effect, small apple nurseries in Western Pennsylvania, Ohio, and Indiana.

Born in Massachusetts, John Chapman chose the frontier life, and in addition to planting apple trees, he disseminated advice on milk and honey as a healthful remedy for almost anything. He preferred bee bread—the yellow stuff in the honey comb—to real bread. Deliberately or not, he added to his own legend by walking barefoot much of the time, wearing a ragged coffee sack as his only garment, and, some say, carrying his cooking pot on his head as a kind of helmet. His life is shrouded in mystery, but the fact remains that through his efforts, thousands of apple trees were planted to give sustenance and pleasure to settlers who never heard of Johnny Appleseed.

Benjamin Franklin, Pennsylvania's Renaissance Man, used apples in his political dealings. He introduced the Newtown Pippin to the British royal

Apples of My Eye

court, where it was received with great favor, and a new export trade began, with one British citizen writing to an American friend, "Your American apples have been an admirable substitute this season, many of our merchants have imported great quantities of them; they sold for two to four pence each."[3]

Although the number of varieties has diminished substantially, it is still possible in Pennsylvania to drive up to a roadside stand in October and admire the brilliant display of locally grown apples. There are baskets of McIntosh, that all-around favorite for cooking and eating, thin-skinned and greenish, blushed with red. The Jonathan is still with us, a bright red apple with tiny white dots, rich and lively flavored, superbly pink when coverted to applesauce. There are Staymans and Rome Beauties for baking, as well as Rhode Island Greenings—tart, smooth, and waxy, unparalleled for pies. I haven't mentioned Red or Golden Delicious, since I consider them nonapples; they are sweet and mealy and good for very little. If I wound your sensibilities, compare the flat-tasting Delicious with the crisp Northern Spy, fine-textured and spicy, its greenish skin lightly striped with red. Or bite into a Rambo, that oldest of Pennsylvania apples, and savor the tangy juice from its crisp firm flesh. It's clear they aren't growing apples the way they used to.

Apples of My Eye

◆ *This delicious apple tart in a cookielike crust makes an elegant ending to a special meal. I use a food processor to mix the dough, but it can be done by hand.*

ELEGANT APPLE TART

PASTRY
1¼ cups all-purpose flour
4 tablespoons sugar
½ cup butter or margarine
2 egg yolks
dash of salt
zest of one lemon, grated

FILLING
5 to 8 medium tart apples
12 oz. jar apricot preserves
2 tablespoons brandy

For pastry, mix flour and sugar; cut in butter. Add egg yolks, salt, and lemon zest. Knead gently and form into a ball, or use food processor. Refrigerate at least 30 minutes. Then roll out ⅔ of the dough to form a bottom crust; place in pie pan. Fill with the peeled and sliced apples, saving a few big slices for the top layer. Spread with preserves moistened with brandy. Roll out remaining dough; using a 3 or 4 inch biscuit cutter, make circles of the dough and arrange them across the top of the apples, either slightly overlapping or with edges just touching. Bake at 425° for 15 minutes, then at 350° for 30 minutes. Serve warm or at room temperture. You may wish to pass a bowl of whipped cream at the table.

Apples of My Eye

APPLE PANCAKES
Use your own favorite pancake recipe, or make them from biscuit mix or buckwheat batter (see p. 151). If you are serving them for dessert, make them a little thinner than you normally would for breakfast cakes.

Peel and core 1 apple for each dozen cakes. Tart ones are tastier. Chop apple coarsely, and after pouring batter onto greased skillet or griddle, sprinkle about 1 or 2 tablespoons of apple on uncooked side. Turn when small bubbles form and cook on other side. Serve with cider sauce.

CIDER SAUCE
- 1 cup sugar
- 2 tablespoons cornstarch
- ¼ teaspoon cinnamon
- ¼ teaspoon nutmeg
- 2 cups apple cider
- 2 tablespoons lemon juice
- ¼ cup butter

Mix sugar, cornstarch, and spices; stir in cider and lemon juice. Cook over low heat, stirring constantly, until thickened. Bring to boil for 1 minute, still stirring. Remove from heat and stir in butter. Serve hot or cold.

Grapes of Diverse Sorts

Although I have visited wineries in the eastern part of Pennsylvania and in northwestern Erie County, I didn't expect to find one in the middle of Lancaster County. But there it was, the Pequea Valley Winery, a few miles south of Lancaster, located in lush Pennsylvania Dutch farm country. Once a large dairy farm, Pequea Valley was purchased by Alice and Peter Wood in the 1970s. They live in the beautiful old white farmhouse and have converted the barns and outbuildings to a small winery, turning out more than fifteen thousand gallons annually.

I toured the winery on a bright October morning when there were very few visitors. Alice Wood, casual and friendly, told us that her husband, an engineer by profession, had become an expert on winemaking during a tour of duty in Europe, then managed a New York state winery before deciding to invest in his own. "We started in 1972 with ten thousand gallons," she said, "and have increased the yield ever year."

I mentioned my surprise at finding a winery in this part of the state. She told me that experiments conducted by pomologists at Penn State University show that the local soil produces grapes with more sugar and less acid than

Grapes of Diverse Sorts

those grown in the Lake Erie region. "This used to be a grape-growing area, back in the 1800s," she told me. When I did my homework, I found she was absolutely right, that York had been the center of the first successful commercial grape-growing industry in Pennsylvania. In 1818 Thomas Eichelberger planted four acres, and by 1826 there were over one hundred fifty acres in the area.[1]

Long before that, however, William Penn had planted European grapes at Pennsbury and instructed his French winemaker, Andrew Dore, to develop two other sites near Philadelphia with an eye toward their commercial possibilities. In 1683 he wrote to English friends: "Here are grapes of divers sorts. The great red grape, now ripe, called by ignorance the fox grape because of the rich relish it hath with unskilled palates, is in itself an extraordinary grape and by art, doubtless, may be cultivated to an excellent wine." But Penn's foreign vines succumbed to disease, and after two years of failures, he gave up his dream of commercial vineyards. One hundred years later, Peter Legaux came from France to plant grapes, but his too died after many years of slowly decreasing yields.[2]

Grapes were first grown in Erie County, now the center of Pennsylvania's wine industry, in 1850. Years of experimentation and research have resulted in hybrid varietals, offspring of two different grape strains. Winemakers in Pennsylvania and New York now hybridize with one European parent and one American parent, resulting in a grape with a more European flavor but a resistance to American disease.

Although Lancaster County may have the better soil, Erie County growers believe that the presence of Lake Erie improves the quality of their wine. It provides the proper chilling temperatures necessary for grapes in the winter,

Grapes of Diverse Sorts

and in the spring the cool water keeps the air cool as well, discouraging spring buds from opening too early and succumbing to a late spring frost. In the summer the lake's surface acts like a giant mirror, reflecting the sun's rays and intensifying the heat during the bulk of the growing season. In the fall the water remains warm, and the growing season is extended by the warmer air produced. The same conditions are present around Lake Kekua in Hammondsport, New York, just across the northern Pennsylvania border, where wineries such as Taylor's, Widmer's, Great Western, Gold Seal, and Bully Hill are located.

No matter what the size of the winery, the winemaking process is essentially the same. Grapes may be harvested by hand, as they are at Pequea Valley, or with a monster machine that literally vibrates the grapes off the vines. The biggest machines, which work night and day, can harvest eight tons in twenty-four hours, while one person can pick up to half a ton daily. Everything is automated in the big operations such as Taylor's in New York. Leaves and stems are taken off, grapes crushed, juice carried hither and yon through glass tubes, conveyor belts speed everything everywhere. There is steel, chrome, glass, and gleaming tile. It isn't difficult to believe the company is owned by Coca-Cola Company.

In Pennsylvania, winemaking is on a smaller scale. Penn Shore in Erie County does some picking by hand, some by machine. At Pequea Valley there are crushing machines, but they are fed by hand; then pipes carry the juice inside the old barn to be strained. Controlled portions of yeast are added to induce fermentation, which takes about eleven days. There is a small lab in a nearby shed where chemical testing goes on. The bottling and corking machines seem primitive compared to Taylor's, requiring constant atten-

Grapes of Diverse Sorts

tion by a real person rather than by another machine. In the same room, a young woman sits at a labeling machine which disgorges a label every few seconds, but she must apply it to the bottle by hand before carefully placing it in a cardboard shipping case.

All the New York and Pennsylvania wineries offer tours and free tastings. Since there is a substantial amount of snobbery concerning eastern wines, it is a pleasure to report that there are some very good ones being made in this part of the world. Many still taste like strong grape juice to me, the grapey or foxy flavor, as the professionals call it, far too pronounced for my personal taste. But in Erie, Penn Shore produces a good dry Seyval Blanc, Mazza Vineyards an excellent Baco Noir, and Presque Isle Wine Cellars a fine Cabernet Sauvignon. Pequea Valley offers a good Seyval Blanc along with a pleasant rosé. All the wineries have excellent selections of Catawba, Delaware, Dutchess, plus some apple wines, if your taste runs to sweet wines.

The tastings vary as widely as the style of the vineyards. At Taylor, the tour and the tasting is highly structured. Buses and well-informed guides move large groups of tourists through the complicated machinery, then lavish hospitality is offered in an attractive room built like an old German wine cellar. Several wines are provided, along with hot hors d'oeuvres that use wine as a major ingredient. At Bully Hill, also in Hammondsport, life is more relaxed. Young guides clad in blue jeans lead guests on foot through the vineyards and vats before offering ample glasses of several excellent wines. If you're lucky, Walter Taylor himself will be there to talk about his difficulties with the "big" Taylor wine company his ancestors began and which, he will explain, will go to any length to prevent him from using his own name on the wines his new company makes. Walter is a self-styled Renaissance man, and

Grapes of Diverse Sorts

his paintings and poems decorate every wall, even those in the excellent restaurant next door. There is a small but informative museum on the history of winemaking on the grounds.

Pennsylvania wineries are less elaborate, but you may taste before you buy at all of them. Penn Shore and Mazza have harvest festivals, where grapes are trampled by barefoot experts and the wine flows freely.

The Pennsylvania wine industry faces some serious problems in marketing and in planning for expansion. The state ranks fifth in production, behind California, New York, Ohio, and Michigan, and the Limited Winery Act, passed in 1968, allows commercial wineries to produce a maximum of one hundred thousand gallons annually. This is probably ample for the foreseeable future, George Sceiford of Penn Shore told me. "One year we actually produced seventy thousand gallons," he said, "and we could do that regularly, but only if everything was going for us; sales, grape production, and of course, the weather." Penn Shore is the state's largest winery and will face expansion problems long before the smaller companies must. But marketing is a serious problem for all of them. "The Pennsylvania Liquor Control Board is not allowed to promote Pennsylvania wines over other wines," he told me, "so people who buy in the state liquor stores never see any promotional literature about our products, and sometimes they never see the wines either. A lot of wine drinkers don't even know we exist. And we just aren't big enough to spend a lot of advertising dollars." He sounded wistful when he talked about California, since that state spends substantial amounts of money promoting its wine industry. Pennsylvania winemakers also have to contend with state stores. "In a free market state, wine consumption per capita is always up," he said. "If we could sell to individual liquor dealers rather than

Grapes of Diverse Sorts

the state, which has laws regulating its business, we could make a big pitch to individual wine merchants and promote our product." Unless the law is changed, Pennsylvania winemakers must rely on other public relations devices, such as their tours and festivals, to make their wines better known in their own back yard.

As I drove away from the Penn Shore winery, I followed a car with a bumper sticker that suggested one way to improve the situation. It read, "Conserve water: drink wine."

Grapes of Diverse Sorts

⁌ *This versatile recipe can be halved, doubled, or increased almost without end to provide easy and delicious party fare. Nothing seems to bother it, including overcooking or a dash or two more of this or that.*

SHERRIED PORK
salad oil for frying
1. teaspoon fresh ginger, minced
¼ cup chopped onion
1. pound lean pork, preferably tenderloin, cut in ½ to 1 inch cubes
2. tablespoons finely chopped orange peel (do not grate)
1. tablespoon soy sauce
½ cup sherry (dry is best)
1. teaspoon sugar

salt and pepper to taste
1. cup chicken stock or bouillon

In a heavy skillet or saucepan, heat salad oil and add ginger and onion. Cook one minute; add pork cubes and brown. Add remaining ingredients, cover and cook over low heat until pork is tender, about 30 minutes. Serves 4 to 6.

Grapes of Diverse Sorts

◈ *This simple chicken and white wine recipe has been a dinner party standby of mine for many years. I am always delighted when someone new comes to town so I can trot it out again.*

CHICKEN WITH WHITE WINE

1 frying chicken, cut up
2 tablespoons olive oil
2 tablespoons butter
1 large onion, sliced
1 large fresh tomato, peeled and cut into eighths, or 2 canned Italian plum tomatoes, drained and chopped
1 large clove garlic, minced
¼ cup chopped parsley
½ cup dry white wine (I have used chablis, Bordeaux, and dry vermouth with good results)
salt, pepper

Wash chicken pieces and pat dry. Heat butter and olive oil; sauté chicken until light brown on all sides. Add onion slices and tomato pieces to pan; sprinkle garlic and half the chopped parsley on top of mixture. Add the white wine, and season to taste. Cover and cook over low heat about 25 minutes or until chicken is tender. Just before serving, sprinkle remaining parsley on chicken. Serve with rice or noodles to enjoy the good juices. Serves 4.

Come to the Fair

There is something very American about a fair. I have attended fairs in other countries, and they were perfectly fine. And I know Americans didn't invent them. But nothing makes me feel more a part of American life than a good fair, whether it is the tiniest neighborhood ethnic street happening or the enormous world-class events in Seattle or New York. At the smaller country fairs, especially, there is a warm sense of sharing and a cooperative effort that one associates with the American frontier spirit. The renaissance of the old crafts, the quilting and canning displays, and above all, the booths dispensing good, old-fashioned foods help us remember all the pleasant things of past generations and draw a merciful curtain across the less attractive aspects of our earlier days.

The really good fairs are disappearing or changing their character drastically, filled as they are with performing motorcyclists and pseudo-country-western singers. But there are still a few standouts, and my favorite is the Kutztown Folk Festival in Kutztown, Pennsylvania. Held annually since 1950, the Kutztown festival is an enormous mélange of exhibits, demonstrations, and lectures, all relating to Pennsylvania Dutch life, and it features some of

Come to the Fair

the best food you could ever hope to taste in or out of Pennsylvania. Held during the Fourth of July week, it lasts for eight days and draws huge crowds, rain or shine.

The festival grounds are big, with ample parking if you don't mind waiting a few minutes to be directed to the proper place. Then you take a short uphill walk to the main area and arrive at a series of permanent buildings and small booths and tents, peopled with pleasant folk who are prepared to tell you about life in the world of the Pennsylvania Dutch. One of the nicest things about the festival is the feeling that real people are running it, displaying the best they have to offer. Everywhere there are women and girls with the little net caps we associate with the Mennonites, serving meals, selling quilts, making apple butter. And there are plenty of bearded men and boys in straw hats and overalls working with tools, demonstrating how to shingle and thatch roofs, or operating the threshing machines in the center of the common.

The food makes a profound impression on the visitor, or at least on this one, for several reasons. First, it's everywhere. You can't turn around without spotting a stand selling iced *wassermelon* on a stick; funnel cake, those jigsaw puzzles of sweet dough, deep-fried, and sprinkled with powdered sugar or drizzled with molasses; corn on the cob dipped in melted butter before it is handed over to you, steaming hot and dripping; deep-fried mushrooms with a hint of cheese in the batter; paper cornucopias of Dutch potatoes, thinly sliced twice-fried chips, glistening with the salt that sticks to their crisp brown sides. There are rows of bakery counters selling apple dumplings; cinnamon bear claws; potato *fastnachts,* those cloud-light doughnuts; peach and apple and apricot and cherry and raisin pie; *shotzels,* cheese-filled pretzels; soft sugar cookies and crisp molasses rounds; witch waffles and corn fritters;

Come to the Fair

cream-filled doughnuts and raisin sticky buns; shoofly pie; potato puffers; and glazed snowballs—and we haven't even reached the meat, the cheeses, and the breads yet.

It is possible to move from booth to booth and sample a few dozen items until you can no longer walk, washing it all down with birch beer or cider. But there is a delicious alternative, a real sit-down meal in one of the big tents or covered shelters where the men and women of the local churches and granges offer *gute esse,* Pennsylvania Dutch for "good eating." Beginning at eight in the morning you can have a simple farm breakfast of eggs, home-cured bacon and ham, home fries, sausage, scrapple, pancakes, toast, juice, and coffee. Or at lunch or early supper there is a baked ham dinner with potato filling, dried corn, lima beans, fruit salad, rolls and butter, coffee or tea, and a nice selection of pie for dessert. At the nearby Pioneer Grange from Topton, there are ham, sausage, and scrapple platters, with cucumber salad, applesauce, shoofly pie, and ice cream. Or at St. Michael's Lutheran Church tent, you can try chicken corn noodle soup; a pork, sauerkraut, and dumpling platter; hot chicken or sausage sandwiches; Dutch salad; and sweet strip lemon pie.

Everything is served family style, and all the bounty is placed on the table at once, so you know exactly what to save room for. The sheer volume of food provided each day of the festival is enormous. Just one congregation, the Zion United Church of Christ from Windsor Castle, serves 16,000 meals during the eight days of the festival. A typical day's order is for 990 pounds of chicken legs, 480 pounds of breasts, 120 pounds of wings, and 30 pounds of gizzards. All the baking is done on the premises during the night, so the pies and pastry are literally just out of the oven. Even the ice cream is homemade.

Come to the Fair

One of the most appealing things about the festival is the cheerfulness of the participants. Everyone works extraordinarily hard, and in the meal tents, the youngest children, some in plain dark pinafores and bare feet, stack up the dishes or set out the chairs. Older girls wait on table, while the men bake hams and fry chickens and the women bake cakes and pies. The older folk get the sit-down jobs, peeling and cutting carrots and celery, dishing up the apple butter and *schmierkäse* or cottage cheese, the pickled beets and pepper salad. You can peek in and watch the dough for the potpie being made or the yeast dough for tomorrow's bread. Most of the participants are delighted to talk with you and never seem too busy to answer questions—even silly ones.

I talked to Dorothy Kresge, who markets a wide variety of pickles and jams under the label Waswit, which means "what do you want?" She raises her own vegetables and each year plants 30,000 cauliflowers, which are blanched and frozen in the fall to make small batches of chowchow all year long. Her chowchow has fourteen different vegetables, and her list of other products includes apple jelly, a delicious bacon dressing, twelve different relishes, and seven fruit butters. Dorothy Kresge is typical of many Pennsylvania Dutch entrepreneurs. "I started out real small," she says, "and just sold to some friends, and then the business began to grow. One day a man from the Department of Agriculture came around and said I had to start labeling my things. I had to list everything and how much it weighed, and I tell you, it was a terrible chore." The business is much bigger now, but she still comes to Kutztown every year—this is her twenty-fifth festival. "I get enough business here so I never have to advertise," she says, "so as a present to the festival, I sell here at wholesale prices."

The cooks are happy to give out recipes, most of which involve "a pinch of

Come to the Fair

this and a dash of that." When I asked a lady from St. Michael's how to prepare dried corn, she said, "Oh, just soak it overnight and next day cook it up with some brown sugar and butter." The Schwenkfelders, a small sect of only twenty-five hundred in America, are a little more precise and hand out samples of their saffron cake along with clear directions for its preparation.

On the main common of the festival grounds there is a re-creation of an old country kitchen where Mary Reclay and a band of industrious ladies cook the way their ancestors did over an iron stove which burns wood and corn cobs. They prepare a complete country dinner each day for the lucky craftsmen and festival workers, and as they cook, they talk and answer questions and hand out recipes for apple butter and cracker pudding and the like. The apple butter I watched simmering in huge kettles was made with two bushels of apples cooked in seven gallons of cider, with about five pounds of sugar, and some cinnamon, cloves, and sassafras. Mrs. George, the woman in charge, said Winesaps or other tart apples are the best, but Yorks and MacIntosh can also be used.

Also near the common is the bread oven. During the week of the festival, about twenty-five hundred loaves are baked in old-fashioned ovens, fueled with wood. The baker knows precisely when to rake out the coals and when to stoke up with more wood. He never seems to open the oven except at the exact moment when the loaves are properly brown and ready to come out. Ellen Zerbe has been making bread dough at the festival for twenty years, and you can watch her mix up the batches and knead the dough in the small screened shed near the ovens. "We have electric warming cupboards for raising the dough now," she told me, "but before that it was terrible. Every little breeze changed the temperature and we never knew where we were."

Walk a little further on and you'll find the honey lady, Mrs. Brininger, who keeps bees and uses honey for just about everything. "The coolest drink there is on a hot day," she says, "is made by dissolving half a cup of honey in a little hot water. Fill up the rest of the glass with cold water and refrigerate, and you'll never find anything more refreshing." She tells visitors to her booth that we're having a bee shortage because of the pollution and the spraying with insecticides. She also shows interested folk the old-fashioned basket bee hive, the kind where you had to kill the bees to take their honey, then go out and catch another swarm and start all over.

You can meet Jane Waible, who will tell you about maple sugar in Pennsylvania; or talk with Daisy Sechler, the chicken lady, who demonstrates the many uses of the chicken foot as well as what she calls "the chick'n fedder." You can have a thick sandwich with slabs of meat cut from the whole ox roasting on a spit. Or sample the dozens of different sausages, or take a slice of cheese from among the numerous varieties. You can watch old-fashioned cornmeal mush being made, sliced, and fried, and have a tasty sample with molasses poured on it. You can do just about anything, except one, at the Folk Festival, and that is diet.

If for some obscure reason you lose interest in food, or when you are too full to contemplate even a morsel of scrapple or a drop of freshly pressed cider, there is still plenty to see: the quilt exhibition, the balloon ascension, the old-time engines that sputter and spit, the glassblowing and the pewtermaking and the weaving and the pottery and the spinning. And should you be a farsighted person, before you leave, you can gather up a bag of *fastnachts* and a few pretzels to take home in the car in case you should be stranded in a July snowstorm without any provisions.

Come to the Fair

☙ *The Schwenkfelders, a conservative German sect, arrived in Pennsylvania in 1734, bringing with them a style of cooking which included the use of saffron. Schwenkfelder cake is a light yeast breakfast bread, delicious as a dessert or snack and perfect for brunch.*

SCHWENKFELDER CAKE
- 2 medium potatoes, peeled and quartered
- ¼ teaspoon powdered saffron
- 1 package dry yeast
- ¼ teaspoon sugar
- ¾ cup lukewarm milk
- ½ cup melted butter
- 2 eggs, lightly beaten
- ½ cup sugar
- 5 to 6 cups all-purpose flour

TOPPING
- 1 cup all-purpose flour
- 1 teaspoon cinnamon
- 1 cup brown sugar, firmly packed
- ½ cup butter or margarine, chilled and cut into small pieces
- 2 tablespoons very soft butter or margarine

Boil the potatoes until soft and drain, reserving potato water. Mash well and let cool. (If there are lumps in the potatoes, there will be lumps in the bread.) Take ¼ cup of the potato water, bring to a boil and pour over saffron. Let it steep 5 to 10 minutes. Dissolve yeast in ¼ cup lukewarm potato water. Add ¼ teaspoon sugar, stir; let stand in warm place about 5 to 10 minutes or until bubbly and almost double in bulk.

Combine milk, melted butter, eggs, and sugar with 3 cups flour. Add mashed potatoes and yeast mixture. Beat in the saffron water and up to 2 more cups of flour,

Come to the Fair

or enough to make a fairly stiff dough. Turn onto a floured board or pastry cloth and knead, sprinkling with flour as needed, between 5 and 10 minutes, or until the dough is satiny and elastic. Place in greased bowl and turn once to grease entire surface. Let rise in a warm, draft-free place until doubled in bulk, about 1½ hours. Punch down, divide in half and with your hands pat each half into a round about 8 inches in diameter. Place in 2 greased 9 inch layer cake pans or pie tins and let rise in warm, draft-free place until doubled in bulk, about 35 to 45 minutes.

For the topping, combine flour, cinnamon, and sugar. With a pastry blender or your fingers, work the chilled butter into dry ingredients until it is the consistency of very coarse meal. Spread the tops of each cake with the softened butter and sprinkle them evenly with crumb mixture. Bake at 350° for 30 to 35 minutes or until the tops are brown. Remove from pans and cool on a cake rack. Cut when completely cold.

Every Pennsylvania Dutch woman has her own recipe for cracker pudding. The ingredients remain very much the same, but the amounts and what you do with them vary enormously. Here is my version of this classic.

CRACKER PUDDING

- 1 quart milk
- 2 eggs, separated
- ¾ cup sugar
- ¾ cup shredded coconut
- 2 cups plain soda crackers (saltines), coarsely crumbled

Heat milk to just below boiling point; add slightly beaten egg yolks; combine with sugar and coconut. Add cracker crumbs, stir well. Cook until thickened, over very low heat, between 3 and 5 minutes. Cool to room temperature. Beat egg whites until they form soft peaks. Fold carefully into cooled cracker mixture. Refrigerate until serving. Serves 4 to 6.

A Pretty Pickle

When I was about twelve, I spent a glorious summer visiting the Great Lakes Exposition in Cleveland, Ohio. It wasn't as good as a real world's fair, but my friends and I spent long hours on the midway, in the replica of Shakespeare's Globe Theatre watching what I still believe were excellent productions, and wandering through the endless exhibits touting Progress. One of the best was the H. J. Heinz Company's 57 Varieties building. I can't recall anything I actually saw in the exhibit, but I clearly remember the booth where smiling ladies offered free samples—tiny paper cups of ketchup, pickles, and baked beans, and best of all, a small pin in the shape of a pickle. I kept that pickle pin for years. I don't know what ever happened to it, I'm sorry to say. But when I visited the national headquarters of the Heinz Company in Pittsburgh, there on the counter beside the soignée receptionist was a little glass bowl of pickle pins. Nostalgia washed over me, and I was curious enough to ask about their origin. Henry J. Heinz thought up the pins himself and began giving them out at the 1893 Chicago World's Fair. About ninety million have been handed out since then.

    I had hoped to see huge vats of boiling ketchup or rows of assembly-line pickle jars, but I was surprised to learn that the Pittsburgh plant—one of

A Pretty Pickle

thirteen in the United States, to say nothing of the worldwide operation—doesn't produce those items. Pittsburgh makes processed foods such as soups, sauces, and baby foods. Not so in 1869, however, when Heinz and his partner opened a factory to bottle and sell horseradish. All would-be tycoons, take heart. Heinz went bankrupt in 1875, but recovered and went on to new glories which included a rapidly expanding world market for his products and a continuing flow of new products. His factory became a kind of workers' paradise, with creature comforts such as dining rooms, locker rooms, and dressing rooms for employees, the first of their kind in the country. Women could take sewing and cooking classes, and mechanical drawing was available for the men. There were rest and recreation facilities, a nurse and a dentist, a swimming pool, gymnasium, and a roof garden. A full-time manicurist was available to care for the hands of women who worked with food products.

Robert Alberts's biography of Heinz, *The Good Provider,* has wonderful pictures of solemn, ruffle-capped ladies hulling strawberries or packing pickles, relaxed family groups at company picnics, and workers resting in the company roof garden.[1] It was undoubtedly a good place to work. But I also like to think of the kind of transformation Heinz and others like him brought to nineteenth-century American housewives, many of whom were spending untold hours of their lives in kitchen drudgery. The beginning of large-scale commercial canning and the invention of the cheap tin can, which made canned goods accessible to almost everyone, was a true revolution, one which is often overlooked by historians in their search for significant events.

Imagine the life of a farm woman, perhaps from Lancaster County, where the very abundance of the land meant continued bondage—caring for

A Pretty Pickle

a large garden from early spring until frost, butchering, salting, smoking, pickling, preserving, churning. And then one day she could walk into the general store and buy a jar of pickles, a can of beans, a jar of jam. The days of scouring the preserving kettle or standing over the boiling iron pot of tomato ketchup, scorching the face and hands and straining the back, were over, if she wished it to be so. Those who yearn for the wonderful smells and spicy odors of canning days clearly never did much canning. Nostalgia for those days can be easily satisfied with a large pressure canner and a few glass jars with foolproof sealing devices.

When the company began in 1869, it was the first commercial processor to produce foods without artificial preservatives. Using clear glass bottles, rather than the green or amber his competitors favored, Heinz exposed the purity of his products to the full view of the consumer. In 1878 he introduced the first automatic pickle sorter, and in 1893 the company secured the first patent for printed labels. In 1899 there was an electric delivery truck in operation on Broadway, followed in 1904 by the world's first electric advertising sign, which proclaimed 57 good things for the table.

Henry J. Heinz would never recognize his test kitchens these days, but he would undoubtedly approve of Chef Ferdinand Metz who presides over the new product development department. Metz is an active professional chef, participating in the international Culinary Olympics since 1968 and heading the team in 1976. A handsome man with a soft voice and a trace of accent from his German background, Metz expresses himself eloquently, replying to any question thoughtfully and precisely. Before coming to Heinz, he worked at Le Pavillon in New York and as banquet chef at the Plaza Hotel when, he says, it was an exclusive society hotel with many elaborate parties.

A Pretty Pickle

He holds a master's degree in business administration from the University of Pittsburgh. At Heinz he puts all his experience together to direct a large staff in the development of new products from start to finish, which in this case means sending a staff member direct to one of the many Heinz factories to supervise large-scale production.

Heinz had more than 57 products even before the founder came up with the catchy slogan. Now the items change continually as recipes are modified, improved, changed, dropped, or new ones added. The name of the game is testing, according to Metz. "The more testing, the less risk," he explained. "Most products are tested about two years, sometimes by region, sometimes nationally. We have many home economists who test as well as ordinary housewives who try the product in their own kitchens." He smiled. "Chefs aren't a bit of good to us when we're trying a new product. If five out of six chefs say it's good, it means nothing. They aren't the people we are trying to please. But if 80 percent of our testing group says it's too spicy, it's too spicy."

The decision to begin developing a new product can depend on many factors, he told me. "Sometimes the idea will be generated from within our own staff," he said, "and a lot depends on the timing. A recipe might turn up again years after it was first discussed and discarded because we didn't think the market was ready for it then. The biggest source for a new product, however, is the market place—market research. When a need is clearly identified, then we are ready to begin."

He pulled an unlabeled jar from the shelf behind his desk. "We've been testing a white sauce for a long time now," he said. "We found out that many women don't like to make white sauce. It lumps, it's an extra step in

A Pretty Pickle

cooking they don't like to bother with. But it's a very versatile sauce when a cook really understands its potential. So we have to educate the consumer as part of our job and induce her to try it." He said that the sauce was in the final stages of testing and would be on the market in limited areas first, along with a brown sauce, an Italian-style sauce, and a cheese sauce.

The kitchens where Metz and his staff of twenty technicians and chefs work look more like laboratories, with computerized scales, large glass jars of potato starch and salt, bottles of oils extracted from various spices. Adjoining the kitchen area is a miniature food production factory, with small-scale food processors, steamers, cookers, and a bewildering array of pipes, gauges, and conveyor belts. "This allows us to observe the changes which take place between the kitchen and the factory," Metz explained. 'A lot of things can happen when you change a recipe, say from twenty pounds in the kitchen to seven thousand pounds in the factory. We have to know what those changes are." I asked him about the need for technical knowledge, and he laughed. "A chef here has to be a mechanic as well as a chef and an engineer," he said. "Most of us have to learn it on the job, but that will change." He introduced me to John DiShetler, a chef just returned from several weeks in one of the Heinz factories, where he was teaching the workers how to make a new product. "The chef has to go right into the factory, know how the machinery works to make sure the final product will be uniform in quality."

Metz is active in a chef's training program he believes will soon be the equal of the famous Culinary Institute of America, long the elder statesman of American schools. Since the program is allied with the Community College of Allegheny County, future chefs get practical training in some of western Pennsylvania's finest hotels and restaurants along with their class work at the

A Pretty Pickle

college. Metz and other practicing chefs encourage young graduates to move around, try different kinds of jobs. "Until you try it out," Metz says, "you'll never know whether you want to work in a restaurant and someday maybe own your own, or work in an institution, such as a hospital or a college. Or maybe even end up in a test kitchen like this one."

As I left the Heinz headquarters I was caught up in the blend of the old and the new. The buildings themselves are an unusual combination of the original red brick factory structures and contemporary cubes of glass and steel. The test kitchens are filled with the latest gadgets, and Metz and his staff are concerned about the impact of the microwave oven on the food industry. But as I left the building, I was reassured by that glass bowl of little pickle pins, for me a real link with the past.

A Pretty Pickle

Heinz and other commercial companies make excellent pickles, but sometimes it is simply more fun to make your own, especially if you have a garden. We are fond of dilled green tomatoes, the kind you can buy in good delicatessens but are difficult to find in the supermarket. Green tomatoes are always available at farmers' markets in the autumn if you don't grow your own.

DILLED GREEN TOMATOES
2   quarts or more small green tomatoes, washed (large ones can be used by cutting into halves or quarters, but they are not as crisp)
garlic cloves
fresh dill, heads and feathery stems
2   cups water
2   cups white vinegar
¼   cup coarse salt

Wash glass canning jars in hot soapy water and rinse. I find that a pint jar is the most convenient size for my family, but you may use half-pint or even quart jars if you prefer. Make sure the jars have two-piece lids, and wash these as well. In the bottom of each jar place 1 large or 2 small garlic cloves and a head of dill; pack jars tightly with tomatoes, trying to avoid large air spaces. Add the feathery dill on top.

    Make a brine by heating water, vinegar, and salt to the boiling point. Ladle into each jar, filling to just below the rim. Wipe jar rim; seal with lids. Place jars on a rack in boiling water to cover; process 5 minutes; remove and check seal according to manufacturer's directions. Let cool and store. Ready to eat in about 2 weeks. They are better when cold. Makes about 2 quarts.

A Pretty Pickle

This slightly offbeat relish is not only good as a pickle relish with hot dogs and hamburgers, it also makes an excellent accompaniment for roasts. If you have a food processor or blender to take care of the chopping chore, it couldn't be simpler.

RED PEPPER RELISH
- 4 small onions
- 15 large red peppers (sweet, not hot)
- 3 cups sugar
- 2 tablespoons coarse salt
- 2 cups cider vinegar

Grind or chop onions and peppers coarsely. Add remaining ingredients and simmer until very thick, about 1 hour. Ladle into pint jars which have been thoroughly washed, including lids. Fill to within ½ inch of top, wipe rim and seal with two-part lid. Process in boiling water 7 minutes. Remove from water and cool on rack or towels. Check seals before storing. Wait 2 weeks before using. Makes 3 to 4 pints.

Note: For a delightful holiday relish, try using 10 red and 5 green peppers.

Early American Travelers

When modern Americans speed over superhighways, the last thing on their minds is the possible difficulty of finding the next meal. Howard Johnson's and McDonald's vie with diners and donut shops, fried chicken or taco stands, and pizza parlors. A truly fine meal may be hard to find, but starvation is virtually impossible in the era of fast food.

This was not so, of course, in the early days of our republic. The ordinary hazards of travel in the eighteenth and nineteenth centuries included the possibility of hunger, discomfort, and even starvation. The traveler had three choices. He could carry a quantity of staples with him on horseback or in his wagon, to be supplemented with whatever wild game he could find; he could depend on the hospitality of farmers and settlers he found along the road; or he could hope to find a reasonably clean tavern or inn where he could spend the night and obtain hot food and good drink.

Before the first roads were built, travel was usually on horseback, and after a long day in the saddle, the weary, hungry traveler accepted whatever food and shelter was available. The American tradition of hospitality stems from these early days when housewives were used to unexpected guests. The

Early American Travelers

food might be the family's simplest rations—corn pone, perhaps, with salt-pork gravy and boiled turnips—but it was offered freely. The traveler brought a change in the harsh routine of the frontier, news of the east, perhaps even gossip of some mutual friend or relative back home.

By 1794, the Philadelphia and Lancaster Turnpike had been completed, and tolls were collected from travelers to provide for maintenance. Soon afterward, more roads were built linking Lancaster with York, Harrisburg, and Pittsburgh. The National Pike, now U.S. Route 40, was begun in 1811, eventually linking Baltimore with Cumberland, Wheeling, Indianapolis, and Vandalia, Illinois. As traffic increased, inns and taverns began to spring up to accommodate the new flow of travelers.

Inns developed along social lines. The most primitive were the drovers' inns, which offered basic accommodations and enclosed lots for livestock. Slightly better were the wagoners' inns, where men slept on the floor on bags of grain. The stagecoach travelers were at the top of the social ladder; their inns were usually the most comfortable and offered the most in the way of amenities. But the old inn that appears so quaint to us today was probably, when first built, filthy, dark, and drafty, serving almost inedible meals. In 1783, Johann David Schoepf, a doctor who had come to America to minister to mercenary troops, traveled from Bedford to Pittsburgh in a two-wheeled chaise. At their first stop there was no food available, so the travelers were obliged to continue several miles further to the cabin of a blacksmith who sometimes kept an inn. Here too there was no food. Finally, at ten o'clock, when the travelers had thought themselves lost in the dark, swampy roads, a farmer took them in, offering bread, butter, and milk, and straw for a couch. The following night was spent in the home of a doctor who was out, looking

Early American Travelers

for pigs gone astray in the woods. "His wife, a good little old woman, and energetic, gave our horses oats for their refreshment and set before us mountain-tea and maple sugar, which as well as her bacon, whiskey, and cakes were the products of her own land and industry." He continued, "Along this road and others like it in America, one must not be deceived by the bare name of taverns. The people keep taverns if they have anything over and above what they need, if not, the traveller must look out for himself."[1]

By 1796, a traveler could go by stagecoach from Philadelphia to Shippensberg, and by 1804 a coach was crossing the Alleghenies to Pittsburgh twice a week. The Philadelphia-Pittsburgh trip, which took six or seven days, cost twenty dollars, including twenty pounds of baggage. Teams of fresh horses waited at the major inns, and the passengers were required to keep to an uncomfortable schedule. Most journeys began at three in the morning, with tavern stops some hours later for breakfast and again for dinner. The roads were crude, and it is not difficult to picture the extreme discomfort of the passengers in a swaying, jouncing, bumping vehicle, arriving after a long and miserable journey at an inn where, if they were lucky, they might find warmth and good food.

The stagecoach lines had lively names—the Pioneer Fast Stage, the June Bug Line, the Pilot Stage, or the Good Intent Stage Line. Taverns frequently served only one line, with the unfortunate result that they would turn away the weary passengers from a competing line.

In the late 1820s Mrs. Frances Trollope, in the course of her travels throughout America, went by stage from Wheeling to Washington, Pennsylvania, and over the Alleghenies to Baltimore. Although not known for her praise of America, she wrote enthusiastically about one evening's meal along the National Pike. After describing the scenic beauty of the Laurel Mountains, she wrote that they had dined at the highest spot on the road, 2846 feet above sea level, and been served wild turkey and mountain venison, with "extremely fine" vegetables. The travelers were told that "wild strawberries were profusely abundant and very fine," while the cows produced superior milk and the climate was "the most delicious in the world."[2]

By the 1830s, things had improved considerably for the stagecoach traveler. Although rooms were still shared and meals served family style, the quality of the food improved as well as the quantity. Philip Jordan in his book *The National Road* wrote that even the poorest mountain house was capable of providing coffee and hot biscuits, chicken, bacon and eggs, corn bread and honey. Western Pennsylvania travelers talked of the ample breakfasts where they rested, platters stacked with venison steaks, fried chicken and ham, preserved cherries and molasses. In winter there were always buckwheat cakes and maple syrup made from the landlord's own maple trees.[3]

Before the Revolution, travelers were customarily charged between seventy-five cents and one dollar per day for lodging, three meals, and beer. Later, meals were about seventy-five cents, breakfast about fifty cents.

Some of the original stagecoach inns are still standing, especially along the old National Pike. Penn Alps, a pleasant restaurant in Grantsville, Maryland, was once the site of such a rest stop. Although the inn has been substantially rebuilt, the huge stone fireplace still remains. Just a few hundred feet further west is the Casselman Hotel, built in 1824, still serving good Pennsylvania Dutch food and offering simple overnight accommodations. Near the Fort Necessity battleground is the Mount Washington Tavern, now a museum owned by the National Park Service. And the Century Inn, in Sce-

Early American Travelers

nery Hill near Washington, Pennsylvania, is a charming hostel which has been operated as an inn continuously since 1794.

Stagecoach was not the only method of travel in Pennsylvania, of course. A network of canals connected Philadelphia to various parts of the state. Horses or mules walked beside the canals along a towpath, pulling the boats. The mountains proved a formidable obstacle to canal transport until the Allegheny Portage Railroad was built, which hauled canalboats over the mountains on rail cars. In many ways, the trip by canal was more comfortable than by stagecoach. But a detailed description of his accommodations aboard a boat on the Pennsylvania Main Line Canal written by Charles Dickens in 1842 raises some doubt. The cabins were tiny and low, Dickens recalled, and in rainy or cold weather, impossibly crowded. "At about six o'clock all the small tables were put together to form one long table, and everybody sat down to tea, coffee, bread, butter, salmon, shad, liver, steak, potatoes, pickles, ham, chops, black pudding and sausage."

Sleeping arrangements were primitive, Dickens wrote, consisting of a series of little shelves which were let down into the main cabin. A red curtain divided the gentlemen from the ladies, and washing facilities consisted of dirty canal water poured into a basin, a towel, and "hanging up before a little looking-glass in the bar, in the immediate vicinity of the bread and cheese and biscuits, were a public comb and hair brush." Then, at eight o'clock, the shelves were taken down, the tables put up, and everybody sat down once again to "tea, coffee, bread, butter, salmon, shad, liver, steak, potatoes, ham, chops, black pudding and sausages." Some travelers liked everything on their plate at once, Dickens tells us, but "as each gentleman got through his own personal amount of tea, coffee, bread, butter, salmon, shad, liver, steak, po-

Early American Travelers

tatoes, pickles, ham, chops, black pudding and sausages, he rose up and walked off." Dinner, breakfast, tea, and supper were all identical.[4]

Conditions of travel have changed enormously since these travelers described their experiences. But despite the modern emphasis on the ease and pleasures of travel, Americans sometimes still eat as if a stagecoach were waiting impatiently at the door. Mrs. Basil Hall, a British gentlewoman, wrote in 1828:

> I do not think I have mentioned one very striking peculiarity of the Americans, which is, I believe, universal, the extreme quickness with which they eat. Mr. Webb told us that he has frequently seen 50 people sit down to dinner in a hotel and in a quarter of an hour every one of them had left the room. They think nothing of lifting a spoon from the potatoes and diving straightaway into the pudding. . . . Indeed, an American breakfast or dinner never fails to remind me of the directions given of old for the eating of the Passover . . . "With your loins girded, your shoes on your feet, and your staff in your hand, and ye shall eat it in haste."[5]

Early American Travelers

⁕ *Whether the early American traveler arrived by stagecoach, canal boat, on horseback or on foot, the chances are that his innkeeper would serve him buckwheat cakes for breakfast. The ubiquitous cake was filling as well as pleasing to the palate, served with melted butter and maple syrup or honey. Many frontier housewives set their batter to rise the night before, and there are buckwheat connoisseurs who swear by this method. I prefer a simpler version which I find equally delicious and considerably easier.*

BUCKWHEAT PANCAKES

- 2 eggs
- 1 teaspoon salt
- 4 tablespoons sugar
- 1 cup buttermilk
- 1½ cups buckwheat flour
- ½ cup cornmeal
- 6 tablespoons melted butter or margarine
- ¼ teaspoon baking powder
- ¾ teaspoon baking soda

Mix eggs, salt, and sugar; stir in buttermilk, flour, and cornmeal. Add butter and mix well. Add baking powder and baking soda. Bake on hot, lightly greased griddle. Thickness can be adjusted by adding more buckwheat flour for a thicker cake, more buttermilk for a thinner one. Makes about 16 five-inch pancakes. Extras can be frozen and reheated in the toaster.

Early American Travelers

Hot biscuits were usually on the table for early travelers, and they still make a hit with family and friends at any meal. Biscuit mix is very convenient, but making your own is not only less expensive but ever so much better tasting. This mix produces fluffy biscuits as well as excellent pancakes and waffles.

BEST BISCUIT MIX
- 6   cups self-rising flour
- 1   teaspoon baking powder
- 1   tablespoon sugar
- 2   cups solid vegetable shortening

Combine all ingredients and mix with pastry blender until the mixture resembles coarse corn meal. Store in canister in refrigerator. Use small amounts as needed. To make biscuits, start with 1 cup, moisten with milk (begin with ¼ cup, add more if needed). Pat dough out about ¾ inch thick, cut with biscuit cutter. Place on greased cookie sheet and bake at 450° for 12 minutes.

The Mysterious Middle East

No one seems to know exactly why Middle Eastern food is so popular in Pittsburgh. There are so few permanent Syrian and Lebanese residents that they appear in the census among the undifferentiated "others." But in the East End alone there are at least eight restaurants serving Middle Eastern cuisine, with others spread throughout the city. I say at least eight because each time I count, someone tells me another new one has opened, serving a slightly different version of *baba ganooj,* that spicy eggplant dip, made to be scooped up into the pocket of a round of the light and airy *pita* bread that is a staple in all of the restaurants. There are also several lively church festivals that offer authentic Middle Eastern specialties.

If you attempt to define the Middle East, you are probably setting the stage for an argument. Historians will discuss one combination of countries, geographers another, politicians still another. But cooks know that, however you draw the political boundaries, the food of the so-called Middle East is distinctive, and boundaries become important only as they reflect attitudes toward the foods native to these areas. There are cultures within cultures, as in the polyglot population of modern Israel; there are subcultures in Turkey and Africa defined by their cuisine. But there are some characteristics common to all, and they remain important whether one is eating shish kebab in the Istanbul Hilton or at a church fair in Oakland, Pennsylvania.

A formal cuisine—a traditional means of preparing special foods—grows up for very good and basic reasons, the most important being availability. No Arab cook will become famous for venison stew or chocolate ice cream. But generations ago, wild sheep were domesticated in the Middle East, and lamb dominates the menus of every household. There is beef, to be sure, but the climate and the lack of adequate pasture relegates it far below lamb in consumption. And there is eggplant, the ubiquitous purple vegetable that most Americans see only when it is french fried in soggy strips. Mashed with onions and garlic, roasted with tomatoes and pine nuts, stuffed with ground lamb and tomatoes, or dressed with lemon juice, yogurt, and sesame oil, it takes on a new life in each dish. There is rice, made into delicate pilafs, cooked in chicken broth, garnished with lamb and nuts. And there is plenty of wheat, sometimes made into bulgur by boiling and drying it, bringing out the nutty flavor of the grain. There are lentils, fava beans, and chick-peas, known as *garbanzos* in the southwestern United States. And there is pastry made of tissue-thin sheets of dough, layered with ground nuts, and slathered in honey syrup. Call it *baklava* or *bakclaw* or what you will, it is sinfully rich and delicious and a perfect ending for a Middle Eastern meal.

I first was introduced to shish kebab and pilaf in Providence, Rhode Island, where a good friend was a member of an Armenian community. My enthusiasm increased watching my one-time landlady, Mrs. Nalbandian, who every Saturday made *baklava* from scratch. Not for her the frozen sheets of *phyllo* dough, referred to in modern recipes for pastry or spinach pies. She

The Mysterious Middle East

had a huge round oak table in her kitchen on which she mixed and rolled the dough, the sheets getting larger and thinner and more elastic, hanging over the table edge, never tearing or breaking until she chose just the right moment to cut them to size. The first time I ever saw this miracle, I incurred her wrath by walking into the kitchen unannounced, creating a draft. "Shut the door!" she screamed at me, she who was always polite and friendly. I scrambled to slam it, creating more draft, and got screamed at again for my trouble. When she had calmed down, she explained that *phyllo* dough is very temperamental. It has to be kept at just the right temperature or you can ruin the whole batch. From then on, I spent many a Saturday morning watching her, peeking around the edge of the door and sliding carefully in so as not to disturb the creation of the masterpiece. For masterpiece it was, when finished. The pans of little diamond-shaped pastries were golden brown and crisp, the ground pistachio nuts bulging from beneath the dozens of thin layers, the honey syrup dripping artistically down the sides. She set a standard for me which has never been equaled. No *baklava* ever tastes quite as good as Mrs. Nalbandian's, nor I hope, ever will.

I thought about Mrs. Nalbandian one August as I watched the men and women of St. George's Orthodox Church in Oakland prepare for their annual Middle Eastern fair and the sit-down dinner that preceded it. Cooking for 350 hungry guests is not exactly my idea of how to spend a hot August afternoon, but the committee at work in the kitchen seemed to be having a very good time. There were as many men as women at work, threading lean pieces of lamb on skewers, cutting and washing fresh green beans, sectioning rounds of *pita* bread so the dips could be more easily scooped into the mouth. Roujina Ilyas, chairman of the event, and her helper, dark-haired,

The Mysterious Middle East

enthusiastic Elaine Moses, showed me the pots of beans cooking with lamb meat, the freezers full of stuffed grape leaves, the committee at work preparing the hors d'oeuvres tray. There would be pickled turnips, pink with vinegar and spices; chunks of white *feta,* the mild goat's milk cheese that goes so well with the strong black olives piled next to it. There were bowls of *hummus,* a spicy dip of garlic, sesame oil, lemon juice, and chick-peas, and of *baba ganooj,* the eggplant dip. Outside I watched the preparations for roasting the skewered lamb. Rows of galvanized iron troughs were filled with charcoal and covered with grills. Elaine told me that the committee asked the parishioners to save their hot water tanks when they were replaced. They were cut in half lengthwise and made fine charcoal pits.

The fair itself is a virtuoso performance. Hundreds of hungry Pittsburghers pour into the church basement at lunch and dinner, forming long, good-natured lines. The rewards are great, for everything is freshly made, and from scratch. No canned grape leaves here for the *dolmas.* There is a committee created just to pick fresh, tender grape leaves, preserve them in brine, then stuff them by hand with the chopped lamb filling. The *pita* bread is freshly baked, hundreds of dozens of round loaves, stacked high, disappearing magically as the hungry visitors continue to come. There are hot Syrian doughnuts, delicate balls of sweet dough deep-fried on the spot to a golden brown, lightly dusted with powdered sugar, and offered to the waiting customer, who moves slowly through the culinary delights, eyes glazed, hoping he can possibly manage another helping of *hummus* before he makes his way back to the office to doze quietly over his desk for the rest of the afternoon.

The dinner, prior to the fair, is noisy and gay. The men of the parish

The Mysterious Middle East

serve as waiters, and they move quickly. The shish kebab and pilaf is piping hot when it arrives on your table, the bread fresh, the hors d'oeuvres tray filled, refilled, and filled again, if you wish. You may arrive as a stranger, but you will soon make friends, since introductions are quickly made around the large tables and conversation is easy. The newcomer is urged to eat more, try a little of this, a bit of that. Wine glasses are filled and refilled, hands clap in rhythm to the music of drums and *ude,* that plaintive stringed instrument that calls up images of camels and sheiks. And the belly dancer arrives, supple and lovely, teasing and flirting with the men while their women watch and laugh at their discomfiture.

There is also a Greek festival in Pittsburgh, every spring and fall at St. Nicholas Orthodox Church in Oakland, where you can eat your fill of *pastitsio,* creamy macaroni and ground beef; *tiropetes,* a mixture of *feta* and other cheeses and eggs, baked between crisp layers of *phyllo;* fish *plaki,* fish baked with tomatoes and onions; and *galatoboureko,* custard baked in pastry; or rich Greek butter cookies topped with powdered sugar. At night, it is easy to imagine yourself in a Greek tavern as there is bouzouki music and the Greek dancers invite you to join them as they circle the room.

Preparations for this fair, or *glendi* as it is called, also begin months earlier, with members of the cathedral and of Philoptohos, the women's auxiliary, using up three tons of ground beef, twenty gallons of *feta,* and six hundred pounds of lamb, to name but a few of the ingredients. State stores are soon cleaned out of Greek wine by the *glendi* planners so that visitors can buy ouzo and other interesting but unidentified wines. As the long line of eager eaters snakes its way down the stairs and into the bright and modern community center, vendors pass by offering glasses of wine to ease the pain of waiting. And once inside, it's worth the wait. The spicy odors of *moussaka* and *spanakopeta,* the rich, buttery smell of the honey puffs called *loukoumades,* and the honey-drenched dark walnut cake, *karithopeta,* blend with music and laughter while visitors are greeted with the Greek version of *bon appétit,* "Kali orexi!"

The Mysterious Middle East

The staple of any Middle Eastern meal is pilaf. It is very easy to make, so easy that it should be taken beyond the bounds of shish kebab and served on other occasions when rice is called for. I make it to serve with almost any chicken dish and it makes an excellent accompaniment to beef and pork.

PILAF
- 1 cup rice
- ½ cup pine nuts
- 2½ cups chicken or beef stock, or add bouillon cubes to water
- 2 tablespoons vegetable oil

Heat oil in large heavy skillet; add raw rice and pine nuts, stirring constantly, taking care not to burn them. Meanwhile have water or stock boiling. When nuts are brown and rice is beginning to look puffy, transfer to boiling stock. Cover; reduce heat to low. Cook 15 minutes and check for tenderness. Serves 4.

The Mysterious Middle East

There are as many different recipes for pita as there are oil wells in Iran. You are admonished to roll them thin or thick or to pat instead of roll; let them rise once, twice, three times; bake them on the oven floor, on tiles, on cookie sheets; let them cool in paper bags or on racks. After several minor failures and one gigantic disaster when not one single pita puffed up, I have devised my own method which I modestly consider foolproof. I personally believe whatever mystique is involved lies in rolling the dough as thin as possible. Even though these are more time-consuming than most bread doughs, you will find them fun to make and delicious to eat.

PENNSYLVANIA PITA

- 1 cup lukewarm water
- 1 pakage dry yeast
- 1 teaspoon sugar
- 3 cups all-purpose flour
- 1 teaspoon salt
- 2 teaspoons sugar
- 1 tablespoon olive oil or salad oil
- 1 or 2 tablespoons water

Mix yeast with sugar and water and stir until dissolved; set aside for about 5 minutes or until it starts to bubble and increase in size. Meanwhile, mix together flour, salt, and sugar. Add yeast mixture and stir well. Add oil; add water, if needed to make a manageable dough. Turn out onto floured board or pastry cloth and knead until smooth and no longer sticky, about 8 minutes. Place in greased bowl, roll around until dough is coated lightly with oil; cover and place in warm spot until doubled in bulk, about 1½ hours. Punch down, mound up again, cover and let stay in warm place again until doubled, about 45 minutes.

Pat dough into long roll, the size of a fat salami. Divide into 12 equal pieces. Make each piece into a fat round ball, then flatten it on the pastry cloth and roll as thin as possible, certainly no more than ⅛ inch. Place each round on an ungreased cookie sheet. If you don't have enough sheets to take care of all 12 pita, cut pieces of heavy foil into squares and place one round on each.

Preheat oven to 500°. Bake as many pita at one time as your oven will hold, but only on the lowest rack. Check after 5 minutes. Pita should be light brown and slightly puffed. Remove and cool on wire racks. If they collapse, don't worry, the pockets will remain inside. Makes 12 pita rounds.

Cloistered in Ephrata

We have reason to be grateful to William Penn for many things, not the least of which was his determination to make Pennsylvania a haven for all religions and sects. One of the many groups that flourished in this state in the eighteenth century was a community of pietists who settled in Ephrata, near Lancaster, in 1732. Under the leadership of Johann Conrad Beissel, a German baker, the members of Ephrata Cloister sought to serve God through lives of simplicity, piety, and austerity, denying themselves all creature comforts. They slept on wooden benches, wore medieval robes of white, worked extraordinarily hard at their simple occupations, spent long hours in prayer and worship, and were sustained by the most meager of diets, the mainstay of which appears to have been bread.

Many original cloister buildings still stand, although they have been extensively restored, and a visit to the site effectively reveals just how these interesting people lived and worked. The structures they built, finished before 1749, were of log and stone, probably like the ones many of them remembered from their German homeland. They are remarkable examples of European medieval architecture in America, modified by frontier conditions but

Cloistered in Ephrata

nonetheless quite unlike the rough log cabins we know their neighbors were building at the same time.

    The grounds are green and beautifully kept. Even though a busy highway is close at hand, the twentieth century seems very remote as you wander through the meeting house, with its high wooden pews and simple pulpit. The starkly simple kitchen in the sisters' house contains only the most basic equipment—a kettle or two, a table and some chairs, a crock, some dried herbs hanging over the fireplace. There are three floors in the sisters' house, each arranged on the same plan: a central kitchen, joined to a common workroom, sleeping cells with wooden benches and wooden block pillows. Only one meager meal a day was prepared in the kitchen. Other buildings housed the main occupations of the brothers and sisters—a print shop, a chandlery, a weave shed, a schoolhouse. There were once ample orchards of apple, peach, and cherry trees and extensive farmlands; only the substantial herb and vegetable gardens remain. Because of their simple tastes and lifestyle, the brotherhood was totally self-sufficient, growing grain, baking bread, cultivating vegetables and fruits, raising cows for milk and cheese, sheep for wool and an occasional meat dish.

    Celibacy was encouraged, although marriage was not forbidden, and married householders lived apart, with a few more creature comforts than the celibate brethren. Since austerity was a way of life, the buildings reflected this attitude—narrow halls to remind one of the straight and narrow path, low doorways to induce humility, lack of adornment to emphasize spiritual over material beauty, and a diet which all but shouted out concern for self-denial.

    The community was always hospitable to travelers, and we are fortunate to have a series of accounts from contemporaries who visited Ephrata. In

Cloistered in Ephrata

1753, for example, Israel Acrelius, a Swedish Lutheran church official, visited and wrote:

> The time came for the brethren to go to their evening meal, and thereupon each one came out of his room immediately, and all went one after another up a pair of stairs into the refectory. This was large enough for 100 persons, with 2 long tables; but now they were mostly seated at 1 table, as the number of the brethren at that time was scarcely 20. Around the hall in the passages were small cases, each large enough to hold a Bible, for which indeed they were intended, and each had a small white linen curtain before it. The cloth was spread on the table, the food placed in deep stone dishes. The courses were pearled barley boiled in milk, with bread broken into it; another course was pumpkin mush, with slices of soft-crusted bread on a plate. Between these was butter, but only for me, as the brethren for themselves had a kind of cheese-curds on platters all around the table. Each one took his place, and I was shown to mine, where the greater part of the brethren were behind my back. After they had sat for some time with downcast eyes, one of the brethren at the table read a passage from the Bible, after which they sat still for some moments; then each one of them took out of his pocket a bag in which there was a wooden spoon and a knife. The spoon and knife given to me were taken out of a drawer under the table. We all ate with a good appetite, first of the barley, then of the pumpkin mush, and finally, of the butter, in which this economy was observed—that when, at the finishing of a dish, one could no longer use the spoon, the remainder was taken up with a piece of bread. There was no other use for a knife than to take the butter and cut the bread; neither was any plate needed, as in fact, none was there. . . . At the close, each one licked his knife and spoon, dried them with a cloth which they had in the

> same bag, and then the knife and spoon were restored to their former place. During the meal not a word was spoken; at its close another chapter was read out of the Bible.[1]

Despite the importance the community attached to their austere way of life, they clearly were seeking reassurance. Acrelius' account of his visit continues:

> After the meal Müller and Eleazar remained with me in the refectory, and then Eleazar asked me what I thought of their arrangements? If I knew what I had eaten? And how long I thought I could live upon such a diet? We agreed that nature is satisfied with a small quantity of food; that both moderation in eating and drinking, and food suitable to the human body, preserves from sickness, makes the body active and the mind cheerful; if that all which might properly be called superfluous in meat and drink and clothing should be used for the suffering, there would be no need of so many hospitals in the old countries, and Christianity would have a very different aspect from that which it now presents. Eleazar said that the English, who could not live without flesh at every meal, wonder at our style of meals; but the German taste is different, many peasants in Germany do not taste flesh 5 times a year. I asked if they regarded the eating of flesh as sinful? Müller answered, "Nay, but the brethren do not incline to the eating of flesh. Our food is usually vegetables, such as cabbage, roots, greens, also milk, butter, cheese and good bread always. At the love feasts, the provision may be somewhat better than usual. We forbid none among us who desire it to eat meat."[2]

The love feasts were religious fellowship meals, a gathering of both sisters and brothers by invitation only, although sometimes the entire commu-

Cloistered in Ephrata

nity participated. There was prayer and worship, symbolic washing of feet, and a meal in which lamb or mutton stew was the chief item.

For all their austerity, the brotherhood excelled in the art of choral singing. This was by no means undertaken for pleasure, since the avowed purpose of the singing schools established for the members of the order was to glorify God and elevate the human soul. In order to do this, Beissel required his singers to deny themselves even more earthly pleasures than the ordinary members of the brotherhood, laying down dietary rules he felt would improve the voice physically as well as spiritually. He demanded that the wants of the body be restrained in order that "the voice become angelic, heavenly, pure and clear, and not become strong and harsh, by a coarseness of the food and consequently prove valueless. But to gain the right tone, so that no unseemingly harsh screeching and croaking be heard in place of the proper melody." Meat was frowned upon, along with other foods which, he mentioned in passing, "we take with great injustice from the animals." These include milk, which "causes heaviness and uneasiness; *cheese* makes one fiery and hot brained, and causes longing after forbidden things; *butter* makes one lazy and stolid, and at the same time satiates so much that one desires neither to sing or pray; *eggs* awaken various and extraordinary desires; *honey* causes light eyes and a cheerful spirit, but no clear voice. Of bread and cooked dishes this is to remark: That for quickening the spirit and natural cheerfulness, nothing is better than wheat and then buckwheat, which although externally different, has the same virtues in its uses, no matter whether used in bread or cooked dishes."

Nothing was more useful, he went on, than the plain potato, but beans satiate and cause unclean desires. As to drink, he wrote, "there is nought that hath greater righteousness than the innocent clear water just as it comes from the well, or is made into a soup to which a little bread is added." He concludes by disavowing any responsibility for "unmannerly paunch stuffing" and exhorts his singers to enter into the spiritual struggle "lawfully and regularly, with no concern for any disorderly or uncontrollable person."[3]

It is not documented whether Beissel's fondness for bread was due to his own skill as a baker, but the bread baked by the brethren, probably rye, was apparently very good indeed. An early governor of Pennsylvania stopped by in 1744 and liked it so much that he asked for extra loaves to take with him on his way to a conference in Lancaster. Many townspeople went out of their way to bring their grain to the cloister's gristmill, one of several commercial enterprises the brethren operated. There was a separate bakery building where dough was mixed in large wooden doughtrays for raising, then shaped in rye straw baskets and left for a second raising. Large baking ovens could be filled with loaves, and the finished bread was stored in large hampers until it was distributed. Adjoining the bakery was a grain storage room, looking like a rough stone jail, with bars across the windows to keep out the animals.

As I walked through the buildings, peered into the bake ovens, and admired the herbs, I found myself thinking about the brothers and sisters as individuals. Weren't they ever hungry? Did they decide to have a love feast because they simply couldn't go another day without the taste of meat? Did any of the women ever decide to go a little crazy and bake a cake or pie, or whip the cream and eggs together for a rich dessert? Their piety and self-denial is a model for us all, but I have a recurring image of one of the sisters, getting up from her hard wooden bench in the middle of the night, and tiptoeing down to the kitchen for a midnight taste of honey.

Cloistered in Ephrata

It is probable that the famous Ephrata bread was a rye loaf. My own favorite rye bread is actually a pumpernickel, a chewy, dense bread that makes superb sandwiches. The members of the brotherhood probably did not have molasses, an important ingredient in this recipe, but rather than have you miss out on this excellent bread, I have chosen to take poetic license and include it here. It just might make you famous.

PUMPERNICKEL BREAD

- 1½ cups lukewarm water
- ½ cup dark molasses
- 4 teaspoons salt
- 2 tablespoons caraway seed
- 2 tablespoons soft shortening
- 3 packages dry yeast
- 2 cups coarse rye meal or 2¾ cups rye flour
- 3½ – 4 cups white flour

Mix together water, molasses, salt, caraway, and shortening. Sprinkle dry yeast on top of mixture and stir until dissolved. Mix in flours gradually, first with a spoon, then by hand or dough hook of electric mixer, until you have a stiff dough. Turn onto lightly floured board or pastry cloth and knead until smooth. Round up, place in greased bowl, and turn to coat all sides. Cover with damp cloth and let rise in warm place until doubled in bulk, about 1½ to 2 hours. Punch down and divide in two parts. Round up each half into a smooth ball and place in opposite corners of a baking sheet lightly sprinkled with corn meal. Cover with damp cloth and let rise until light, about 30 to 45 minutes. Brush tops of loaves with cold water. Bake at 450° for 10 minutes, then reduce heat to 350° and bake about 30 minutes longer. Cool on rack. Do not slice until completely cold.

Cloistered in Ephrata

🌀 *Since the brothers had rye flour, one wonders if they ever varied their somewhat monotonous diet with other forms of rye products. Many nineteenth-century cookbooks include recipes for rye cakes, calling them flannel cakes, Indian rye pancakes, or rye flapjacks. In her handwritten cookbook, Mrs. Boggs of Pittsburgh, (see pages 13–15 above) notes the following rye cakes: "1 quart cold milk, four eggs and a little salt stirr stiff flannel cakes, with rye flour—let them stand they will be light without yeast—in a few minutes." This recipe makes a very heavy pancake, so unless you are prepared to spend an uncomfortable morning after breakfast, I recommend a few changes. Miss Leslie suggests using part Indian meal and part rye, in whatever proportions you like, and this indeed makes a lighter, more palatable cake. The following recipe is my version of rye cakes, incorporating everybody's advice, including my own.*

RYE PANCAKES

- 1 cup rye flour
- 1 cup corn meal
- 1 teaspoon salt
- 1½ teaspoons baking powder
- 1¼ – 1½ cups milk
- 2 eggs, beaten
- 2 tablespoons butter or margarine, melted

Combine flour, corn meal, salt, and baking powder. Add 1 cup milk, eggs, and melted butter. If the batter is not thin enough to suit you, add more milk. Bake on medium hot griddle until bubbles form on top; turn and cook briefly until done. Serve with maple syrup or powdered sugar and jam. Makes 8 to 10 eight-inch cakes. The pancakes are, I believe, better when the batter is quite thin.

Toiling in the Nutrition Wasteland

Observers from other planets might well report back to their leaders that Americans eat only pizza, cheeseburgers, and sugar-frosted cereals. Even a casual survey of fast-food establishments and the shelves of supermarkets would result in the overwhelming impression that technology is carrying the day when it comes to our diet. Yet the constant yammering about cholesterol and saturated fats may be making some slight impression on us. A study by the Center for Science in the Public Interest tells us that although we continue to feed our sweet tooth and eat large amounts of red meat, we are listening, at least with one ear, to some of the experts' warnings.

The survey covers the years between 1910 and 1976, and in that period we reduced our consumption of butter by 76 percent and increased that of margarine by 68 percent. We have also cut back on other high cholesterol foods such as heavy cream, eggs, and whole milk. We eat more chicken (+179 percent), turkey (+820 percent) and fish (+42 percent), but we eat less cabbage (−65 percent), and fewer apples (−70 percent) and other fresh fruit (−33 percent). The bad news is that our sugar consumption is appalling, with soft drinks increasing by 157 percent, corn syrup by 224 percent, and

Toiling in the Nutrition Wasteland

straight sugar or other caloric sweeteners by 33 percent. And fat provides more than 42 percent of our daily calories, 27 percent more than our grandparents were eating in 1910.[1]

All this is by way of pointing out statistically what you already know in your heart and stomach. We eat, generally speaking, precisely what we want to eat, and since the endless goodies set out before us in supermarkets and gourmet shops are completely accessible, helped along by sophisticated and attractive advertising, the battle is a losing one everywhere except at the waistline.

To most of us, nutrition is a boring word. It reminds us of interminable sessions in the third grade, peering at charts about the basic four food groups. Nutrition suggests dull diets, high in everything except pleasure. If something is called nutritious, most Americans avoid it. But let us once determine to eat sensibly or embark upon a diet to lose weight and the media, equally determined to tell us everything, confuse and upset us. There is no one more skilled in the department of cross purposes than the editor of a women's magazine. Scientific articles on the cardiovascular sytem and the dangers of cholesterol are followed by lavishly illustrated features on sinfully rich chocolate desserts or pages of French sauces you too can make to please your fat family.

The American marketplace, especially the food industry, is stronger than any individual. We are, in a sense, at their mercy. In 1928, the number of items offered in a typical supermarket was 900. Now the number is in excess of 12,000 and rising every day. Yet since there are just so many basic foods one can offer, the increase is primarily in the area of highly processed foods.[2]

I spent a day being painfully educated into the world of processed foods

Toiling in the Nutrition Wasteland

when I attended a food distributors' exhibit at the Seven Springs Convention Center. An annual event, the show was hosted by Sky Brothers, Inc., a food distributor with warehouses in Harrisburg and Altoona that serves eight states. About one hundred fifty vendors set up shop in the huge convention hall and proceeded to cook up instant homemade bread, genuine imitation bacon, and preroasted, presliced, individually portion-packed roast beef. Some three thousand restaurant owners and food store employees milled about, asking questions, tasting, buying. The ingenuity of the food processors was mind boggling.

I saw fully cooked pie fillings which by various instant devices could be turned into pancake syrup, parfait toppings, or Danish pastry fillings. There was a multipurpose, instant onion product, "re-hydrates in minutes . . . fresh crisp look, large random pieces have old-fashioned 'cut from raw' appearance, the crunch and texture of freshly prepared onion." Great for hamburgers, the brochure continues, pizza, tacos, soups, salads. They come in a foil-lined, waxed cardboard carton, as do the frozen, shell-less diced or wedged hard-cooked eggs. I suggested to the gentlemen in charge of the booth that the egg already came in the perfect biodegradable container, its own shell. He looked puzzled. "But you don't have to *cook* these," he explained, as if to a slow child. "We do that *for* you."

I moved on to the Old South baked buttermilk biscuit booth, where large serrated blocks of baked dough were being unloaded from cardboard packing boxes and popped into microwave ovens. Nearby small loaves of yeast dough were thawing, ready for baking in the same ovens, each with its own small wooden board so the restaurant owner could promise individual loaves of homemade bread with each dinner. Cases of whipped topping were

Toiling in the Nutrition Wasteland

at the ready to squirt on cakes, pies, pastries, "a perfect ingredient for fillings, icing, salads and puddings," since the formula contains no milk but plenty of additives to help coagulate the fluffy stuff.

I sampled a chicken hot dog, which tasted just as rubbery as the beef and pork varieties, but the salesman assured me solemnly that his company has taken the burp out of the hot dog. There were several kinds of gravy mix, which could easily be mixed by the gallon, and single serving boil-in-the-bag hot fudge sauces for absolute portion control—no guessing, no messy cleanup, and judging by my taste, no flavor. Frozen potatoes appear to be one of the most versatile of products, with offerings of shoestring, crinkle-cut, hashed brown, puffs, mashed, and so forth. Yeast doughs run a close second, the emphasis being on basic doughs the chef can manipulate for himself to provide a variety of "homemade" products for his discriminating client.

I am accustomed to the large number of prepared frozen entrees in the supermarket cases for home use, but I had never given much thought to how the same principle could be applied in the restaurant business. Fully cooked lasagna, noodles Alfredo, turkey Tetrazzini, and manicotti were spread out before me, making me wonder if the "homemade" Italian dishes in my favorite restaurant might not be created by the Italian chef as he took off the wrappings and placed them in the microwave oven.

Such an exhibit is educational and, for me at least, deeply depressing. The lack of concern with real food, the emphasis on cost per portion, extended shelf life, ease of preparation all seemed to me to be the exact opposite of where I think the world should be heading.

Fortunately, however, there are a few strong voices who are making themselves heard to those who choose to listen. The Cooperation Extension

Toiling in the Nutrition Wasteland

Service at Penn State University has been concerned with nutrition for many years, and their expertise is available to help you can properly, freeze correctly, plan your meals, and cook your food. They send home economists and nutrition specialists to groups and clubs and write and mail out pamphlets on dozens of food-related subjects, including gardening. Marketing and agricultural experts are based in every large city, checking the weekly best food buys for the newspapers. They have been at work so long and with such quiet zeal that people tend to forget about them until there are budget cuts and they aren't there any more.

Marie Kieffer is a friendly, outgoing Somerset County home economist who has been with the Cooperative Extension since 1961. She works with 4-H clubs as well as specializing in canning and freezing demonstrations for groups. Currently, she is trying to spread the word about the unsuspected dangers lurking in what we once thought were safe preserving techniques. Paraffin, for example, is out if you're putting up jams and jellies. "Always use a two-piece lid and process the jar for ten minutes to make sure of the seal," she explained. "Paraffin seals leak, get moldy, and they're very dangerous." Everything should be processed, she continued, even pickles. Penn State experiments have shown that all kinds of unpleasant things can grow in your pickle jar if it hasn't been properly processed. Since my own favorite pickle recipe has always involved merely packing the sterilized jars with vegetables and filling with boiling brine, I was stunned. "You've been very lucky," she told me. "Don't take the chance again."

Marie likes to concentrate on information about additives, sugar content, fast food, plus better quality basic meal preparation. But there is a large segment of the population she serves that knows little or nothing about basic

Toiling in the Nutrition Wasteland

nutrition, and the Expanded Nutrition Education Program has been developed to help them and others like them around the country. If you read the folder about the program, you can, of course, learn the facts. ENAP increases knowledge of "the essentials of good nutrition, preparing and serving satisfying meals, managing available resources, including food stamps, better practices of food storage, and improving the diets and health of families, especially pregnant women, infants, preschool children, teenagers and the elderly." It sounds simple and, somehow, sterile, like all nutrition information. But when you listen to Marie Kieffer talk about the rural poor and their needs, the program comes alive.

"We serve about one hundred fifty families," she said, "and since our budget was cut, we have only five aides to serve them. Fifty-seven percent of the families are on food stamps. They live all over the county, on top of mountains, hidden away in valleys, in ex-mining pockets or flood-damaged areas where almost everyone has left but there may be two or three shacks left."

The aides are local women, trained by Marie and other Penn State staff to offer assistance in any of the areas relating to food and nutrition. They help in meal planning, food buying, gardening, cooking. "But the aides do much more than that," Marie said. "Sometimes they're a lifeline. There are women living in complete isolation from any other person. Maybe the husband has had to go out of the county to find work and she's totally alone, or with little children. There's no one to talk to, no one to help out. One of the aides tells about a woman who had a pretty messy house, but after the aide began to visit regularly, there was great improvement, because for the first time, 'company was coming.'"

While the rural poor suffer from isolation, the exact opposite is true in a

Toiling in the Nutrition Wasteland

city like Philadelphia, where the urban poor are crammed together in substandard housing. What they have in common is their poverty and their inadequate diet. I visited the Cooperative Extension office in Philadelphia where home economist Justine Olive runs ENAP. She looks on the program as an opportunity for one-to-one teaching.

"We have fifteen paraprofessionals," she told me, "trained intensively for three weeks in the basics of nutrition, kitchen sanitation, safety, etc. Then they go out into the neighborhood and literally knock on doors to find people who need help." The aides are indigenous to the neighborhood, which is mostly black and Puerto Rican. In most cases, aides are genuinely welcomed for the help they give and for their friendship. "Sometimes, though, people are very suspicious," Justine said. "One aide spent three months talking to a woman on her front porch before she was invited into the kitchen."

It's no wonder that suspicion is there, since many of these clients have been exploited by local merchants who take advantage of their ignorance and inability to speak English. Aides try to encourage shopping at large supermarkets rather than at small corner stores where prices are higher. At the bigger markets, the merchandise is cheaper and more varied, but the shops are usually further from home, they don't give credit, the signs are in English, and the clerks don't—or won't—understand Spanish.

The target population is the young family with children, since aides hope to set up good food patterns before the children learn bad ones. It is difficult to steer families away from what they have always eaten, perhaps an exclusive diet of rice and beans, plus high-priced avocados. The aides help the family buy food stamps, plan meals, and prepare many basic foods, including bread. But aides are frequently pulled into other areas of the family's life.

Toiling in the Nutrition Wasteland

"We're supposed to make referrals to other agencies like the welfare office or social security," Justine explained, "but sometimes, the aides just go with them to make it easier. Bureaucrats can be very unkind."

The most difficult task, according to both Marie and Justine, is to change the eating habits of the elderly. Their patterns have solidified over the years, and they have no inclination to change. If you are handicapped by age and ill-health, it's easier to reach for a snack out of a box or bag than to go to the trouble and pain of cooking a proper meal, even once a day. Since most elderly people live on fixed incomes, often alone, a program like Meals on Wheels can be a true lifesaver.

Started in England during World War II when food services were almost totally disrupted, the concept of feeding elderly and shut-in people in their own homes developed into an extraordinarily successful program, spreading to many other countries, including the United States in 1954. By 1976, there were more than 276 programs in Pennsylvania alone, over half of them located in the western region of the state.

I spent a remarkable morning observing the volunteers at work at St. Francis Church in the Lawrenceville section of Pittsburgh as they prepared to deliver meals to each of their fifty-five clients. The church kitchen and adjoining hall is home base for the Bloomfield-Lawrenceville program five days a week. An interesting ecumenical example, the program is one of fifty-seven kitchens administered by the Lutheran Service Society of Western Pennsylvania. There are others run by different service organizations. For eleven dollars a week, Meals on Wheels will provide two meals each day, five times weekly.

When I arrived at St. Francis, volunteers were setting up for delivery. Both daily meals are delivered at the same time, one cold, one hot. Today's cold

Toiling in the Nutrition Wasteland

supper consisted of a sandwich, fruit or jello, juice, milk, crackers, tea bags, hard-boiled eggs, and cookies. The hot meal included homemade soup, fish, macaroni and cheese, and broccoli. Brown bags were spread out on a long table ready for filling with the cold food, each marked with a name and special instructions: no salt, diabetic, bland, and so on. In the kitchen, bricks were heating in the oven and would later be placed in the metal containers to keep foods warm. The cook, Mary Malovich, was putting the finishing touches on baked fish sticks. Volunteer assistant cooks filled sectional foil containers with the hot fish, macaroni, and broccoli, passed them to other helpers who sealed and stacked them inside metal picnic hampers, along with cups of steaming vegetable soup. Brown bags ready, they were packed into large green plastic laundry baskets, and the volunteer driver and assistant prepared to load their car.

Helen Zinsser is assistant director of the Lawrenceville-Bloomfield Meals on Wheels as well as an intake worker, a volunteer like everyone in the program except the cook. She told me that when a new client is added to the roster, the intake worker visits to find out if there are special diet problems or doctor's instructions, and if the client can afford the weekly fee. "Almost everyone pays the eleven dollars," she told me. "We have one or two who can only manage eight, but at the moment, everyone pays something. They don't like to think they're receiving charity, you know."

Meals are planned by the cook in consultation with dietician Margery Gann, employed by Lutheran Services. Old-timers like Mary Malovich and Helen Klingenberg of the North Side have been with the program many years and need little assistance in their job of providing nutritious, tasty meals every day, but dietician Gann encourages cooks to share their favorite recipes through the monthly newsletter.

Toiling in the Nutrition Wasteland

I watched with interest as Mary and her helpers filled the plates that needed special attention. One client wanted no fish, so she received beans, carrots, and peas along with the broccoli, plus a small piece of meat. A "no starch" label found them substituting beets for macaroni. In the brown bags, cookies were omitted from a bag labeled "diabetic."

The special diets slow up production, Helen Zinsser admitted, "but after all, that's what we're here for." The biggest problem St. Francis finds is one which all the programs seem to share—a lack of dependable volunteers. "We need three or four to pack bags, assist the cook, and clean up," Helen said. "Then we need five drivers who can use their own cars, plus five to assist them. We deliver five days a week, and most drivers come in once a week. So that means we need at least fifty people who can be counted on, rain, hail, or whatever." Even as we talked, a crisis over drivers arose. A regular phoned in to say her mother was in the hospital and she couldn't come in. Helen and another volunteer started calling around town, including their own relatives. Finally, on the fifth try, a neighborhood church member agreed, arriving in less than ten minutes. When I congratulated her on her quick response, she said, "The trouble with this group is, I answer the phone and as soon as I've said hello I'm in deep trouble!"

Even with the skill and expertise of the cook, it is impossible to provide two meals daily for only eleven dollars. Additional funds come from the county, the federal government, donations from local restaurants and stores, and contributions from groups and individuals. I visited on Friday, collection day, and the envelopes went right into the baskets along with the brown bags. Clients may pay by cash, check, or food stamps, and they are strongly encouraged to pay regularly unless there is real financial hardship.

Toiling in the Nutrition Wasteland

Meals on Wheels services vary from community to community across the state and across the country. In Center County, Pennsylvania, for example, Meals on Wheels volunteers serve three meals daily three times a week and are proud they have never accepted federal funding.

Statistics and annual reports cannot convey the kind of service Meals on Wheels is providing. The food is, of course, the main objective, but as in all food experiences, there is a fringe benefit, a caring, a nurturing experience for both the client and the volunteer. The personal touches, the importance of human relationships, the contact with the outside world for many unable to leave their homes is difficult to measure. The program provides a check list of canned goods to keep on hand for emergencies, for example, and the volunteer is instructed to make sure the food is still there from time to time, or to see that it is replenished. There is a list of emergency telephone numbers kept up-to-date, a flashlight with fresh batteries, a can opener. Clients become friends, and volunteers often return to visit, even when they have no delivery to make. They help with referrals to other agencies, run small errands, help to deal with, as one of the bulletins reports, "the multiplicity of concerns and problems ever present in the lives of the elderly and shut-in." If you're feeling cynical about the world, or if you're wondering whether your tax dollars ever do any good, why not volunteer a few hours a week in your own community's Meals on Wheels? They can use your money, but they would rather have you.

Toiling in the Nutrition Wasteland

Many of us have discovered how delicious granola can be—and how expensive. There are any number of recipes for making this nutritious cereal at home, and you might like to experiment with ingredients and quantities. Here is the version we like the best.

GRANOLA

- 1 pound rolled oats (regular, not instant)
- 2 cups wheat germ
- 1 cup brown sugar, firmly packed
- 1 cup shredded or grated coconut
- 1 cup chopped nuts (walnuts or filberts)
- ½ cup sesame seeds
- ½ cup sunflower seeds, shelled
- 1 cup corn or peanut oil
- 1 teaspoon salt
- 1 cup raisins or dried apricots and prunes, chopped

Mix all ingredients except the fruit. Use your hands. Bake the mixture in a large roasting pan until golden brown at 325° about 45 minutes. Stir with a wooden spoon every 15 minutes. Cool; add fruit. I keep mine in a glass canister in the refrigerator, but it also freezes well if properly wrapped in plastic bags.

Toiling in the Nutrition Wasteland

If you and your family enjoy homemade bread, this unusual recipe is sure to please everybody. It tastes good right from the oven but stays fresh for two or three days if wrapped in plastic. It makes excellent toast.

BRAN BREAD

- 1 cup milk
- ¼ cup honey
- 1 teaspoon salt
- 1 package dry yeast
- ½ cup lukewarm water
- 1 teaspoon sugar
- 2 tablespoons butter or margarine, melted
- 4 cups all-purpose flour
- 2½ cups bran (buy this in a health food store—do not use packaged bran cereal)

Scald milk and honey, add salt, and cool to lukewarm. Dissolve yeast in water with sugar; add to milk, along with melted butter. Add half the flour and beat until smooth. Add remaining flour and bran and mix to make an easily handled dough. Turn out onto floured board or pastry cloth and knead until smooth and elastic, about 6 to 8 minutes. Grease a large bowl, roll dough in it to cover with thin film; cover and keep in a warm place until doubled in bulk, about 2 hours. Punch down, divide into two loaves, or make rolls, if preferred. Place loaves in greased loaf pans and rolls on greased cookie sheets. Cover and leave in a warm place until doubled in bulk, about 40 minutes. Bake at 350°, 30 minutes for loaves, 20 to 25 minutes for rolls. Makes 2 small loaves or 24 dinner-sized rolls.

American Cuisine

In 1874, two years before America was to celebrate her one hundredth birthday, the editorial page of the Philadelphia *Ledger* took note of the fact that Grand Duke Alexis of Russia had visited America and been rebuffed in his search for an American cuisine. It appears that the duke made a point of querying every hotel proprietor whom he met, but received only a series of shrugged shoulders, raised eyebrows, and puzzled looks. According to these gentlemen, there was no American cuisine and all of the best cooks were French.

The *Ledger* printed a long essay in response to this calumny, written by James W. Parkinson, the caterer who had arranged "The Thousand Dollar Dinner" in Philadelphia in 1851 (described on pages 205–07 below).[1] Mr. Parkinson was not surprised to learn that American hotelkeepers would not admit to the existence of American dishes because, he wrote, the men that the duke would be apt to meet were a very different class from the keepers of small inns in Europe. English and Continental innkeepers, he wrote, were born and bred in the business, serving in the most lowly capacity on their way up the ladder of hotel life, cleaning, serving, marketing, cooking. American innkeepers, on the other hand, knew little or nothing of the kitchen mysteries, being gentlemen capitalists with a talent for organizing and directing a large business.

Parkinson continued by discussing the so-called heritage from France and deploring the insecurity of Americans who demanded French names on their restaurants and French language on their menus. This delusion is fostered, he declared, by the "butterflies and noodles" from America who visit France and return to demand "French pastry, French bread, French twists . . . French everything!"

To celebrate America's forthcoming centennial properly, Parkinson suggested, what better way could there be than to promote an American bill of fare, starting, of course, with American fish. Shad, for example—the Germans had just stocked the Rhine with shad scooped up from the Connecticut River—or bluefish, smelts, silver eel, and red bass, American shrimp, mascalonge *(sic),* pompano, or the great varieties of magnificent trout. He wrote in praise of the oyster, the lobster and crab, the turtle and terrapin, moved on to fowl, wild game, cereals and vegetables, to the beasts of our fields, lauding our lamb and pork, our beef, caribou, antelope, and buffalo, "whom to get a shot at, and a taste of, English sporting lords by the dozen travel three thousand miles by sea and nearly as many more by land."

Parkinson wished that the duke had been allowed to sample "made" American dishes other than the Boston pork and beans which pleased him so much that he imported "the notion" to Russia.

> But where is our New England chowder (in the art of making which the great Daniel Webster was as proud as of his knowledge of the Constitution);

> and where our pumpkin pies, "hail fellow well met" with the Thanksgiving turkey himself? Add to these American triumphs the glories of buckwheat cakes and Jersey sausages . . . made of sound and wholesome corn-fed pork. In the art of making butter who denies that Americans may challenge comparison with the best? Who doubts that our Chester county butter, which commands a dollar a pound all the year round, has no superior in the world? And that American cheese has its own distinctive excellencies, is evident from the fact that while hundreds of tons of it are annually imported into Europe, there are Englishmen who prefer some American cheeses to the cheese of their own Chesire and Gloucester.

Parkinson makes his way through fruits, nuts, confectionery and finally, that all-American dish, ice cream. He concludes with a summary of the wonders of American food and a very modern and most prophetic statement.

> It must be made patent to all mankind, that America is not only blessed by Providence with enough of the richness and the fat of the land with which to feed her own people, but with a generous superabundance also with which to help support the starving populations of Europe. I remain, Mr. Editor,
>
> Very Respectfully Yours,
>
> James W. Parkinson,
> Philadelphia

American Cuisine

◈ *Even Mr. Parkinson would agree that few foods are more American than the cranberry. Unfortunately, most of us never see it on the table except at holiday times. Try making this bread when cranberries are in good supply and freeze several loaves for other times of the year.*

CRANBERRY NUT BREAD

- 1½ cup coarsely chopped cranberries
- ¼ pound butter or margarine, softened
- 1 cup sugar
- 3 eggs
- 2½ cups all-purpose flour
- 1 tablespoon baking power
- ½ teaspoon salt
- 1 teaspoon cinnamon
- ½ teaspoon nutmeg
- ¾ cup milk

Sort the cranberries, discarding bruised ones as well as any of the little twiggy stems which sometimes appear. Wash and pat dry; chop coarsely. (The food processor or blender is ideal for this task.) In a bowl by hand or with an electric mixer, cream the butter and sugar; beat in eggs one at a time. Combine flour, baking powder, salt, and spices, and sift together. Add the flour mixture and milk alternately in three parts, beating as little as possible but making sure the flour is incorporated into the batter. Stir in berries. Pour into 2 greased and floured loaf pans (9 × 5 × 3), or smaller foil pans (6 × 3½ × 2) if you prefer dainty loaves. Bake at 375° for 40 to 50 minutes or until a toothpick inserted in the center comes out clean. Tops will crack slightly. Cool completely before slicing.

For an excellent variation which produces a crumbly coffee cake, make the same batter, but spread in a 13 × 9 × 3 inch baking dish or two 8 inch layer cake pans. Make the following topping and spread evenly over the batter. Bake 35 to 45 minutes until crusty and a toothpick comes out clean. Cool before cutting.

American Cuisine

TOPPING
- ¼ pound butter or margarine, chilled
- ¾ cup all-purpose flour
- 1 cup sugar
- 1 teaspoon cinnamon

Cut the chilled butter into small pieces and combine with remaining ingredients. With a pastry blender or your fingers, work them together until the consistency of coarse meal. Sprinkle on batter and bake at 375° until done.

American Cuisine

❧ *Although many cultures cultivate the pumpkin or its close relative, I always associate this vegetable with the Pilgrims and the first Thanksgiving. What could be more American than that celebration? Here is a recipe for an unusual pumpkin pancake, equally delicious for breakfast with maple syrup or Cider Sauce (see page 120) or as a dessert pancake, spread with apricot jam or simply dusted with powdered sugar, or a cinnamon and sugar mixture.*

PUMPKIN PANCAKES

- ½ cup dairy sour cream
- ½ cup canned pumpkin, or fresh cooked and pureed pumpkin
- ½ cup water
- 1 cup all-purpose flour
- ¼ cup wheat germ
- 1 teaspoon baking soda
- ½ teaspoon salt
- 2 tablespoons sugar
- 1 teaspoon powdered ginger
- 2 teaspoons cinnamon
- 1 tablespoon salad oil
- 1 egg, slightly beaten

Combine all ingredients, stirring gently until well blended. Drop by ¼ cupfuls, or less if you prefer small cakes, on a moderately hot griddle, turning when small bubbles begin to appear on top. **Makes 8 to 10 six-inch pancakes.**

The Food Is Simply Wild

I tend to be very suspicious of people who tramp about the countryside extolling the virtues of wild foods. When they talk about the extra vitamins, the beauties of nature, and the freshness of the field products, I don't listen, because I know that what motivates them is not health but greed. I know because that's what motivates me. What can possibly give anyone more pleasure than a bucketful of blueberries picked in nobody's woods? Or applesauce made from an apple tree gone wild in the meadow? Or discovering that tart young grapes are growing wild just up the road from your camp?

If one must confess to greed, I suppose it is better to covet my neighbor's berry patch than his gold. But there is a special satisfaction in knowing the day's labors have cost nothing but my time. I will work harder digging ramps out of a rocky hillside or batting away gnats and mosquitoes on a sweltering day while picking blackberries than I ever would consider doing in a *real* job. I have never been one to hike just for fun. But let someone say, "I know where there are some ripe strawberries," and I will grab my bucket and take off at a brisk pace, walking twice as far as I would ever consider civilized on a simple pleasure jaunt.

The Food Is Simply Wild

Thus far I haven't been especially adventurous. It is not for me to lasso a snapping turtle for the evening steak, nor do I search for the tender shoots of milkweed and poke. Wild mushrooms terrify me. I am content to harvest familiar old friends. I am a dedicated apple stealer and blueberry picker, a fine thing to be in the state of Pennsylvania, since the land abounds with both. People tend to talk about huckleberries here rather than blueberries, and there are continuing arguments about which is which. Even expert botanists disagree about numbers of seeds and colors and varieties. I really don't care, because they both taste good. Most people use the words interchangeably, and I intend to do just that.

Pennsylvania has many large stands of huckleberries, including the most famous one of all, near New Bloomfield in Perry County. The Department of the Interior has designated the Box Huckleberry Natural Area as a registered natural landmark. In 1919 a federal botanist declared the huckleberry patch to be more than one thousand years old. The nine acres contain a single plant because it spreads by underground rhizomes rather than seedlings. Just thirty miles away, near Losh Run, another stand of box huckleberry is calculated to be over twelve thousand years old, possibly the oldest living plant in the world. Whether you believe it or not, the area is all now part of the Tuscarora State Forest so you can't pick the berries to make a twelve-thousand-year-old pie. But the thought of all those berries blooming year after year since before recorded history provides a comforting continuity with the past.

For me, blueberries pass the ultimate test. Not only are they succulent and sweetly tart, oozing juice and staining the mouth and tongue a delicious shade of blue, but eaten without cream and sugar, they can also be eaten

The Food Is Simply Wild

without guilt. Healthful they are, and low in calories, but even if they cost one hundred calories apiece, I would still adore them.

One of my very earliest childhood memories concerns blueberries. Our family used to visit an old friend in Kingston, Massachusetts, which was then a charming, small New England village near the shore. The house was surrounded by woods, thick with blueberry bushes, and I can remember walking along what seemed a dark and mysterious path but was in reality a sandy road. In those long ago days, peanut butter sometimes came packed in little tin buckets, and the empty pails were ideal for berry-picking expeditions. I clearly remember picking lots of blueberries, eating a fair share of them, and then somehow becoming absolutely terrified of real or imagined *things* lurking in the woods. I fled back down the sandy road, berries flying madly around me as the bucket turned over and over in my flailing hand. I sank down on the doorstep, panting and sobbing, my empty bucket beside me. I'm still not certain if I was crying from fright or from disappointment over the loss of those marvelous blueberries.

Berry pickers are a special breed, and they divide themselves according to berry. Strawberry pickers tend to be of sunny disposition, devil-may-care, eternally optimistic, always certain the tiny, elusive wild strawberry is lurking in large numbers under the next leaf or over the next hill. Raspberry pickers are determined but friendly. Wild raspberries are found amid brambles, but once the picker is inside the berry patch, legs bleeding and torn, the raspberries fall easily into the basket or the mouth, pure liquid sunshine. But the picker of blueberries tends to be solitary, unfriendly, even hostile. Competition for the best bushes is fierce, and determined pickers have little time for idle conversation or friendly exchanges.

The Food Is Simply Wild

I have observed this singleness of purpose in myself as well as in other dedicated blueberry pickers. The task does not lend itself to socialization. Blueberries were meant to be picked, otherwise God would have put padlocks on the bushes. A real blueberry picker will go to any length to find and pick berries. We all have favorite spots, kept darkly secret from anyone else. It is a challenge to arrive before the birds or the bears or whatever wild rival your particular section of the world contains.

I remember spending a summer not too many years ago waiting patiently for the berries to ripen to perfection. They were slow that year, and I was absolutely terrified that I would have to leave for home before I had eaten my fill. Finally, the day before departure, I knew I had to take action. Armed with a galvanized two-gallon bucket, I set forth dressed in my berrying costume—husband's old white shirt, blue jeans, sneakers, and a battered cloth tennis hat to keep off the mosquitoes and gnats. It was a muggy day and the bugs were out in force, but I found some high bush berries which were absolute gems, bursting with fat blue berries, berries that had spent the summer getting ready just for me. I picked feverishly, stripping the berries into the bucket as thunder rolled and crashed in the distance. As the first drops fell, my bucket was half-full. Then the heavens opened and the deluge really began, a summer storm of magnificent proportions. The harder it rained, the faster I picked, totally unmindful of the rain streaming down my back, my glasses steaming, my sneakers soggy. The bucket filled with water as well as berries, so I poured and drained and picked some more. Finally, when the pail would hold no more, I set out for home, slogging happily down the path, squishing into the house before an astonished and incredulous family. They could never understand all this. No one could, except

The Food Is Simply Wild

another dedicated berry picker. I did notice, however, that everyone seemed to enjoy the stream of pies and hot cakes and muffins filled with plump and juicy blueberries that poured magically from the freezer all winter long.

Next to blueberries, perhaps apples are the most rewarding harvest for the single-minded scrounger. Since I love tart apples and enjoy making applesauce, no tree is too old, no apple too worm-laden for me to ignore. Even the most gnarled and knobby of apples has a few good bites in it, and with the worm holes carved out, it is very suitable for sauce. My greedy nature is totally satisfied when I gaze at the neatly stacked packages of pink apple sauce in my freezer. Never mind what I spend on sugar. The apples were free.

The closest I have come to stalking the exotic is in my newly developed passion for ramps, or wild leeks. I would still be ignorant of their powerful attraction, had not my partner in many a wild food foray, Josie Stanton, discovered them growing near our summer cottage in Somerset County. Josie can always spot the apple trees, the berry bushes, the watercress, the morels, long before anyone else. And she was delighted when she identified the wild leeks in our woods.

Allium tricoccum lilaceae resembles a small onion with leaves like lily of the valley and a smell and impact that makes garlic as fragrant as lavender. The ramps we pick in mid-April grow on a steep, wooded hillside, seemingly right out of the rocks. It is not possible to pluck the ramp by simply grasping the top leaves. One must dig under the root with a stick or knife and pry it out. It takes dozens of ramps to make the broken fingernails worthwhile. Eaten raw, they are dynamite, and some say just one will remain on your breath for two months. I don't really believe that, but I have seen people

The Food Is Simply Wild

move away from me uneasily in a theater or bus. Chopped and cooked in stews and omelets or simply sauteed in butter, they are delicious; ramp soup is similar to vichysoisse. There are spring ramp festivals in West Virginia and Tennessee, where sometimes they have to dismiss school if some of the children haven't consumed any. They can't stand to be in the same room with their breathy friends.

Even though my wild food forays are modest compared with the real experts, I read the books of Euell Gibbons with admiration and respect. His farm in Beaverton, Pennsylvania, was the headquarters for his enormously successful campaign to make the world aware of wild foods. Even if you are not about to sally forth to find the makings for cattail meal pancakes and Japanese knotweed pie, you can enjoy his food-gathering expeditions as an armchair explorer. And who knows, maybe you will be the first on your block to prepare pigeon pie, mayflower marmalade, terrapin stew, and birch beer.[1]

The Food Is Simply Wild

This easy-to-make jam will keep indefinitely in the freezer, up to a month in the refrigerator.

BLUEBERRY FREEZER JAM
1   pint fresh blueberries, preferably wild, rinsed and drained
½   cup powdered pectin
1 to 1¾ cup sugar, depending on sweetness of berries
¼   cup clear corn syrup
¼   teaspoon cinnamon
rind of one lemon, grated
½   cup lemon juice

Whirl berries in blender or food processor. Mix pectin with ¼ cup sugar and stir into blueberry pulp. Transfer to bowl of electric mixer and mix at lowest speed for 7 minutes. Add remaining ingredients and continue mixing 3 more minutes. Pour into freezer containers or jars—small ones are best—and let stand at room temperature 24 hours, then freeze. Thaw as needed, but store thawed container in refrigerator. Makes 2 pints.

The Food Is Simply Wild

Those of you fortunate enough to know about a stand of wild leeks, or ramps, will enjoy this tasty soup. It is wonderful on a cold day, and all that is needed for supper is a big tossed salad and some crusty bread. If you can't find ramps, you may substitute leeks, but it won't be quite the same. It may also be served cold.

RAMP SOUP

enough ramps to fill two cups, when trimmed and chopped
- 2 cups potatoes, pared and diced
- 3 tablespoons butter
- 1 quart chicken broth
- 1½ teaspoons salt, or to taste
- 1 cup milk

Trim the ramps so that there is only a short green tail left above the small white bulb. Wash very well, drain, and chop into small pieces. Sauté ramps and potatoes in butter until limp but not brown. Add chicken broth and salt and cook until potatoes are soft. Puree in a food processor or blender; return to pan, add milk and heat but do not boil. Serves 4.

A Story with a Twist

The next time you reach for a handful of pretzels in a cocktail lounge, stop a moment and reflect. You are undoubtedly eating one of the most famous products of Pennsylvania, which has a virtual monopoly on pretzel production: Of the eighty-eight pretzel bakeries in America, sixty-six are in Pennsylvania. They range from highly automated factories, where sixteen hundred pounds of pretzels are taken from the ovens every hour, to small, family-owned operations, where each pretzel is bent and baked by hand.

If you think a pretzel is merely a pretzel, and what's all the fuss about, think again. Pretzels are big business, since Americans consume some 300 million of them every year. There are traditional twists, large, small and medium; thick Bavarian sticks; and pencil-slim sticks. They come salt free, fat free, soft, hard, chocolate covered, Kosher, round, square, long, short, light and dark. Whatever you want, someone in Pennsylvania is undoubtedly making it at this very moment. And if you think the regional arguments over chili and clam chowder are vociferous, try eavesdropping on a Philadelphia pretzel lover sharing his thoughts with someone from Pittsburgh, or worse yet, California, where they have never heard of soft pretzels, and wouldn't

A Story with a Twist

dream of eating them with mustard. I once saw a woman and her little boy, obviously strangers, stop dead on a downtown Pittsburgh street where a pretzel vendor was doing a brisk business. "Mama!" the child cried, unbelieving. "It's pretzels. He's selling pretzels!" Mama was also dumbfounded.

"Imagine," she murmured, like a Victorian lady, "on the public street."

Despite the chauvinistic insistence of certain Pennsylvanians, the pretzel was not invented in this state or even on this side of the Atlantic. A number of authorities refer to it as a savoury biscuit from Alsace and Germany, and the *Dictionary of Gastronomy* says it has been known since Roman times.[1] Another story dates the first pretzel from the year 610, when a monk from southern France or northern Italy is supposed to have used some leftover bread dough to form a crossed strip representing children's arms folded in prayer. When the children knew their prayers properly, he gave them the little cookie as a present, using the Latin word *pretiola*, meaning little reward. A woodcut from 1483 shows a traveling pretzel bakery, the bakers shoveling their wares in and out of an oven on wheels, then hanging them on a wooden dowel to cool. And there is the legend of the heroic pretzel bakers in Vienna, who in 1510, while working at night, detected the invading Turks digging tunnels under the city. The pretzel makers picked up their baking shovels and spoons and engaged the fierce Turks in hand-to-hand combat, annihilating them, so the story goes, and averting a threat to all of Europe. Their reward, aside from an increase in business, one hopes, was a coat of arms bestowed on them by the Austrian emperor, complete with scrolls, flowers, a crown, a heraldic beast, and one pretzel, rampant.[2]

The Pennsylvania Dutch brought the art of pretzel making from Europe, and the first commercial bakery opened in Lititz, Pennsylvania, in 1861. The

A Story with a Twist

Sturgis Pretzel Bakery uses the recipe that a tramp offered in exchange for a good meal, back before the Civil War. The bakery is still owned and operated by descendants of Julius Sturgis, and tourists troop through by the hundreds to watch a demonstration of pretzel twisting and to try a few turns themselves.

Pretzel dough made at home is a simple paste of flour and water, baked in a very hot oven until brown and hard, then glazed or sprinkled with coarse salt. In the old-time Sturgis bakery, the dough was a yeast dough, mixed by hand and kneaded with a long piece of wood called a riding rail. It took twenty-five to thirty trips of the rail to condition the dough for the next step, pulling it apart into baseball-sized chunks. These were rolled into sausage shapes and cut into many little discs which were in turn rolled into slim cylinders and then twisted into the traditional pretzel shape. After about an hour's raising, they were dropped into a pot of hot water, to firm them up before baking. Wood ovens were heated to 550°, and in ten minutes, the pretzels were crisp and golden brown. The moisture was removed in a kiln drier, and the old-time baker could tell when they were done by squeezing one. If it talked back, or crackled, he knew it was ready.

Another bakery that continues to make pretzels mostly by hand is Martin's in Akron, Pennsylvania, where Mennonite women prepare twenty-four hundred pretzels a day. They have two house specialties, one made from whole wheat flour and dipped in caustic soda before baking. Another is the somewhat softer health pretzel, dipped in soda ash.

Bachman's in Reading does a huge mail order business and specializes in soft pretzels. Wege Pretzel Company in Hanover is famous for the beer drinker's friend, a thick, hard, and salty pretzel. The Anderson Bakery in

A Story with a Twist

Lancaster is an automated giant, rolling out sixteen hundred pounds of pretzels every hour. Visitors who watch the highly sophisticated operation from an indoor catwalk can see the huge dough masses turned into strips, the eighteen machines twisting thick Bavarian sticks into shape, the dozens of varieties of pretzels moving swiftly by on separate conveyor belts. As in all of the bakeries, there are plenty of free samples to help you make up your mind what to buy.

There seem to be a number of superstitions associated with pretzels. People once wore them around their necks to ward off evil spirits—the three divisions of the pretzel representing the Trinity—but they ate them later.[3] They were hung on trees in the hope that the trees would bear well. And one custom persists to this day: Each person grabs a piece, like the halves of a turkey wishbone, and pulls until it breaks. Whoever gets the knot presumably gets his wish.

Despite their coat of arms, the workers in a pretzel factory did not have an easy life. The Sturgis Bakery records show that the old-time pretzel baker received about one dollar a day and worked 6 days a week in the boiling hot bakery. He got twenty-five cents for each 1000 pretzels twisted, and he also worked in every other operation of the bakery, from two in the morning until noon—ten hours a day. He received only half his pay in cash. The rest was in the form of a credit slip, made out for family necessities such as groceries, clothes, or shoes. His full salary—six dollars—only came to him on rent day, when he had to borrow for life's necessities. At Sturgis, the bakery workers ate with the family at lunch, but no mention is made of whether they had to pay or if this was an early employee fringe benefit.[4]

Today, you can buy pretzels in numberless flavors—cheese, rye, car-

A Story with a Twist

away, beer, butter, garlic, chocolate, pizza—and shapes—thin pencils, thick sticks, nuggets, rods, big boys, loops, and cocktail sticks. Pretzels without salt are called baldys and are used for babies' teething. Publicists would have us believe that pretzels are a good diet snack, since they contain little or no fat. They are easily digested and have even been used to alleviate motion sickness. You can find recipes for pretzel crumb pies, poultry stuffing, soup, dips, meat loaf, oyster dishes, salads. When I was very small, I enjoyed our midwestern Sunday night suppers, which consisted of pretzels and ice cream. My New England husband is horrified at the thought, but I commend it to you. The creamy coolness of the ice cream is a delicious contrast to the crunchy, salty texture of the pretzel. And if you're looking for something a little different this year, you can trim your Christmas tree with pretzels, either real ones or pretzel-shaped cookies decorated with icing and nuts and candies.

    I find it curious that although we have songs about Pennsylvania pawnshops and polkas, we lack a musical tribute to the Pennsylvania pretzel. Perhaps this is an idea whose time has come.

A Story with a Twist

Don't expect these pretzels to taste like the ones you buy on the street. They are rolls in pretzel shapes, but if you try very hard you can imagine you are eating a real soft pretzel.

SOFT PRETZELS

- 1 cup warm water
- 1 package dry yeast
- ¼ cup sugar
- 1 teaspoon salt
- 2 tablespoons butter or margarine
- 1 egg
- 4 to 4½ cups all-purpose flour
- 1 egg yolk
- 2 tablespoons water
- coarse salt

Measure warm water into large warm bowl; sprinkle yeast over it and stir until dissolved. Add sugar, 1 teaspoon salt, butter, egg, and 2½ cups flour. Beat until smooth, then add enough flour to make a stiff dough. Cover tightly with aluminum foil and refrigerate from 3 to 24 hours.

Turn dough onto lightly floured board or pastry cloth. Divide in half; cut each half into 8 equal pieces. Roll each piece into a pencil-shaped piece about 20 inches long. Make into pretzel shapes and place on a lightly greased cookie sheet.

Fill a shallow skillet or baking pan with about 2 inches of water and bring to a boil. Reduce heat and keep water just under the boiling point. With a spatula or slotted spoon, slide one pretzel at a time into the water and let cook not more than 2 minutes. Remove, drain, and return to baking sheet. Never have more than 2 pretzels in the pan at the same time.

Blend egg yolk and water; brush mixture on each pretzel and sprinkle with coarse salt. Let rise in a warm place about 20 minutes or until doubled in bulk. Bake at 400° about 12 to 15 minutes or until light brown. Remove to baking rack to cool. **Makes about 20 soft pretzels.**

Here Let Us Feast

Surely there is a streak of masochism in all of us, since we continue to give and attend banquets. Who among us has not blanched at the sight of yet another platter of creamed chicken, the isolated pieces of old hen slowly congealing into a glutinous white mass? How many stale rolls have we crumbled while waiting for the needless, boring speeches to finish? What horrors of limp salads, ancient green peas, and soggy cake with "whipped topping" have we endured in the name of some favorite charity? Although the politicians' aptly named "rubber chicken" circuit goes on, there is a faint ray of hope. A senator recently held a $100-a-plate benefit: in return for $100, he would send you a plate, empty of anything except his autograph. And a few years ago, nondinners became a popular fund-raising technique—you were asked to contribute $50 or $100 to the worthy group and were not required to go to a dinner at all.

I suppose someone in antiquity discovered that if people must gather on business of whatever kind, they might as well eat. Did the Romans give Julius Caesar, or perhaps Brutus, a testimonial banquet? Did the Egyptians hold little dinners for their pharaohs and assistant pharaohs, honoring them for fifty years of faithful service?

Here Let Us Feast

In recent history, say the last two hundred years, records abound with stories of famous dinners and banquets. The gourmands of the Victorian and Edwardian eras did themselves especially proud in numbers of courses and quantities of food and wine consumed. A glance at some of the menus provided for state occasions confirms the fact that these folk really knew how to eat. Charles Fracatelli, chef to Queen Victoria, often served banquets with seventy or more dishes. The habits of excess survived the trip across the Atlantic, and the bounty of America may have even improved upon the practice. A menu from the Revere House in Boston detailing a dinner for the Boston Light Infantry in 1852 shows forty-two dishes, plus punch, coffee, and liqueurs. The allegedly wild west was sufficiently civilized in 1876 to produce a menu engraved on a silver plate at the San Francisco Palace Hotel listing eleven courses, each with a different wine or champagne.[1]

In Pennsylvania, banquets have enjoyed great popularity as a means of celebrating special occasions, to honor a famous guest or merely to mark the passing of another year. Multicourse dinners, usually with French menus, were common in the larger cities. At the annual dinner of the Pittsburgh Chamber of Commerce in 1898, 398 guests ate their way through ten courses of superb food and wine, and if still awake, could listen to a speech by Andrew Carnegie. Fresh oysters were served with a glass of Rudesheimer Berg, followed by clear green turtle soup and Amontillado sherry. Next came halibut with hollandaise, cucumber salad, and sweetbreads à la Bohemian, accompanied by Veuve Clicquot. Terrapin à la Maryland arrived with Thistle Punch, whatever that may be; then roast quail and red-head duck salad à la Josephine and potatoes duchesse, with a Chambertin. Desserts were *gelée au Madeira,* pudding à la Romanoff, and petits fours; then cheese and coffee, fruit and liqueurs.

Here Let Us Feast

The seating plan for this banquet reads like a directory of Pittsburgh city streets, parks, and schools—Frick, was there, as were Dalzell, Taylor Allderdice, Magee, Craig, Bartlett, Wightman, Phipps, Heinz, Brashear, Westinghouse, and four Mellons.

In 1911, when William Howard Taft was the guest speaker, the chamber of commerce dinners were still French in style and long in courses. The oysters were replaced by caviar, the clear turtle soup by *velouté de terrapin au Xeres,* a thick soup with sherry. Then came *filet de poulet aux truffles; mignonettes d'agneau aux fines herbes; cèpes à la moscovite,* wild French mushrooms, probably in some kind of mold; *salade japonaise,* with artichokes; peaches; a sweet biscuit glazed with hazelnuts; puff pastries *aux trois couleurs;* demi-tasse; Apollinaris water; cigars and cigarettes.

By 1923, the dinners had become more American and considerably lighter. The fish course was gone, leaving grapefruit maraschino, cream of chicken soup, filet mignon with mushroom sauce, green beans and potatoes, lettuce hearts, and frozen Melrose pudding with layer cake jubilee. And a 1970 celebration honoring the seventy-fifth anniversary of the Carnegie Library in Pittsburgh, and catered at the library, has become comfortingly spartan, serving only consommé; boned, stuffed, Cornish game hen with asparagus and bibb lettuce; French pastry and coffee.

One of the most interesting accounts of a lavish Pennsylvania banquet comes to us from a New Yorker, R. B. Valentine who was invited to Philadelphia in 1851 for a special dinner at the restaurant of James W. Parkinson, a famous caterer. There were seventeen courses, Valentine wrote, "each a perfect banquet in itself." In addition to the food, there were rare wines and liqueurs with every course. "Behind every one of the thirty guests was a

Here Let Us Feast

wine-cooler," and each guest had his very own waiter. "We sat so long at the table that the sun in the meantime had both set and risen again. It was precisely six o'clock in the evening when we sat down and it was high six in the morning when we arose." The menus were highly prized as mementos, and one of the group took his back to New York and threw it down "before the proprietor of the then most famous hotel in New York, and said: 'There, Charley, go to Philadelphia and learn how to get up a dinner.' "[2]

The menu was indeed unique. Each of the seventeen courses had its own selection of wines. The banquet opened with Morris River Cove oysters; green turtle soup; fresh salmon and baked rock fish; turkey with celery and oyster sauce, chicken in egg sauce, and beef tongues for the "boiled" course; a selection of salads and cold meats for the "cold" course. Entrees began with roast beef and veal, lamb chops, and chicken croquettes and proceeded through braised pigeon, turtle steaks, and fricassee of chicken. More chicken appeared with the "roast" course, along with capons and spring lamb. There was an inexplicable ninth course called "Pièces Montées" which included Moorish Fountain, Flora's Offering, and Indian Temple, probably the spectacular molded creations Victorian chefs often prepared for table ornaments.

Then came the vegetables, eleven in all, followed by sherbets; then game—snipe, duck, plover, woodcock, and rice birds. After diamond-back terrapin came several dessert courses: first, pastry, including peach pie, charlotte russe, Italian cream, a variety of cakes and puddings; then "confectionery," with Chinese almonds, cream candy, brandy drops, and nougats. Ice creams and water ices—caramel, harlequin, strawberry, lemon, and champagne—were followed by fruits and nuts, then a selection of liqueurs. Twelve different wines were offered, ranging from "Marcobrunn of 1834,

Here Let Us Feast

specially obtained from the cellar of the Duke of Nassau," to an 1841 Medoc, to "rare old cask Amontillado pale sherry." And there was 1821 cognac before dinner; madeira, port, maraschino, and curaçao after.

The Philadelphia papers spoke of this entertainment as "The Thousand Dollar Dinner," but Valentine wrote: "The fact is that our Philadelphia entertainers paid the caterer fifteen hundred dollars for the banquet—fifty dollars a plate." [3]

I wonder if at the close of the evening's festivities the exhausted chef and his colleagues were called in to take their well-deserved bows, a time-honored tradition. I can remember church banquets in Lakewood, Ohio, when plump ladies in flowered cotton dresses, their faces still flushed from kitchen heat, were called into the dining room to be applauded by their friends and neighbors, as they shyly wiped their hands on their aprons. One wonders if all chefs would agree with Jules Harder, chef of the San Francisco Palace Hotel in 1874 when he said, "The most discouraging experience I have is to get up something extra in the way of a sauce or flavor for some big man and to have . . . it make no more impression than a baked potato." [4]

Here Let Us Feast

༄ *Sometimes its's fun to go all out for friends and family and produce a modern banquet. The following menu and recipes include some of my favorite dishes for an elegant autumn or winter dinner party. And if you are looking for a change from the traditional holiday turkey, this menu might be the answer. An asterisk indicates that the recipe is printed below; consult the index for the remaining recipes.*

Hors d'oeuvres
Bologna Roll-ups   Oyster-stuffed Cocktail Tomatoes*

Potage
Cream of Walnut Soup*

Entree
Stuffed Roast Pork*
Pilaf   Zucchini Casserole
Cheese Batter Bread*

Dessert
Fruit Cup with Champagne*
Brownies   Kolacky

OYSTER-STUFFED COCKTAIL TOMATOES

Allow 3 to 4 cherry tomatoes for each guest, making sure they are ripe but firm. Allow 1 tin of smoked oysters for each 24 tomatoes. Cut a tiny slice from the top of each tomato and gently scoop out the pulp. A grapefruit spoon with serrated edges makes it an easy task. Turn tomatoes upside down to drain. Fill each tomato cavity with one or two smoked oysters. Sprinkle tops with parsley and arrange on a plate with more parsley sprigs. Chill until serving time.

Here Let Us Feast

◈ *The walnut soup comes to you directly from Poland, where I spent several weeks attending a cooking course under the supervision of Andrzej Dalikat. This soup was served at our welcome-to-Poland banquet, and the students persuaded him to share it with us.*

CREAM OF WALNUT SOUP
½	cup walnuts, coarsely chopped
¼	cup butter or margarine
2	tablespoons tomato paste
2	tablespoons all-purpose flour
1½	quarts boiling meat and/ or vegetable stock
1	cup light cream
	salt and pepper to taste

Fry walnuts in butter. Add tomato paste and flour. Add mixture to boiling broth and cook until slightly thickened. Drop meatballs into soup (recipe below) and when they rise to top, remove pot from heat, add cream, salt and pepper. Serves 6.

MEATBALLS
1	pound ground pork or beef
1	teaspoon salt
¼	teaspoon pepper
½	teaspoon marjoram
1	egg, lightly beaten

Combine all ingredients and make into very small meatballs, about the size of marbles.

Here Let Us Feast

STUFFED ROAST PORK

2½ to 3 pound pork roast, boned and rolled
1   medium onion, coarsely chopped
½   cup dried apricots and/or prunes, cut in small pieces
½   cup raw apple, peeled and diced
½   cup walnuts, pecans, or pine nuts, coarsely chopped
½   cup coarse, stale bread crumbs or small bread cubes
salt and pepper to taste

Unroll pork roast and spread flat. Mix all other ingredients. Moisten with a very little hot water to "glue" stuffing together. Turn out onto pork roll, spreading evenly. Carefully roll meat and tie securely in several places. Place on rack in roasting pan. Roast at 350° for about 1½ hours or until done. Cut strings before serving. At table, slice into thick chunks. Serves 6.

CHEESE BATTER BREAD

1	cup milk	1	cup warm water
3	tablespoons sugar	2	packages dry yeast
1	tablespoon salt	1	cup grated sharp cheddar cheese
1	tablespoon margarine	4	cups unsifted all-purpose flour

Scald milk; stir in sugar, salt and margarine; cool to lukewarm. Measure warm water into large warm bowl and sprinkle the yeast over it, stirring until dissolved. Add lukewarm milk mixture, cheese, and flour; beat until smooth. Cover and let rise in warm place until doubled in bulk, about 1 hour. Stir batter down and beat vigorously about 30 seconds. Turn into 6 small greased loaf pans (approximately 6 × 3½ × 2) or deep dish pie dishes (10 oz.). Bake at 375° about 35 to 40 minutes or until done. Makes 6 small loaves.

FRUIT CUP WITH CHAMPAGNE
Allow approximately ½ cup fruit for each serving. Any seasonal combination will do, but melon balls with grapes, or strawberries, raspberries and blueberries, or apples, pears, and peaches are especially nice. Canned or frozen fruit can be used if necessary. Spoon fruit mixture into parfait or champagne glasses. Just before serving, pour chilled champagne into each cup to fill it. One split of champagne will serve 4.

The Cup That Cheers

As the years go by, it becomes more and more difficult to find really good apple cider. If you have the right kind, without preservatives, after a few days in the refrigerator or on the back porch it begins to fizz and tingle and you have to drink it quickly before it turns to vinegar. A lot of people seem to be making their own cider recently or buying someone else's and going through that laborious but rewarding process of making hard cider. Like so many of the skills once taken for granted in early America, we are discovering not only the pleasures but the pain and persistence required to create a perfect barrel of cider, a fine loaf of bread, a yard of excellent cloth.

Americans come by their affection for cider honestly, since it was by far the most popular drink in the earliest days. "Cider is the common drink of this country and very plentiful and easy to be procured," wrote Robert Proud in 1760. Even before that, Captain John Smith reported that the Virginia colonists, suspicious of New World water, preferred "most excellent and comfortable drinks."[1] As soon as their first orchards yielded bountiful crops, fruit was converted to liquor, with apple cider the favorite. Considered to be at its prime when it was a year or two old, cider was the family drink, with foaming

The Cup That Cheers

pitchers on the table at every meal. Even the children had their share, sometimes diluted with water. Almost every farm had an orchard and a cider press or mill, enabling the family to produce between fifteen and forty barrels annually.[2]

After cider, beer was perhaps the most popular alcoholic drink. Early Swedish settlers had their own malt houses for making home brew. William Penn wrote to an English friend in 1685: "Our Drink has been Beer and Punch made of Rum and Water. Our Beer was made mostly of Molasses, which, well boyled with Sassafras or Pine infused into it, makes a very Tolerable Drink; but now they make Mault and Mault Drink begins to be common."[3]

Commercial beer production began before the Revolution. In 1774, Philadelphia's City Tavern received the first barrel of Philadelphia-brewed, English-style ale, made by one Robert Smith, who had learned his trade at the famous Burton-on-Trent brewery in England. A short time afterward, Fitzgerald Steven, a Tory, wrote to his wife in Maryland from the Penny Pot Tavern in Philadelphia. "A well-favored Inn. . . . Minced collops to my Breakfast, or eggs with bacon, or a pasty or pigeon Pye, with bread and chese and a quart of Master Smith's proper Ale, and so to the day's business. . . . The Delegates rage windily against the King's Blessed Majesty, which shall stand firm as the House that was founded on the Rock. The sloop Welcome Home beareth thee six barrels of Master Smith's Brew. I kiss thy hands."[4]

When the Scotch-Irish arrived in Pennsylvania, they brought with them a taste for stronger stuff and began distilling whiskey from rye and corn. By 1780, cider had fallen to second place as a national beverage, and by 1800 there were more distilleries in Pennsylvania than there were grist mills.[5] Men

The Cup That Cheers

engaged in hard physical labor ate enormous quantities of food and were able to drink large quantities of whiskey regularly. The whole family drank whiskey, as they had once drunk cider, with the little ones given bread dunked in liquor instead of milk. Visitors were expected to have a drink when they arrived and also when they left, even the minister. During the harvest season, farmers provided whiskey for their field hands several times a day. Although some reminiscences of the period indicate that the heavy work dissipated the stupifying effects of the whiskey, other farmers discontinued the practice because of accidents, rowdy fights, and the growing influence of the termperance movement. Despite strong threats of desertion by their laborers, many farmers stood fast, and the custom gradually died out.[6]

Before 1800, when roads were still primitive, if they existed at all, whiskey was almost the only farm product that could profitably be carried across the Alleghenies to eastern cities. Four bushels of grain was all the ordinary packhorse could carry. But when grain was converted to whiskey, a horse could carry the equivalent of twenty-four bushels. In 1790 in Washington County, there were more than five hundred stills on the farms. In 1793, the capacity of all known stills in the state was over 2 milllion gallons, and only eight years later, 9 million. Two or three farmers, if they found themselves with a surplus of rye, would combine their resources and start a distillery wherever the best spring water could be found. When they had enough booze for thirty or forty packhorses to carry, they set out for the east and a tidy profit.

Revenue-hungry governments have always kept a thirsty eye on the makers of alcoholic beverages. Pennsylvania, where every fourth or fifth farmer was running a copper still on his premises, was clearly rich territory for

The Cup That Cheers

the bureaucrats. In 1791, the federal government looked into the future, saw the potential revenue, and slapped an excise tax on whiskey. All hell, as they say, broke loose, especially in western Pennsylvania, where settlers felt they were being discriminated against.

The tax seemed to many farmers to infringe on their personal rights and liberties. They said in one of their petitions, "that we are supplied with this necessary article, much upon the same conditions that our mills furnish us with flour, and why should we be made subject to a duty for drinking our grain more than eating it, seems a matter of astonishment to every reflecting mind."[7]

There were ample grievances in addition to this. Stills were taxed according to their capacity, and yet another tax was imposed when the whiskey was sold. If found guilty, the defendant was forced to stand trial in the eastern part of the state, an expensive, time-consuming trip many miles from home. All of the dissatisfactions of the western settlers seemed to focus on the excise tax. It was a clear-cut issue around which they could organize.

So the Whiskey Rebellion was born. Meetings were held, petitions mounted, resolutions passed, societies organized. Liberty poles bearing radical mottoes appeared; threatening letters were received by men who were not vocal enough in their opposition to the hateful tax; and the stills of those who paid the tax were "mended" by Tom the Tinker's men, meaning they were shot full of holes. There was violence, confusion, charges and countercharges. Federal troops were sent to subdue the unruly Pittsburghers, and ultimately the westerners lost their political battle. But the excise tax, far more important than the revenue it generated, served to consolidate the power of the federal government. The United States were indeed united under a government with power and authority.[8]

The Cup That Cheers

All this occurred in the name of whiskey, essentially a simple beverage that requires only good grain, good water, and some expertise. In 1753, John Shenk, a Swiss Mennonite farmer, was producing grain of excellent quality in the central Pennsylvania community of Schaefferstown. He began converting the excess into whiskey along the banks of Snitzel Creek, a clear stream fed by deep limestone springs. He founded the distillery which later became Michter's, the first in America, which continued to operate until Prohibition shut it down. In 1950, some workmen found a boarded-up room in the old distillery building and discovered records which allowed the restoration of the original plant. Although Michter's now contains modern equipment, that first distillery has been carefully restored to its original specifications and becomes, in fact, a small distillery within the context of the larger one.

If you would like to tour the distillery, you are welcome. The waiting room is a miniature museum, with a fine collection of old bottles and distillery equipment from bygone days. I overheard a conversation between two gentlemen reminiscing about their youth. "We used to make our own stuff," one of them said. "I used to take the buggy into town and buy a big batch of sugar and some Mason jars, and the storekeeper would say, 'My, your mother's going to do a lot of canning, isn't she?' "

Visitors begin by hearing a brief but informative lecture on the distilling process. Then you are taken through the modern plant to observe the milling method of grinding grain, similar to the stone grind of old grist mills. The milled grain is cooked in limestone water and the resulting stillage put in an open mash tub somewhat like a huge pressure cooker. Yeast is added, inducing fermentation, and the liquidified sugar is converted to alcohol. The spirit is separated out by distillation, then aged the proper time—six years in the case

The Cup That Cheers

of Michter's. All very interesting, but for me the highlight was the last stop on the tour. Visitors walk across Snitzel Creek and enter the smallest legal distillery in America, which turns out one barrel a day just exactly the way it was done in the eighteenth century. The stills are hand-hammered copper and the three large fermentation tubs—where you can watch the yeast working and hear the plup-plup of it—are made of cypress. It is an operation handled with tender, loving care, with concern for the past, and respect for a good drink of whiskey.

The story of ardent spirits in Pennsylvania would not be accurate without some mention of the powerful temperance movement in the nineteenth century. The caricatures of grim-faced ladies wielding axes in barrooms persists to the present day, yet the temperance movement grew out of a real need for reform. Whiskey, beer, and cider were drunk by everyone, and in 1837 a farmer's newspaper characterized cider drinkers "as the most brutish and cruel of all the unhappy tribes of inebriates."[9] There was plenty of public tippling as well, so that William Cobbett wrote to English friends from Philadelphia in 1818: "All the materials for making people drunk or muddle-headed are much cheaper here than in England.... Come on, then, if you love tippling, for here you can drink yourself blind at the price of a sixpence."[10]

There were stories of ten-year-old children found drunk in the gutter, of families pauperized by the father's spending on drink. The little daughter pleading with her father to leave the barroom is a modern cliché, but there is ample evidence that there was much tragedy as a result of excessive drinking.

The Darby Association for Discouraging the Unnecessary Use of Spiritous Liquors was organized in 1819 in Delaware County, the first such society

The Cup That Cheers

in Pennsylvania. Between 1820 and 1840, temperance societies appeared all over the state, sending out dynamic, crusading speakers who made many converts to the cause. Then in 1854, T. S. Arthur of Philadelphia published *Ten Nights in a Bar Room,* a moral tale about the evils of drink. Later dramatized, it played all over the country, pointing out the tragic consequences of intemperance, particularly among the young. The "hero" eventually kills his father, also a drunkard, in a barroom brawl.[11]

At the 1876 Centennial Exposition in Philadelphia, one of the largest and most popular exhibits was the Brewers' Building, which had mechanical demonstrations of each step in the brewing process and "samples of malt liquors constantly on draught." The brewers sought to put their industry in the best possible light before the world since they were aware, they said, that there were many enemies who classified them "willfully or ignorantly . . . with productions inimical to the welfare of society." Their brochure presented facts and figures about the investment in the nation's breweries: $88,806,290 in breweries, $24,094,500 in malt houses. They emphasized the amount of land under cultivation with barley and hops, 1,639,639 acres, and the annual wages paid out by malt houses and breweries each year, $6,858,500. They likened their brewing process to that of making bread, "both equally necessary to our well-being," and suggested that since temperance means "the truest medium between total abstinance and excess," beer is the ideal beverage, since this is the medium between ardent spirits and water. They conclude with statistics on American expenditure for whiskey, wine, and other liquors, showing only half as much money spent on malt liquors as on whiskey. Therefore, they reasoned, "pauperism spreads mainly among the whiskey-drinking population."[12]

The Cup That Cheers

If an industry as large and powerful as the brewers felt it necessary to defend its product against the temperance folk, I find it easier to understand how our country moved toward Prohibition. The ladies with the axes finally triumphed, if only for a short while. Bereft Americans who wanted booze had to steal it, smuggle it, or make it in the bathtub, until the eighteenth amendment to the Constitution was repealed in 1933 and the cup that cheers was once again legally full to overflowing.

The Cup That Cheers

❧ *My mother has been making these for many years during the holiday season. They are very simple, require no cooking, and make a fine addition to the winter cookie jar.*

BOURBON BALLS

1 small package vanilla wafers, crushed (1 to 1½ cups)	3 tablespoons white corn syrup
1 cup ground walnuts	½ cup bourbon
2 tablespoons cocoa (not instant)	1¼ cups powdered sugar
	½ teaspoon cinnamon

Mix all ingredients except ½ cup sugar and the cinnamon. Drop by scant teaspoonful on a cookie sheet and chill well, at least 2 hours. Form into marble-sized balls; combine cinnamon and sugar and roll balls in it. Chill well and roll once again.

❧ *This is a versatile sweet sauce with a distinctive tang. It goes very well with fresh fruit, such as peaches or nectarines, and I especially recommend it with Sherry Rice Pudding (page 19) and Apple Charlotte (page 75).*

WHISKEY SAUCE

½ cup butter or margarine	1 egg, beaten
1 cup sugar	2 oz. blended whiskey or bourbon

Melt the butter and beat in sugar. In a separate small bowl, beat the egg and add a teaspoonful or so of the hot butter-sugar mixture to stabilize the egg. Then pour into butter and sugar and beat vigorously with a wire whisk until well blended and creamy. Cool to lukewarm. Stir in whiskey. Serve warm or at room temperature over puddings or cakes; cold over fruit.

Dollhouses

Miniature objects have always had a special fascination for me. I remember being given a bracelet as a child which had five tiny colored glass bottles hanging on a gold chain, and each bottle had its own miniature cork. Even as an adult I have always enjoyed looking at miniature pots and pans, small tea sets, and dishes. Some of them are truly museum pieces.

The Sandwich Glass Museum in Sandwich, Massachusetts, for example, has a fine collection of miniature objects, apparently used as salesmen's samples. The Museum of the City of New York has a permanent dollhouse collection on display which delights me with its period furnishings. And in Pennsylvania, there is a museum devoted entirely to dolls and their houses. In 1963, Mary Lesher Merritt built a museum in Douglassville, near Reading, to house her enormous collection of dolls, toys, and doll houses. Today it contains more than thirty-five hundred dolls dating from 1725 to 1900, along with all the things necessary for a doll's well-being. There are small shops, elegant town houses, masses of china and silver, fans, wardrobes, and even dolls for dolls.

What, you may well ask, has all this to do with food? Well, dolls have to eat, and any dollhouse worth looking at, let alone worth exhibiting, is bound to have a very special kitchen and dining room.

Dollhouses

The Merritt Doll Museum is not a place for people who like their exhibits tidily arranged and clearly marked. The dollhouses are rarely dated, and there is scant descriptive material. The dishes, silver, and other artifacts are arranged almost carelessly in their glass cases, with little attempt to differentiate between periods and styles. But this very disorganization contributes to my pleasure. It's like rummaging in someone's attic, not knowing exactly what treasure will turn up next.

There is, for example, a huge dollhouse labeled simply Towne House. It is probably from the eighteenth or early nineteenth century, with a Lancaster County grandfather clock on the staircase landing. The dining room is beautifully furnished with a curio cabinet and a red satin Récamier sofa. There is a tiny Wedgewood tea set in deep blue, all ready for an elegant tea. The kitchen is typical Pennsylvania Dutch, complete with Gaudy Welsh pottery on the shelves of the Dutch cupboard, a wooden dough tray, scenic Leeds and Derby china pieces, a painted tin coffee urn, and Pennsylvania Dutch wooden chairs. There is a tiny electric chandelier, made for candles but "modernized" for the rich doll residents. A basket of doll bread is set to raise in front of the marble fireplace, and a tin kettle on a brass trivet sits on the edge of a hand-hooked rug.

Nearby is another country kitchen, the huge (doll-size huge, that is) cast-iron stove dominating the room, its coal scuttle nearby, complete with doll-size coal. There are two wee Ball canning jars, complete in every detail, sitting on a glass-front dish cupboard which is jammed with tiny pottery crocks, striped glassware, and bowls of miniature fruit. A little food grinder is attached to the wooden table, on which we can also see one-inch cookie cutters for gingerbread men, tinware, a rolling pin the length of a matchstick, a wooden

Dollhouses

butter mold smaller than a dime. There are hand-braided rugs, cast-iron frying pans and kettles; and the dainty bisque lady who cooks in her striped dress and calico apron has a faithful china dog at her heels.

One large area of shelves in the museum is devoted to china and glassware. It's as if the dolls had attended a going-out-of business sale at the local doll pottery, for there are masses of dishes crowded into a small space— spatterware and Spode, Gaudy Welsh and ironstone, Crown Derby and primitive Pennsylvania ceramic ware. There are sturdy English cheese dishes, dozens of fluted brown ceramic cake and pudding molds in every imaginable size. There are complete sets of English china in soft green, light blue, pure white; tureens and four-compartmented serving dishes; berry bowls and tea sets; swan and stock designs; pictures of old English homes; and Chinese willow patterns. Copper chafing dishes two inches high sit atop cast-iron kettles and brass coffee pots. Red coffee grinders are piled beside half-inch tin canisters and button-sized baskets. There are gold-rimmed meat platters and fluted china baskets, no bigger than a thimble; silver toast racks; hand-blown vases decorated with gold leaf, ready to hold one very small violet. In one room there is a complete bar, with bottles of Scotch, balloon brandy glasses big enough to hold six drops, decorative blue and white glass bottles as slender as a pencil, and an elegant coffee service for teetotalers.

An unusual feature of the museum is a series of miniature shops, including two very English, very primitive, butcher shops. One represents the British Christmas season, with festoons of greens and a sign wishing you Merry Christmas and exhorting the doll customers to ask God to Save the King. Sides of wooden meat hang from the tiny rafters; pigs and cows are arranged for display. There are plaster-of-paris chops and chickens and a row of sturdy butcher blocks, each manned by a dour butcher, cleaver in hand. There is also a fine old grocery store, with huge scales on the counter and barrels in front of it, along with sacks of Pillsbury's Best Flour. It has a cashier's cage with an accountant at the desk; a tall ladder to reach the groceries on the top shelves; bins attached to the walls labeled tea, cinnamon, coffee, and such.

The pottery and glass shops will send any child into raptures of joy, and many adults too. The pottery store also stocks pewter ware, and shelves are laden with wonderful crocks and pitchers, some in that fine blue-gray color which distinguishes the best work. There are fluted pottery cake molds, pewter candlesticks, vases, and plates. The china and glass shop has well-dressed customers being attended to by neat salespeople, ready to sell their elegant stock of Bristol hand-blown glass goblets and pitchers of red and blue, some striped with white; silver and brass bowls; teapots; complete sets of English china, and vases and other items we would call "gift shop" stock.

Another exhibit contains a small replica of a village market from Mexico or South America—stalls laden with bright plaster bananas, cheeses, tomatoes, peppers, carrots, and apples, presided over by a diminutive lady in a shawl who will weigh your purchases on her primitive scale. Just down the row of displays you will find an old English pub, heavy with oak furniture, stocked with pitchers, tankards, and mugs, and a genuine barrel of beer no bigger than your thumb. The publican and his wife stand before the roaring fire, along with their dog, to make their tiny customers welcome.

Further along there is a bake room delightfully equipped with open shelves that are stocked with bread and rolls, muffin tins and cake pans; napkin-covered baskets sit on shelves above the cast-iron stove, presumably holding bread dough. There is a lovely copper urn with a spiggot; a flour

Dollhouses

barrel; and spoons, bowls, and rolling pins—all under the watchful eye of a white-capped bakery chef.

Perhaps the most dazzling individual items are the tea sets, scattered throughout the dollhouses, and the china. There are delicate Imari cups and saucers, with matching plates; Spode teapots; English "portrait" plates in delicate pinks and blues with Gainsborough-like ladies; and china plates the size of a bottle cap, decorated with tiny hand-painted flowers. There are Chinese teacups without handles, cruets, and long-handled coffee servers in china, pottery, silver, and copper. There are thimble-sized Toby mugs and an eighteenth-century tea service on a piecrust, tilt-top table, just next to a Duncan Phyfe banquet table that bears a silver cake stand and a decorated, three-tiered cake.

Miniatures and houses for dolls have been popular since the seventeenth century when the salons of Europe took a fancy to these small curiosities. But miniatures were also common in the Orient; Chinese and Japanese art have long reflected an interest in tiny representations of human and animal forms. Collecting miniatures is today one of the most popular of hobbies, on a par with collecting stamps, shells, or coins. Once you begin, there is no stopping, for the acquisition of these tiny replicas of real objects becomes a compulsion that is hard to resist. Perhaps we like them because we can arrange and rearrange them to find pleasing patterns absent in our daily life. Or perhaps we can order them as our own life can never be ordered. Whatever the reason, there are few adults who can resist the fascination of these charming miniatures.

Dollhouses

◈ *This shortbread makes a delicious cookie for tea time, for dolls or people. In our family, it has become a popular holiday sweet as well and makes a big hit as a gift from our kitchen.*

FILBERT SHORTBREAD
1   cup butter or margarine, softened
1   teaspoon vanilla
½   cup sugar
2½   cups all-purpose flour
1¼   cups toasted and skinned filberts (hazelnuts), finely chopped or ground

Cream the butter and vanilla and add sugar gradually, beating until light and fluffy. Beat in 1½ cups flour, then stir in the remaining cup, or use your hands to blend it. Stir in one cup filberts. Divide dough in half and shape each half into a 6 inch square, about ½ inch thick, on an ungreased cookie sheet. Crimp the edges with a fork, as you would for pie dough, and prick the square all over. Sprinkle the ¼ cup filberts on top and bake at 325° for 25 to 30 minutes or until very lightly browned. Cut into small squares while still warm, but let cool completely on the baking sheet.

Note: To toast and skin filberts, spread whole nuts on a baking sheet and place in a 350° oven for about 10 minutes, stirring once or twice. When they are cool, the nuts need only to be rubbed briskly to shed their skins. A blender or food processor is ideal for chopping.

Dollhouses

⁕ This is an old-fashioned pound cake recipe similar to one my Aunt Stella made, similar in turn to one her mother, my Polish grandmother made. It is delicate and buttery and should be served without frosting, cut in very thin slices.

POUND CAKE
- ½ pound sweet butter
- 1 pound powdered sugar
- 6 eggs, separated
- 3 cups all-purpose flour
- 1½ teaspoons baking powder
- ½ cup milk

Cream butter and sugar until very light and fluffy. Add egg yolks and mix well. Sift flour and baking powder together and add alternately with milk. Fold in stiffly beaten egg whites gently until no trace remains. Pour into large ungreased loaf pan (9 × 5 × 3) and bake at 350° for 1 hour. Turn off oven and leave cake in another 15 minutes. Cool in pan.

An Herbal Tea Party

I have been experimenting recently with herb teas, steaming cups of beverages fragrant with flavor and history as well. These teas have been used to cure minor aches, pains, and indispositions for centuries. Although their reputation is medicinal, they have probably survived since medieval times because most of them are so pleasant to drink. In a world that relies on over-the-counter pills for instant relief, there is something very soothing about the idea of sipping sage tea or imbibing an infusion of linden flowers to calm the nerves.

It used to be traditional in the spring to "thin the blood" with a cup of sassafras tea. After the rigors of a New England winter, many Americans found this rite invigorating and pleasant, a sure sign that spring was indeed on the way. Sassafras was a great lure to many colonists, as English apothecaries paid high prices for the roots, and it was considered a profitable venture to outfit a ship and set sail for the New World in search of, not gold, but sassafras.

When imported tea was boycotted during the Revolution, colonists brewed their own tea from the leaves of strawberries, sweetbrier, raspberries, and home-grown herbs. It was patriotic to drink herb tea, and it probably didn't taste all that bad. John Gerard's *Herbal,* published in 1597, said that the leaves of the raspberry "boiled in water, with honey, allum, and a little white wine added thereto, make a most excellent lotion or washing water, and the same decotion fastneth the teeth."[1]

The French call herb tea *tisane,* and it is still possible to order it in some French restaurants. Agatha Christie's famous detective, the impeccable Hercule Poirot, is fond of a tisane, and drinks it with great style. Until recently, my idea of an herb tea was that childhood favorite, catnip tea. Whenever I wanted a tea party for my dolls, my mother would brew up a weak concoction of catnip leaves and hot water for me to pour into the tiny cups. (Perhaps that's the reason all the neighborhood cats found our backyard so attractive.) The tea tasted rather minty and pleasant. The Pennsylvania Dutch drink it cold, before meals, as a tonic to stimulate jaded appetites, and hot afterwards, to prevent gas. Taken hot at bedtime, catnip tea is said to ensure a good night's sleep and to prevent nightmares. Even today catnip is listed in various pharmacopoeias as a tonic, a mild stimulant, and an antispasmodic to reduce fever. Country people used to believe that catnip tea could prevent colds if taken immediately after exposure to drafts and dampness. It is certainly warming and soothing, and as Euell Gibbons suggests, until some dedicated scientist sets up a rigidly controlled experiment, giving hot catnip tea to large numbers of people after exposure to cold, and refusing it to an equally large number of people, we cannot truly estimate how many colds have been prevented.

My own experiments have concentrated on sage and mint. Where else could I begin, having read in Gerard's *Herbal* that sage is "singular good for the head and braine; it quickneth the sences and memory, strengthneth the

An Herbal Tea Party

sinewes, restoreth health to those that have the palsie; takes away shaking or trembling of the members; and being put up the nostrils, it draweth thin flegme out of the head."[2] As if that weren't enough, sage tea is reputed to cure headache, head colds, dyspepsia, delirium, nervous excitement, and lethargy. But after having brewed it in my small earthenware pot, I think I would drink it for its flavor alone. The tisane can be made of either fresh or dried sage leaves, and the result is a stimulating, refreshing, and strangely delicious tea. Sweetened with maple syrup, it is a traditional drink in Vermont, or a dash of rum can be used for variety. I've been told it is unequaled for treating a scratchy sore throat, and I shall certainly try it next time that particular disaster strikes.

If you have a backyard, you probably have mint—more of it than you need. A heady infusion of fresh mint tea is an excellent way to utilize all that excess herb, since it takes a good many leaves to make a proper pot of tea. Few herbs have been so universally esteemed since ancient times as the many varieties of mint. As tisanes, they are refreshing either hot or iced, and they mix easily with other herbs, such as sweet marjoram, lemon verbena, or thyme. The tea is far too good to be considered merely a medicine, but it does contain large amounts of vitamin C, and has been known to cure the hiccups, giddiness, upset stomach, colic, chills, colds, and influenza. Gerard suggests it will prevent the watering of eyes, can be laid against the stinging of wasps, or mixed with salt to soothe the bite of mad dogs. Generally, he says it "is marvelous wholesome for the stomach."[3] An 1883 volume called *Common Sense in the Household* suggests the tea for averting "the unpleasant consequences of a sudden check of perspiration, or the evils induced by ladies' thin shoes."[4]

An Herbal Tea Party

I have a long list of tisanes I plan to brew. Wild thyme tea, for instance, sweetened with honey, is said to be a superior cure for hangover. Then there is rosemary, the pungent herb with foliage like prickly pine needles. The *Herbal* says the distilled water "made from the flowers of rosemary, being drunke at morning and evening first and last, taketh away the stench of mouth and breath and maketh it very sweet."[5] And Shakespeare apparently knew his pharmacopoeia when he has Ophelia say, "There's rosemary, that's for remembrance," for early herbalists assure us that the constant use of this herb will cure forgetfulness and comfort the brain. When infused in white wine, the resulting lotion is said to comfort the brain and keep the hair from falling out. Perhaps it is not so surprising, then, to find rosemary listed as an ingredient on modern hair tonic and lotion bottles.

Next spring when the first yellow flowers of the coltsfoot make their appearance, I will wait patiently for the leaves to follow, pick and dry them, and brew a cup of coltsfoot tea. It is reputed to be good for coughs, colds, and asthma, but I look forward to the pure pleasure of the taste.

In revolutionary days, many a housewife must have invented wild and wonderful potions to replace the tea that lay at the bottom of Boston harbor. Giving up tea was a great sacrifice, but not too great for a true patriot. As for me, when summer comes around again, I shall take to the meadows and forests to find new leaves to brew.

An Herbal Tea Party

TO MAKE HERBAL TEA

Tea can be made from bee balm, speedwell, horehound, goldenrod, borage, vervain, ground ivy, mint, red clover blossoms, tansy, coltsfoot, and camomile. Any good book on herbs will give you many other suggestions as well as cautionary advice about the ones that don't taste all that good.

No matter what dried leaves you use, the method is the same. Use a porcelain or earthenware teapot, rinsed with hot water. Add about a teaspoon of dried leaves or flowers for each cup, plus one for the pot. Fill with boiling water and steep no more than five minutes.

The strength of the tea should be judged by taste, not color, as these leaves will make a paler brew than the black teas you are accustomed to drink.

Fresh rather than dried leaves may be used (mint leaves are especially good fresh) and should be gently crushed in a cloth before infusing. Use more fresh than dried leaves, perhaps three teaspoonsful for each cup.

Glorious Gadgets

I once lived in a house with five fireplaces, including one in the kitchen. Most of the time they were a charming adjunct to the efficient oil heating system. But one cold January night we had a fierce snow storm, with rapidly dropping temperatures and high winds. The electricity failed, and with it the oil burner and the kitchen stove. During the next two days, I discovered firsthand what colonial housewives had done with their time. They kept the fires going. I moved from one room to another, tending the fireplaces. As soon as I had completed my rounds, fire number one needed attention again. I tried to cook over the fire and was finally forced to grill hot dogs on a stick like any Girl Scout on a picnic. My face was scorched, my back aching, my clothes sooty, and I felt a new kinship with past generations of women who had toiled this way every day of their lives.

I think about this sometimes when I see a restoration of an old Pennsylvania farmhouse. The kitchen is always the showpiece, with a large fireplace, an array of interesting pans, hooks, and cranes. A guide in colonial costume usually sits by the cold fireplace and talks about the artifacts, sustained by twentith-century plumbing and vitamins.

I suggest that the next time you visit such a site you consider those

Glorious Gadgets

utensils carefully, not as curiosities but as real tools. Put yourself in the place of the woman who used them. Look at the large cast-iron kettle hanging from the crane and remember that this was her major food container, the pot in which she cooked mush and stew and soup. Filled with meat, vegetables, and liquid, the heavy pot could weigh as much as twenty pounds. The stubby, three-legged pot with a tight-fitting cover was a Dutch oven for baking corn pone and biscuits. There is usually a spider on display, a three-legged cast-iron frying pan for cooking meat directly over the coals, and sometimes a grill, not unlike the modern version, used for broiling. There are long-handled toasting forks, toasting irons, and waffle irons which turn out crisp cakes in interesting shapes and designs. And with such simple tools, the housewife and her daughters had to prepare three meals a day for hardworking men and women. In addition, they had to dry, salt, pickle, and preserve produce for the winter; make butter, cheese, apple butter, jams, and jellies; bake bread, cakes, and pies. Small wonder that each new labor-saving device was welcomed, after a natural period of suspicion, and eagerly added to the meager stock of available utensils.

A primitive pickle grinder, for instance, with handmade grinding rods, cranks, and latchets, shortened the many hours of cutting and chopping. A cast-iron apple peeler appeared in the late 1800s that could peel the skin of an apple, a peach, or a pear in mere seconds. An Erie iron manufacturer cast muffin, biscuit, and corn-stick pans in beautiful shapes and designs, some resembling flowers and leaves as well as the traditional rounds, squares, and oblongs. The heavy iron heated evenly and retained warmth, requiring less time in the oven. In 1858 a large sausage stuffer was patented, a strange contraption with an iron handle and a graduated bowl, which speeded up the process and made

Glorious Gadgets

more uniform sausages. There was a variety of cabbage cutters, an important item for households that ate a lot of sauerkraut and slaw. One ingenious device had a handle like a pump which, when raised and lowered, allowed a cutting blade to chop cabbage into the box below. Another design featured a square box fitted over a crock or barrel. A cylindrical crank rotated the blades, shredding the cabbage. A rectangular cheese grater had a removable drawer below; a cast-iron nut cracker improved on the hammer, increasing the quantity of nuts a family could crack during a long winter evening.

The art of making butter seems charming to us as we look back now, our twentieth-century vision blurred by nostalgia, but it was considered a fatiguing chore by almost everyone required to do it. Women, as they got older, spoke of how they had dreaded butter day when they were young. One old gentleman I know who made butter for years and sold it as a major source of income was astonished to think that anyone could be interested in how it was made. He was just glad he didn't have to do it any more.

There were dozens of different kinds of churns, all designed to make the task easier. In the old-fashioned broomstick churn, the dasher moved up and down while the cream slowly turned to butter. There were pump churns; animal-powered devices, using either dogs or horses; barrel churns with handles for turning; and paddle churns in lidded glass jars, still on sale in country stores and gourmet cooking shops. After churning, the butter had to be "worked," the excess moisture pounded and rolled out of it, another time-consuming chore. Lettie Smith of Newtown, Bucks County, in 1853 designed and patented a Labor Saving Butter Worker, featuring a working tray which could be raised and lowered and a drawer below to store ice and keep the butter in better condition.

Glorious Gadgets

Wooden butter molds, popular now as decorative items, were used to enhance the looks—and consequently, the price—of butter. Some of them are works of art, products of the Swiss and German wood-carvers who brought their skills to Pennsylvania. The designs range from simple stars and flowers to elaborately detailed representations of animals and people, delicate flowers and vegetables, hearts, swans, wheat, and religious symbols.

The fireplaces in early American homes vary in depth and width. Some will have an oven built into the back or side wall of the hearth, which required extra coals inside to bring the oven temperature to the proper baking level. Then the coals were raked out and the pies, cakes, and breads put in. If the oven was too hot, the bread burned on the outside, but remained doughy within. Too cool an oven resulted in heavy, soggy bread. The housewife frequently judged oven temperatures by putting her hand inside for a count of twenty or thirty. If she had to remove her hand before the count was finished, the oven was too hot for the bread.

Some homes had summer kitchens to avoid heating up the entire house on hot days, and the addition to the house also served to expand the kitchen facilities. Outdoor ovens were common in Pennsylvania. They were substantially larger than those attached to the fireplace and could accommodate the larger amounts needed as the family grew or when hired hands had to be fed during threshing and harvest times. The oven generally had a little roof extension over the mouth end to protect the baker from the weather, for neither snow nor sleet prevented the baking of bread.

Although Benjamin Franklin had invented an iron stove in 1742, stoves were not widely used for cooking until commercial iron furnaces became more common. Increased size and more intense heat from the furnaces encouraged

Glorious Gadgets

the manufacture of cheaper and more efficient stoves. By 1840, householders were beginning to board up their kitchen fireplaces and install stoves for both cooking and heating. At first, of course, farmers were suspicious of the new contraptions, and stoves were installed directly in front of the fireplace: In case of failure, they could be removed and the hearth reactivated.

One of the earliest advertisements in Pennsylvania for a cookstove appeared in the Pittsburgh *Gazette,* December 8, 1818. Charles Postly's Patent Cooking Stove was recommended because it was useful for "extensive cooking, [and] is a handsome piece of furniture, for the sitting room." It came with removable boilers, in case you wanted just to sit by the fire; ovens for baking; and a wooden vessel to boil the washing water. Steamers attached to the boilers cooked vegetables, utilizing the steam created while the meat was cooking. It had been in use for three years in New York City, boasted the manufacturer, and on the largest size you could cook a dinner for seventy or eighty persons.

In the June 1865 issue of *Godey's Lady's Book,* Mrs. Sarah J. Hale noted in her "Editor's Table" column that "Mechanical Science is giving important aids to the labor of Cookery; one of the best of these we commend, *Spear's Anti-Dust, Gas-Burning, Cooking-Stove.* (James Spear 1116 Market Street, Philadelphia) We advise our friends to send for a circular, if not able to call and see the curious and complete invention, which *consumes its own gas, makes no dust, economizes fuel, and has conveniences for every kind of cooking.*"[1]

By the late nineteenth century, stoves of all shapes and sizes abounded. In October 1900 the Majestic Manufacturing Company advertised the Great Majestic Combination Range in the *Ladies' Home Journal.* Judging by the

Glorious Gadgets

accompanying drawing, it was indeed majestic, with what appear to be five ovens, some eight or ten burners, and an assortment of warming shelves. The blurb reads: "Would it be an object to you to reduce your fuel bill at least one third; own a range that will cook for one or forty; heat water for the kitchen, bath and entire house; require no interchanging as the seasons change; burn natural or fuel gas, hard or soft coal, or wood; and rightly used, last a lifetime?"[2] It must have sounded as revolutionary and desirable to the housewife of 1900 as the microwave oven does to the modern cook.

The same magazine advertises a variety of other household gadgets, including the massive kitchen cabinets we have come to call Hoosier cabinets. The Hoosier Manufacturing Company in New Castle, Indiana, called theirs "A Kitchen Piano. Everything at her fingers' ends. Nothing to walk or long for. Sugar, flour, salt, spices, milk, eggs, molasses in this self-cleaning cabinet." Or perhaps you would prefer a Victor Instantaneous Water Heater, using gas or gasoline. Or even, in 1892, a Stevens Dishwasher, which "washes, rinses, dries perfectly in 5 minutes from 60 to 100 pieces at one time."[3] From there it's just a step to electric woks, bacon cookers, and doughnut guns.

Glorious Gadgets

◈ *My maternal grandmother was a busy lady, raising five children, working as a professional nurse full time, and providing goodies for a substantial part of the neighborhood as well. This bread recipe requires no kneading, probably because she didn't have time. My mother has made it for years, supplying family and friends and substantial parts of* her *neighborhood, too.*

MOTHER'S BREAD
1	yeast cake or 1 package dry yeast
2	cups warm water (110°–115°)
½	cup sugar
½	teaspoon salt
1	egg, beaten
6	tablespoons butter or margarine, melted

6 to 7 cups all-purpose flour

Add ½ of water to yeast and dissolve. Add sugar, salt, egg, and 3 tablespoons melted butter. Add remaining water. Work in flour until dough is easily handled and not sticky. Use remaining butter to grease a large bowl. Roll dough around in it to coat with butter. Cover and let rise in warm place until doubled in bulk, about 1½ hrs. Punch down. Divide into 2 loaves (use pans approximately 9 × 5 × 3 inches), or make rolls or small loaves (6 × 3½ × 2). Add poppy, caraway, or other seeds if desired. Let rise again until doubled, about 45 minutes. Bake at 400° for 20 minutes for loaves, 8 to 10 minutes for rolls. Remove from pans to cool on rack.

Glorious Gadgets

ↄ❦ *Gingerbread turns up with regularity in old cookbooks, including the manuscript copies. Some of the recipes are for rolled gingerbread, or what we would call cookies. There are others for the soft variety, similar to cake. I like this particular recipe because the measurements are easy to remember and it makes a light, spicy dessert that keeps well.*

MY SOFT GINGERBREAD

⅔ cup butter, margarine, or vegetable shortening	1⅔ cups all-purpose flour
⅔ cup sugar	1 teaspoon ginger
1 egg, slightly beaten	1 teaspoon soda
⅔ cup dark molasses	⅔ cup boiling water

Cream the butter and sugar; add egg and molasses. Sift dry ingredients together and combine with egg mixture. Into the cup in which you measured the molasses, pour the boiling water. Combine gently. Pour into buttered 10 × 10 inch pan. Bake at 350° for 40 to 45 minutes or until the center is done. Let cool slightly and serve, or serve when cold. This gingerbread will always fall slightly in the middle as it cools because it is so soft and light, so don't be disturbed when this happens. It is excellent for breakfast, served with a little butter.

Kitchens: Restored and Reconstructed

I love to look in other people's kitchens. I don't care what century they represent. So I always head for the kitchen in any restoration or museum that I visit, whether it is as elaborate as Williamsburg or as simple as the local historical society. There are a number of excellent sites in Pennsylvania where one can observe the kitchen habits of an earlier day, but to me, three are especially good.

At the Pennsylvania Farm Museum of Landis Valley in Lancaster you can see the changes in rural village life from the early days of our nation up to the 1890s. The Landis brothers, George and Henry, collected farm implements and household furnishings for most of their lives and put them all in a museum that now belongs to the commonwealth. Set in one hundred acres of lush farm country, the village buildings have been restored with great charm and accuracy and surrounded by a group of other complementary exhibits.

You can walk through a general store; visit a fire house and a school house; stop by the restored 1856 Landis House hotel and have a snack; enjoy the print shop, the seamstress's house, the pottery shop. There are

Kitchens: Restored and Reconstructed

exhibits of spinning, weaving, gunsmithing, harness-making, and tools. But the re-created nineteenth-century roadside tavern has the big beautiful fireplace, with all the proper utensils hanging in place. And in the settlers' cabin, a re-created simple log shelter, there is a tiny kitchen and a shallow fireplace where a real person demonstrates how to cook a real meal—pork and sauerkraut the day I visited—using the same techniques the settler's wife did in 1760. Outside you can look at the barn, the bake oven, the well, the animal pens that house real animals during the summer months. If you follow the path to the lovely Federal farmhouse, restored from the early nineteenth-century original, you'll find that the kitchen fireplace is deeper, the seven-plate iron stove is a decorative as well as a practical adjunct. The pump and the brick bake oven are still outside the back door, ready for use. Just down the road is the Landis House, originally the home of the museum founders, now furnished as it might have been in 1870. Housewives had more conveniences by then—the pump had moved to the back porch. The dining-sitting room is a cozy, cheerful place with a magnificient cast-iron stove, and the pantry is just a step away, its shelves lined with newspapers, the edges cut in fancy designs.

Perhaps my favorite historical museum in Pennsylvania is another village, Old Economy, in Ambridge, a few miles west of Pittsburgh on the Ohio River. This settlement, like the Ephrata Cloister, was a product of William Penn's policy of tolerance for all religious groups. Father George Rapp, a peripatetic German pietist, had led his band of followers from Europe in 1804 to a farm in Butler County, then on to Harmony, Indiana, then back to Pennsylvania in 1825 to build their permanent home on the present site of Old Economy.

Kitchens: Restored and Reconstructed

The members of the Harmonist Society were Christian communists, pooling their resources and working without wages for the good of the community. Members practiced celibacy and were divided into households, with from three to eleven people living in each house. One male was selected as head of the household and was responsible for the conduct of all in his group. One woman was chosen to cook and care for the house, drawing needed supplies from the village store and farm stocks. Other householders worked in the society's various commercial enterprises or in the garden and fields. Although there was some freedom within the community as long as members refrained from becoming too worldly, it was generally a restrictive society.

Pat Reibel, who guided me through Old Economy, explained that the Harmonists, unlike the brothers and sisters at Ephrata, lived very well. Their many commercial ventures prospered—a hotel; mills for linen, wool, and even silk; farm products; pottery; furniture—providing sufficient money for them to maintain a high standard of living. Father Rapp's home and the adjoining home of Frederick, his adopted son, are beautifully furnished with fine furniture, glass, and china. One room, used as an office, contains a large vault which, I was told, once held $500,000 in emergency church funds.

The dining room and kitchen are of special interest, since this house served as the corporate headquarters of the society. There were many visitors, most of them on business, who had to be entertained and given lodging. Consequently, the kitchen, with its ample fireplace and more floor space than was usual, served to feed the household as well as the continuous procession of guests.

Among the early visitors was Friedrich List, an emigrant German econo-

Kitchens: Restored and Reconstructed

mist, who wrote of the "clean and comfortable homes . . . the wonderful garden in back of [Rapp's] house consisting of several acres with a vineyard, all kinds of flowers, orange, lemon and fig trees, all kinds of American plants, cotton, tobacco, and the finest kinds of small espalier fruit trees." After dining with Rapp, he commented on the society's good beer, the excellence of the food (served on imported porcelain), and spoke admiringly of the "satisfaction, cheerfulness, purity, and consideration of the members."[1]

The kitchen in the Rapp house illustrates open-hearth cooking in 1830. The traditional utensils are there: a trammel and ratchet instead of a crane, a large stew kettle, trivets, and spiders. Cooking pots are set over small, individual fires rather than one roaring blaze, an interesting distinction. "It makes sense," Pat Reibel said, "to think that the cook would want different temperatures for different foods, so she would arrange her pots on the hearth as we do ours on the stove—with different temperatures on the burners." We also talked about the hazards of cooking over the open fire, especially in a long dress. She told me some women wore aprons which could wrap around flowing skirts and literally button them up, creating a tidy "bag" which helped prevent accidents. When stoves came along, the apron buttons disappeared.

On our way to the Baker house we stopped to inspect the community kitchen and the large outdoor bake oven. Originally there had been ovens at each corner of the property, I learned, but only one remains. There are now volunteer bread bakers at Old Economy who bake three times a week during the spring and summer. Fires are started at 9 in the morning, and by 10:30 the bakers hope the soot from the last go-round has fallen from the brick interior, one of several ways to test for proper temperature. When the oven is the right heat, the floor is dusted with a wet mop and the loaves are put in with a long-handled wooden peel to bake for half an hour or so. When questioned about their techniques, the bakers respond as cooks have throughout the centuries. "After a while," they say, "you just get to *know* when it's right." The kind and condition of the wood—hard burns hotter than soft, dry better than wet—wind, outside temperature, and the state of the oven itself all help to determine the length of time the bread should bake.

Since the Economists led a communal life, all the bread was baked in the central ovens and distributed to householders. Other community cooking projects, such as pickling, or making apple butter or jelly, were carried out in the Feast Kitchen, where twelve huge black iron cauldrons are sunk into ovens, with overhead hoods and vents to allow hot air to escape. The Feast Kitchen is so named because the meals for the Love Feasts were prepared there. As described by the curator of Old Economy, Daniel Reibel, "the feast was the closest thing to a sacrament [the society] had. The feast was called *Liebsmahl*, love feast. The whole community gathered at noon on the day of the feast. . . . Men sat on the right (south) side and women on the left side (north). . . . There was a regular meal of stew, noodles, bread, fruit in season, salad, beer, and wine. After the meal there was a service. Since the love feasts were partly secular in nature, a portion of the service was of secular music; perhaps there was some other entertainment as well."[2]

The Baker house is a home typical of the Harmonist householder. It contains furniture made in the community's cabinet shop, and much of the pottery in the double cupboard is also homemade. There are attractive brown and green dishes, some decorated with tulips; the mugs and crocks have personal thumbprints, a sure sign that the item was made in Old Economy. The community imported Wedgewood and other china from Europe, some

Kitchens: Restored and Reconstructed

for their own use, but the bulk of it they sold in their store, an import sideline that demonstrates once again their business acumen.

We walked up to the top floor of the Rapp house, now used for special design exhibits and lectures. There I met Charles Bashaar, a skilled cabinetmaker. Retired three times, he is still working at top speed and apparently enjoying himself enormously. His grandmother was a Harmonist, working in the community's hotel. "Besides that," he told me, "she got up before 4 A.M. every day and baked four or five pies. Her son took a bucket to the mill for lunch, and he always had fresh pie." His grandmother was "a little bit of a thing, but she was the boss," he said emphatically. "She never got over the fact that food in Germany had been scarce, and she just couldn't stand waste. There were six of us grandchildren, and if we didn't eat everything on our plates, it was still there for the next meal."

Among the visitors to Old Economy in 1828 was Mrs. Basil Hall, an intrepid British lady who traveled throughout America with her husband and infant daughter by stage, private carriage, and from New Orleans to Pittsburgh by steamboat.

> Last night we stopped in a place called Economy, one of those eccentric establishments of which there are so many in this country. The founder and manager of this one is a German of the name of Rapp. . . . All that we could view was the exterior of the buildings, which had a very cheerful appearance. I cannot pretend to tell you under what kind of management the place is, but I believe that Mr. Rapp is a clever man and tolerably despotic, so that it will probably continue to flourish during his life and fall to pieces at his death.[3]

Kitchens: Restored and Reconstructed

Mrs. Hall's prophecy was very astute. Although the society continued under other leadership after Rapp's death in 1847, the momentum declined. Around 1868 there was a second short burst of growth under Jacob Henrici, but by 1880 the average age of the members was about seventy and it was impossible to maintain the property. The society was officially dissolved in 1903.

My final choice for old kitchens to visit is the Colonial Pennsylvania Plantation in Ridley Creek Park, near Philadelphia, where the Bishops Mill Historical Institute administers 112 acres containing a farm and outbuildings that have been in continuous use since the early 1700s. Its goal, pursued with both anthropological and archeological zeal by the staff of professionals and volunteers, is to re-create a working farm of that period.

The staff of the plantation welcomes visitors, but in a far more casual way than at comparable restorations. I arrived on a cool spring day, made my way past the empty admissions booth, walked up the path past the barn, crawled over a fence because I didn't see the gate, stared down two horses in the front yard, and walked up the steps of a beautiful stone and wood farmhouse in varying stages of repair. I heard voices from behind a closed door, but no one appeared. I poked around, looking at the large fireplace clearly being restored, peered into a huge bake oven, wandered out into the yard again, and found a small girl dressed in homespun, cap, and shawl, sitting on the steps crying.

"Are you all right?" I asked tentatively. She blew her nose and wiped her eyes.

"Yes," she said, "but there's a terrible downdraft in the chimney and the kitchen's full of smoke. And I've been chopping onions for the stew. Do you

Kitchens: Restored and Reconstructed

want a tour?" I said I did and was taken upstairs to see the bedrooms and downstairs to see the root cellar, where last winter's vegetables had survived well. My guide, Marian, confessed she had used the last of the carrots for the stew. She unwrapped an unpleasant looking object, covered with mold, from some old rags. "It's our cheese," she said proudly. "We never know what we're going to get until we taste it." She peered at it. "It doesn't look too good, does it?"

We went into the spring house, where the cooler temperatures keep food from spoiling during the summer months. There was nothing there but a large earthenware crock. Inside was a large tin can of lard. "Pretend you didn't see that," Marian suggested. "We're only supposed to use things here that might really have been available in the eighteenth century."

The concept of the plantation is that of a working, participating museum. Staff and volunteers live here during the day just as a farm family might have lived in the 1770s. The garden is planted with "authentic" vegetables such as turnips, onions, carrots, lettuce, beets, and pumpkins. There are herbs both for flavor and medicine. Farm animals are kept on the premises, and the women of the "family" cook, spin, weave, sew, and dress in the traditional manner. It is an exciting, ambitious project, and the people I met seemed to be having a very good time.

Marian took me in the kitchen to check on her stew, as well as the biscuits that were baking in the Dutch oven set over the coals, with more hot coals on the lid for even heat. I talked with Shirley Lighton, a volunteer whose special interest is colonial foods. She was working on a standardized cookbook for the volunteer cooks, based on the utensils they actually have in the kitchen. When a recipe calls for "one tin cup of," that tin cup will match

Kitchens: Restored and Reconstructed

their tin cup, or "one pewter spoonful" will be the same pewter spoon. She uses recipes from the cookbooks of the time, mostly those by Hanna Glasse and Susannah Carter, English women who wrote cookbooks the settlers might have brought with them.

As I was leaving, the horses somehow got into the garden, and all hands turned out before they trampled everything in sight. While two of the animals were being coaxed away, a third arrived and pranced happily in to see his friends. There was a good deal of advice exchanged, along with considerable giggling, but the horses were ejected before too much damage had been done. As I walked out to the parking lot, two yellow school buses were disgorging large quantities of squirming children. I watched the staff square their shoulders and put on welcoming smiles. I couldn't help but think that this was one hazard eighteenth-century settlers did not have to endure.

Kitchens: Restored and Reconstructed

Sarah Yeates's cookbook[4] *has a wealth of kitchen wisdom in it, some of it sounding very modern. Her "Observations on Puddings," for example, indicate that bread and custard puddings "require time, and a moderate smart oven, which will raise and not burn them." When it comes to making cakes, she suggests, "be careful to have everything in readiness, for should you be kept waiting for any particular Article when near the finishing of a Cake, it will grow sodden and not rise in the baking, and so lose one of its chief excellencies." I have found to my sorrow that she is absolutely right when she says, "When butter is used, take care to beat it to a fine cream before you put in your sugar, as afterwards if you were to take ever so many pains it would not answer so well."*

Here is her recipe for a loaf called Diet Bread Cake, an odd designation when you consider the number of eggs and sugar. Perhaps she uses the word diet *to mean* healthy. *And even with the amount of sugar used, it is not especially sweet. Whatever the reason, the recipe makes a dense loaf, similar to pound cake. It is very good toasted and buttered with cinnamon and sugar or jam. My own adaptation follows her original directions.*

TO MAKE DIET BREAD CAKE
The yolks of 12 eggs with only 6 whites, well beaten till it forms a cream, add to which 1 pound lump sugar pounded fine, then by degrees add 1 pound fine flour; the peels of 2 lemons with the juice of 1 or 2 according to your palate the whole to be beaten up well for more than an hour to be baked in a quick oven.

Kitchens: Restored and Reconstructed

DIET BREAD CAKE A LA BARTLETT

12 egg yolks	2 cups flour
6 egg whites	zest of one lemon, finely grated
2 cups sugar	juice of two lemons

Beat egg yolks lightly. Whip egg whites until they are frothy and begin to stiffen slightly. Mix egg yolks and whites together until they are creamy. Add sugar gradually, then flour and lemon zest. Stir in lemon juice. Pour into well-greased loaf pan, 9 × 5 × 3 inches; bake at 375° for about an hour or until a toothpick inserted in center comes out clean. Cool slightly and turn out on rack to complete cooling.

The Pennsylvania Historical Society in Philadelphia has a number of manuscript cookbooks in their collection, among them one written by Jane Janvier, kept between 1817 and 1837. She too has a recipe for Diet Bread, as well as a number of meat recipes, an unusual addition to manuscript books. The assumption usually was that every good housewife knew how to cook meat and vegetables. It was that special cake or cookie or pudding recipe from a neighbor that was noted down for future reference. In any case, my favorite recipe from this collection is one which foretold the use of the freezer in modern households. I have seen recipes for snow ice cream, for maple syrup spozas dropped on snow or ice, but this is the first I have encountered that actually tells you to freeze the dough. First, Jane Janvier's original directions; then my very slight adaptation which you may find a little more convenient.

JANE JANVIER'S SCOTCH CAKES
Take ½ lb of butter, melt it, stir into it 1 lb of brown sugar, break 2 eggs into it, stir into it ¾ lb of flour, a little cinamon and rose water, put it out of doors and let it freeze very hard then thaw a little sugar and flour on the board and roll them out very thin and bake them in a moderate oven.

SCOTCH FREEZER COOKIES

½	pound butter or margarine, melted	1½	cups all-purpose flour
2	cups firmly packed dark brown sugar	1	teaspoon cinnamon
2	eggs	1	teaspoon vanilla

Mix ingredients in order to form a stiff dough. Pat into a flat rectangle; wrap in wax paper or foil and place in freezer until frozen solid—not less than 1 hour. Cut off small chunks and let thaw slightly, just enough to roll out. Sprinkle flour and a little sugar on a pastry board or cloth and roll dough very thin. Cut into squares with a sharp knife or into fancy shapes with cookie cutters. Place on ungreased cookie sheets and bake at 350° for 4 to 5 minutes or until crisp. Watch carefully as they burn easily. Cool on wire rack. Dough may also be shaped like a sausage, frozen, and then sliced, similar to icebox cookies.

There's No Place Like Homestead

When you drive over the Homestead High Level Bridge just outside Pittsburgh and look at the vast steel mills spreading across the valley, it isn't hard to visualize the way Homestead must have looked in 1909. That was the year sociologist Margaret Byington went house-to-house collecting information for her study of the mill town, sitting in kitchens, talking with housewives and mill workers about life in a steel town. For many, that life was grueling—uncertain, unhealthy, unrewarding. Workers, she said, "turn daily from twelve hours in the din of the huge mills to home, supper, a smoke and bed."[1] The methodology of Byington's study has been both praised and criticized, but I find her observations on the routine of the mother-housewife not only enlightening but strangely moving as well.

First, a few statistics. In 1909, Slavic day laborers were earning about twelve dollars a week, compared with the fifteen or twenty dollars earned by more skilled workers. Generally, Byington found Slavs spending a greater percentage of their income on food than were native whites and English-speaking Europeans. A look at one Slavic family's food purchases for a week shows a high proportion of bread, meat, butter, and coffee, with fruit and

There's No Place Like Homestead

vegetables lower down on the shopping list. This family of five depended on the father's weekly $9.90 as their sole income. Total food costs came to $5.19, a built-in deterrent to riotous living. In other, slightly more affluent homes, the menu was more varied and nutritious, with oatmeal, milk, bacon and eggs, a greater selection of fruit and vegetables, and even an occasional pie or cake.

One important consideration for the family planner was the inevitable dinner bucket. Byington was impressed with the care each woman took to make the bucket pleasing to her "mister." "Most of the men, as they are not given regular time for eating, snatch a bite between tasks, though some, whose work permits, stop for a leisurely meal. I even heard of men who took steaks to cook on the hot plates about the machines. But they usually rely on the cold meal, and the women take great pains to make it appetizing, especially by adding preserves in a little cup in the corner of the bucket. They try to give the man what he likes most, apparently half from pity at the cold food and hard work that fall to his lot."[2]

Margaret Kuzma, now over eighty, remembers the bucket very well. "Meat was very important," she said. "Even in the bucket there was substantial meat—not just cold cuts, but pork chops and ham." Mrs. Kuzma has lived in Homestead all her life and worked for most of her eighty years. She started as a meat cutter in her father's butcher shop when she was a young girl. Later she became his bookkeeper, moved on to her own business, and still goes to work every day in her own shop. And she is an active member of the Slovak community.

"My mother and father came from what was then the Austro-Hungarian Empire," she told me. "My father had been in the Prussian army and had

There's No Place Like Homestead

made a lot of friends who later came to Homestead, and Braddock, too. He and his two brothers came first to Lebanon and later western Pennsylvania. They were all butchers, and my father opened his own shop here." She explained that the store was more than just a meat-cutting establishment, "although we did that, too, of course. But we made our own headcheese and paprika bacon and smoked bacon. We had our own smokehouse right there. And *klobasy,* we made that. And *pirohy,* with cheese and cabbage filling. Not potato. Potato was Polish, my father used to say."

There was a constant supply of young men available to work in the butcher shop and learn the meat-cutting business, she told me. "They would come here to visit or live with a relative, and pretty soon someone would say, 'We have a new boy from the old country,' and my father might take him on. Lots of our 'boys' are still here, retired mostly now. They always lived with us, too, two or three at a time. And we always had a maid, a Slovak girl we would bring over. My mother would teach her to cook and she'd stay until she got married, and we'd get another one."

In those days, workers got up at 5 A.M. and ate a hearty breakfast—steak, potatoes, bread. Then at noon those whose schedule permitted came home to a cooked meal. "We always had more meat than other places," Mrs. Kuzma explained. "But all the men expected meat at noon in the boardinghouses, too. Every man got a pound and a half a day, divided over the three meals. Supper always included soup, usually with homemade noodles, and the meat was in one big half-pound chunk. It was weighed out every day."

Byington visited some of the Homestead lodging houses. At one, where the two rooms measured a mere twelve by twenty feet, she found the wife of

There's No Place Like Homestead

the boarding-boss in the kitchen getting dinner, "some sort of hot apple cake and a stew of the cheapest cuts of meat. Along one side of the room was an oilcloth-covered table with a plank bench on each side; above it a rack holding a long row of handleless white cups and a shelf with tin knives and forks. Near the up-to-date range, the only piece of real furniture in the room, hung the 'buckets' in which all mill men carry their noon or midnight meals." In the second room, double iron bedsteads were lined up for the twenty men, the boss, his wife, and two babies.

Mrs. Kuzma told me that at the usual boardinghouse, each man paid a fixed amount—usually three or four dollars—for a place to sleep, cooked meals, and laundry. Then the total cost of the food purchased was divided among the men on "pay Friday." Usually the cook's food was included in the total, "free" food for service rendered, if you will.

In 1909, most families lived on credit, carrying accounts at local stores and paying up every two weeks or monthly on pay Friday. A majority of the lower income families never caught up, Byington tells us, and although credit was convenient, many of the women she interviewed were sure it was more expensive in the long run. Grocers tended to overcharge, and "it is much easier to be extravagant when no cash is paid out and the price is simply jotted down in the 'book.' A woman who tried this method once, found it so expensive that at the end of two weeks she threw the book into the stove and would never use one again."[3] Mrs. Kuzma confirms this. "Everybody had a credit book with the different shops," she said, "the butcher, the milkman, the grocer. When they paid up, we would enter it in their book. We had more than a thousand accounts at the butcher shop." During the Depression, merchants carried accounts for long periods. "We had over fifty

There's No Place Like Homestead

thousand dollars in unpaid bills," she remembered. "And we owned some houses, and one tenant never paid a cent for seven years. Of course, everybody was in the same boat, and people were very kind to one another."

The butcher shop was also a social center, according to Mrs. Kuzma. "We didn't have telephones, so people came in to order. Lots of them didn't know English, so they would ask us to translate." She shook her head. "Some of them never learned English at all, even when the kids went to school. The parochial schools all taught in Slovak, you see."

Despite the slender resources of many Slavic families, a tradition of good cooking developed in Homestead. Mrs. Kuzma learned to cook from her mother, who was very good, she says, especially at pie. "She made crusts like nobody else ever has," she sighed. "And noodles, they were special. All the women tried to cut theirs as fine as possible, but my mother's were like angel hair." Although there was little time and less money for recreation, Sunday traditionally was devoted to relaxation. Extra meat was bought on Saturday for a Sunday roast, and even though the men usually had to work on either Saturday or Sunday evening, there was more leisure to sit down and enjoy a hot meal, often with married sons and daughters at home for the day. Family favorites included chicken paprikash with dumplings; *holubky,* stuffed cabbage; and soups of all kinds. "Nut tortes, too, and Dobosh torte, which everybody thinks is Austrian but is really Slovak. Oh, and *patica,* that's a raised dough filled with nuts and poppy seeds." For holidays there was sour mushroom soup made with sauerkraut juice; and *bobalky,* a sweet egg bread with poppy seeds; as well as roast lamb and beef, with special stuffing for a beef or pork filet.

Christmas Eve is a special time for Slovaks. "No excuses accepted for

There's No Place Like Homestead

Christmas Eve," Mrs. Kuzma said firmly. "Everybody in the family comes." There is always fish; *kolacky,* sweet dough filled with nuts or cottage cheese or jam; and *hrata,* a sweet wine which everyone samples, even the children, after it is heated and mixed with brown sugar and butter. Easter means more good food—ham; *klobasy;* the egg cheese called *cirak; pascha,* a special Easter bread; and of course, dyed eggs.

Even the poorest Slovak families took notice of special holidays. Thanksgiving Day in 1909 was a regular working day, but on the Fourth of July and at Christmas, "the great mill stops. Everyone who can goes home, some to families in Homestead, others to neighboring towns, and there are Christmas trees in many homes. Some of the women who kept budget accounts took care to explain that their unusual expenses in December, both for food and extras, were for Christmas festivities."[4]

Slovak women were slow to "go American" in Homestead, Mrs. Kuzma said. "You still don't find boxed potatoes around. We always make dumplings on Friday with sweet cabbage or sauerkraut or cottage cheese in them. And there's plenty of beef and veal goulash. And bean soup with *lechki,* little noodle squares. I don't think I'd be wrong in saying about 95 percent of the people around here eat the same things—always have and always will. A lot of things about Homestead haven't changed much at all since I was girl."

There's No Place Like Homestead

❧ *Hearty beef and veal stews have always been the mainstay of Pennsylvania kitchens. Hungarians, Czechs, Poles, and Slovaks all add their special touches — sour cream, paprika, or dumplings. This recipe has no particular ethnic background but is rather a little bit of everything, just like Pennsylvania. You may find it tastes better the second day, after the flavors have had time to blend.*

HEARTY VEAL STEW

- 2 pounds lean veal cubes (shoulder or breast)
- 2 tablespoons sweet Hungarian paprika
- 2 tablespoons all-purpose flour
- 2 tablespoons shortening or vegetable oil
- 2 onions, coarsely chopped
- salt and pepper
- 1 green pepper, seeded and diced
- 1 very ripe tomato or 2 canned Italian plum tomatoes, drained (reserve juice) and chopped
- 1 cup sour cream
- chopped parsley

Mix paprika and flour in a paper or plastic bag and shake veal cubes until well coated. Brown in heavy skillet or Dutch oven in shortening or oil. Add onions and cook briefly until onions are well mixed with meat. Add salt and pepper to taste; add green pepper and tomato. Let mixture cook over low heat, covered, in its own juices, checking occasionally to make sure there is still liquid in the pan. You may need to add tomato juice or hot water to prevent sticking. Simmer until tender, about 30 to 45 minutes. Before serving, stir in sour cream and check for seasoning. Sprinkle with chopped parsley. Do not boil after cream is added. If you reheat it the next day, bring to just below the boiling point or cream may curdle.

There's No Place Like Homestead

◈ *Homestead men were hearty eaters, and the pork chop recipe which follows will supply your own family with a substantial and nutritious one-dish meal.*

LAYERED PORK CHOPS
4   pork chops, approximately 1 inch thick
1   medium onion, sliced
1   fresh tomato or 2 firm canned plum tomatoes, sliced
1   green pepper, seeded and sliced into rings
½   cup rice
1   cup chicken stock or bouillon
salt and pepper to taste

Brown the chops quickly, in little or no fat, in a large heavy skillet. On each chop place a slice of onion, a slice of tomato, a slice of green pepper. Sprinkle rice around bottom of skillet and add broth. Liquid should come to the top of chops; add water if necessary. Cover tightly; cook over low heat until liquid has been absorbed by rice and chops are tender, about 45 mintues. Check every 15 minutes or so to make certain liquid has not evaporated too quickly. Add more if needed. Check for seasoning before serving. Serves 4.

Festivals for Many Folks

Scarcely a month goes by without some kind of festival appearing on western Pennsylvania's calendar of events. There are Middle Eastern and Greek festivals in Pittsburgh, buckwheat and maple syrup celebrations in dozens of communities, a Pennsylvania Dutch folk festival in Springs. Pittsburgh's Kennywood Park is the scene of Polish and Slovakian days, there are international fairs in McKeesport and Ambridge, and the biggest gathering of them all is the Pittsburgh Folk Festival. At each event, food plays a major role.

There is a tradition of good ethnic cooking in western Pennsylvania. By ethnic, most area residents mean people of Eastern European origin, since first and second generation Slavs far outnumber representatives of other nationality groups in this part of the state.

Unfortunately for the adventurous eater, however, there are few opportunities to sample the delights of Slavic cooking, since restaurants featuring dishes from these countries are rare. One can cultivate the friendship of a good cook and hope to be invited for dinner. The alternative is to move from festival to festival, knowing that the food sampled is the next best thing to home cooking.

Festivals for Many Folks

Since it is now "in" to be ethnic, fairs and festivals have proliferated. Americans, discovering new pride in their ethnic origins, enjoy wearing the traditional costumes, showing off their skills at folk dancing and singing. And nowhere can the discriminating diner find a greater variety of foreign foods than at the Pittsburgh Folk Festival, held annually in June at the huge Civic Arena downtown. For three glorious days it is possible to feast on food as well as culture, pausing only long enough for a brisk walk past the many food booths to make sure nothing has been overlooked.

The Folk Festival is one of the highlights of my year. If the days are clear and warm, there are few things more satisfying to me than spending a long evening at the arena. First, of course, one must walk slowly past all the food booths set up around the outside of the auditorium. Strolling musicians play exotic instruments and sing gay songs. Festival participants and dancers, costumed in kilts and saris and richly embroidered blouses mingle with the visitors and add to the brilliance of the scene.

The booths selling food are busy from the moment the doors open for business, and the smells of barbecuing kielbasa, roasting chicken, stuffed cabbage and *pirohy* can drive one mad with hunger. Decisions are difficult. Like a greedy child, I want to sample everything. First, perhaps, I may have a Scandinavian hors d'oeuvre—a bit of *sillsallad*, herring spiced with apples and beets. Then I may proceed to Latvia, where the *kumpls* attracts me, a huge and succulent pink ham encased in rye dough and baked a golden brown. Since I'm right next door and the line isn't too long, I decide to try Slovakian *haluski*, noodles with sweet cabbage. Looking ahead to possible late night hunger pangs, I also buy a cruller, called *ceregi*, and a generous slice of nut roll, *orehovnik*, to eat later.

Festivals for Many Folks

There are conveniently located stands selling ice cold beer on tap, and I discover I must eat the nut roll in order to balance the beer as I walk. Before it is gone, I buy a grilled sausage from Hungary which comes with a side order of sauerkraut and is called, so the menu says, *kolbasz savanyu kaposzlaval.* I allow myself just one piece of Croatian strudel, made with apples and cheese, before I go inside to enjoy the crafts booths and demonstrations. And more food.

I remember the first year the festival was held at the arena, having moved to larger quarters from Oakland's Syria Mosque where all the food was contained in one large room. I wasn't aware that there were additional food specialties inside the arena, and I happily stuffed myself with the goodies of the group outside. I was chagrined to walk inside and discover the wonderful delicacies from the Philippines, Ireland, India, China, Lithuania, and a host of others, delicacies which, due to my premature greed, had to remain unsampled until the following year. Now that I know better, I pace myself, like a runner in a long distance race, saving just enough room for an English scone, a Polish doughnut, a dish of Italian *gelata.*

The Pittsburgh Folk Festival began in 1956 and has been continuously sponsored by Robert Morris College and directed by Charles Cubelic, with a big assist from Nicholas Jordanoff. More than thirty-five hundred people participate in putting on the festival, considered a model for other events throughout the country. I know people who plan their vacations around the festival dates, as well as their business and social engagements.

The Folk Festival motto, Unity in Diversity, is reenforced by the program's credit list. The Ladies Philoptochos Society of St. Nicholas Orthodox Cathedral, for example, helps to ensure the authenticity of the *spanakopita* (spinach pie) and the performance of the *kritikos,* a Cretan dance. El Club Cultural Español provides the chicken in *escabeche* sauce, the demonstration of mantilla making, the dances from Peru and Venezuela. Egg rolls and fortune cookies, as well as demonstrations of Chinese calligraphy, are supplied by the Tri-State Organization of Chinese-Americans. The Tamburitzans, that incredibly talented group of young musicians and dancers from Duquesne University, are everywhere—cooking, eating, dancing, singing, strolling through the crowds playing tamburitzas and accordions. There are Polish Falcons, Scandinavian Folk Dancers, Gordon Highlanders, the League of Ukrainian Catholics, *I Campagnoli,* the Hindu Temple and Indian Association, the Irish Knights of Equity. They perform the dances of their own cultural tradition, enjoy the dances of their friends, and everybody eats—sitting, standing, walking, running, strolling, staring. It is a study in cross-cultural pleasures, where kilted young Scotsmen devour juicy slices of pizza and a dancer in a heavily embroidered Yugoslavian blouse eats chicken *adobong* from the Philippines with his fingers.

If you are interested in the origins of food, the Folk Festival offers fertile ground for informal study. All the European countries seem to specialize in sausage, firm and spicy. You can spell it *kobase,* knockwurst, *kolbasz, kielbasa, klobase, kolbassi, kowbasa,* or salami. Nut pastries originate in the Ukraine (*rohalky*), Slovakia (*rozki* and *poteca*), Serbia (*crehnjaca*), Lebanon (*baklava*), Germany (*nusskipfel*), Greek (*katalfe*), and Bulgaria (*torte ot orihl*). Meat wrapped in cabbage or grape leaves turns up in Croatia as *sarma,* in Greece as *dolmades,* in Hungary as *toltott kaposzta,* in Lebanon as *mikshee warab-inib,* in Lithuania as *antkiotas parsukas,* in Poland as *golabki,* in Slovakia as *holubki,* and in the Ukraine as *holubsti.* And every country wraps up meat, vegetables or cheese in their own specialty, from the *manicotti* of Italy to the Cornish pasties of England to the enchiladas of Mexico.

Even the most cynical of political observers, thrust into this festive atmosphere, begins to think there may be something to this one-world notion after all. Friendships have been formed and serious quarrels settled over the dinner table. I find it entirely possible to think that future generations of diplomats may discover the only thing on which we can all agree is food.

Festivals for Many Folks

Although almost any kind of food may be found at Pennsylvania festivals, you are certain to discover an abundance of cookies, pastries, and other sweets which can be eaten out of hand as you wander among the various booths. This recipe is a little unusual because it came to me via one of my Polish aunts, yet kolacky is not a traditional Polish sweet—rather it is associated with Hungary or Czechoslovakia. Perhaps my aunt got it from one of her Chicago neighbors. But since her Italian husband enjoyed it, along with the mini-United Nations her friends represented, it is an appropriate recipe for a chapter about ethnicity.

AUNT STELLA'S KOLACKY

- ½ pound butter or margarine
- ½ pound cream cheese
- 2 cups all-purpose flour
- 2 tablespoons sugar
- 2 tablespoons baking powder
- jam or other filling

Cream the butter and cream cheese until light and fluffy. Sift dry ingredients together and add to creamed mixture to make a dough stiff enough to handle. Roll out on a lightly floured board or pastry cloth to ⅛ inch thickness. Cut into rounds with a 2 to 3 inch cookie or biscuit cutter. Make a small impression in the center of each cookie with your thumb. Fill with a scant teaspoon of jam—apricot or raspberry is good—or other filling, such as poppy seeds, nuts, or stewed dry fruit. Place on ungreased cookie sheet; bake at 350° for 15 to 18 minutes or until lightly browned. Remove to rack to cool. Sprinkle with powdered sugar when completely cool. Makes about 4 dozen.

Festivals for Many Folks

꩜ *This coffee cake, with its fluffy nut filling, is similar to many of the nut tortes and rolls you will find at the Pittsburgh Folk Festival. It is probably closest to the Slovakian poteca or patica.*

NUT-FILLED COFFEE CAKE

½ cup dairy sour cream	1 teaspoon sugar
1 tablespoon milk	¼ cup warm water
⅓ cup sugar	3 cups all-purpose flour
½ teaspoon salt	2 egg yolks, well beaten
1 package dry yeast	¼ cup very soft butter or margarine

Combine sour cream, milk, ⅓ cup sugar, and salt in saucepan over low heat. Stir until mixture just barely bubbles. Pour into large bowl and cool to lukewarm. Dissolve yeast and 1 teaspoon sugar in ¼ cup water and stir until well blended. Allow to sit 5 to 10 minutes until bubbly. Combine sour cream and yeast mixtures. Beat in 1½ cups flour until smooth. Cover and place in warm spot 45 minutes. Beat down. Add very soft butter to beaten egg yolks; combine with yeast mixture. Add enough of remaining flour to make soft dough. Turn out on floured board or pastry cloth and knead until smooth and elastic, about 8 minutes. Place in large greased bowl, rolling the dough so all sides are covered with oil. Cover and keep in warm place until doubled in bulk, about 1 hour. Punch down, knead briefly, and let rest while you make filling (see below).

Roll dough into a rectangle, approximately 24 × 12 inches. Spread filling over entire surface; roll up like a jelly roll, starting with the long end. Pinch seam to seal. Place seam side down on well-greased cookie sheet or in angel cake tube pan. Cover and let rise in warm place until almost doubled in bulk, about 45 minutes. Bake at 350° for 35 to 45 minutes or until light brown. Cool in pan

Festivals for Many Folks

about 15 minutes, then remove to wire rack to finish cooling. Loaf may be spread with simple confectioner's sugar icing, or glazed with honey and decorated with nuts and candied fruits or raisins.

FILLING
- 2   cups walnuts, finely chopped or ground
- 2   egg whites
- ⅓   cup sugar
- dash of salt
- 1   teaspoon grated lemon rind

Grind or chop walnuts; beat egg whites until foamy and double in volume. Carefully beat in sugar, one teaspoonful at a time, then salt, until peaks are formed. Fold in lemon rind and nuts.

Notes

Subject Index

Recipe Index

Notes

Collector's Items

1. Mary Plumsted's Cookery Book, dated 1776, is in the collections of the Pennsylvania Historical Society, Philadelphia.
2. Mrs. Sarah Yeates's cookbook is in the library collection of the Pennsylvania Farm Museum of Landis Valley, Lancaster.
3. The cookbook begun in Waterford, New York, dated 1790, is in the collections of the Western Pennsylvania Historical Society, Pittsburgh.

Maple Sugar

1. Helen Nearing and Scott Nearing, *The Maple Sugar Book* (New York: Schocken Books, 1971), p. 4. Quotation from Louis, Baron de la Honton, *Nouveaux voyages dans l'Amérique septentrionale,* 1703.
2. Ibid., p. 61. Quotation from Patrick Campbell, *Travels in the Interior Inhabited Parts of North America,* 1793.
3. Ibid., p. 41. Quotation from Benjamin Rush, *An Account of the Sugar-Maple Tree of the United States,* 1792.
4. Jean Maust Mann, "Sugaring on Negro Mountain," *Casselman Chronicle* (Springs Historical Society of the Casselman Valley), 1 (Spring 1961), 2.

5. Ibid., pp. 3–5.

6. Nearing and Nearing, *The Maple Sugar Book,* p. 120. Quotation from Joseph François Lafiteau, *Moeurs des sauvages ameriquains,* 1724.

7. Ibid., p. 4. Quotation from John Burroughs, *Signs and Seasons,* 1886.

At Home with William Penn

1. Evelyn Abraham Benson, ed., *Penn Family Recipes* (York, Pa.: George Shumway, 1966).

2. Ibid., p. 72.

3. Ibid., p. 65.

4. Ibid., p. 29.

A Pennsylvania Paradox

1. Doris Janzen Longacre, *More-with-Less Cookbook* (Scottsdale, Pa.: Herald Press, 1976).

2. Ibid., p. 22.

The Ladies from Philadelphia

1. Sarah Josepha Hale, *The Ladies' New Book of Cookery: A Practical System for Private Families in Town and Country* (New York: H. Long and Bros., 1852), pp. 450–53. Also titled *The New Cook Book* in some editions on outside cover.

2. Ibid., p. iii.

3. Frank Luther Mott, *A History of American Magazines: 1885–1905* (Cambridge, Mass.: Harvard University Press, 1957), p. 545.

4. Sarah Tyson Rorer, *Mrs. Rorer's New Cook Book* (Philadelphia: Arnold and Co., 1902), p. 3.

5. Ibid., p. 12.

6. Emma Seifrit Weigley, *Sarah Tyson Rorer* (Philadelphia: American Philosophical Society, 1977), pp. 131–32.

7. Ibid., p. 92.

8. Eliza Leslie, *Directions for Cookery in Its Various Branches* (Philadelphia: Carey and Hart, 1848), p. 375.

9. Ibid., p. 334.

10. Ibid., p. 210.

11. Eliza Leslie, *Miss Leslie's New Cook Book* (Philadelphia: T. B. Peterson and Bros., 1873), p. 413.

12. Sarah Josepha Hale, *Woman's Record or Sketches of All Distinguished Women from the Creation to A.D. 1868* (New York: Harper and Bros., 1870), p. 722.

13. Rorer, *New Cook Book,* pp. 497–98.

14. Hale, *The Ladies' New Book of Cookery,* pp. 299–300.

Magic Mushrooms

1. Waverly Root, *The Food of France* (New York: Alfred A. Knopf, 1958), p. 70.

2. Elizabeth Pennell, quoted in "The Well-Bred Mushroom," *Gourmet,* 26 (February, 1966), 64.

Life in a Bologna Factory

1. Marion Cabell Tyree, *Housekeeping in Old Virginia* (Louisville, Ky.: John P. Norton and Co., 1879), p. 152.

2. Richard Gehman, *The Sausage Book* (New York: Weathervane Books, 1969), p. 33.

Springs Comes in the Fall

1. Alta E. Schrock, "The Schrocks of Strawberry Hill," *Casselman Chronicle,* 17 (1977), 3–4.

2. Rhoda Miller Maust, "My Memories of the Children's Home," *Casselman Chronicle,* 17 (1977), 1–2.

Notes to Pages 101–38

Trains

1. *American Heritage Cookbook and Illustrated History of American Eating and Drinking* (New York: Simon and Schuster, 1964), pp. 329–30.
2. J. C. Furnas, *The Americans: A Social History of the United States, 1587–1914* (New York: G. P. Putnam's Sons, 1969), p. 353. Quotation from Edward P. Alexander, *The Pennsylvania Railroad: A Pictorial History*.
3. Ibid. Quotation from Theodore Dreiser, *A Book About Myself*.

As We Sow

1. David B. Burpee, "Looking Back—100 Years," *Burpee Seeds* (catalogue) (Warminster, Pa.: W. Atlee Burpee Co., 1975), p. A-5.

Apples of My Eye

1. Stevenson Whitcomb Fletcher, *Pennsylvania Agriculture and Country Life,* Vol. I (Harrisburg, Pa.: Pennsylvania Historical and Museum Commission, 1950), 207.
2. Ibid., p. 208.
3. Ibid., p. 210.

Grapes of Diverse Sorts

1. Stevenson Whitcomb Fletcher, *Pennsylvania Agriculture and Country Life,* Vol. I (Harrisburg, Pa.: Pennsylvania Historical and Museum Commission, 1950), 225.
2. Ibid., pp. 222–23.

A Pretty Pickle

1. Robert Albert, *The Good Provider* (Boston: Houghton Mifflin, 1973).

Early American Travelers

1. George Swetnam, *Pennsylvania Transportation,* Pennsylvania History Studies, No. 7 (Gettysburg, Pa.: Pennsylvania Historical Society, 1964), p. 11.

2. Frances Trollope, *Domestic Manners of the Americans* (Barre, Mass.: Imprint Society, 1969), pp. 151–52.

3. Swetnam, *Pennsylvania Transportation,* p. 19.

4. Ibid., p. 46.

5. Una Pope-Hennessy, ed., *The Aristocratic Journey* (New York: G. P. Putnam's Sons, 1931), p. 49.

Cloistered in Ephrata

1. Israel Acrelius, *A History of New Sweden, or the Settlements on the Delaware River* (1753), pp. 58–59.

2. Ibid., p. 59.

3. Julius Friedrich Sachse, *A Critical and Legendary History of the Ephrata Cloister and the Dunkers* (Philadelphia: n.p., 1800), pp. 152–54.

Toiling in the Nutrition Wasteland

1. Letitia Brewster and Michael F. Jacobson, *The Changing American Diet* (Washington, D.C.: Center for Science in the Public Interest, 1978), pp. 3–5.

2. Tracy Westen, "Food Technology and Nutrition Ignorance: Is There a Connection?" Speech before the Community Nutrition Institute, Washington, D.C., June 1, 1978.

American Cuisine

1. James W. Parkinson, *American Dishes at the Centennial* (Philadelphia: King and Baird, 1874).

The Food Is Simply Wild

1. Euell Gibbons, *Stalking the Healthful Herbs* (New York: David McKay, 1966), and *Stalking the Wild Asparagus* (New York: David McKay, 1962).

A Story with a Twist

1. Andre L. Simon and Robin Howe, *Dictionary of Gastronomy* (New York: McGraw-Hill, 1970), pp. 310–13.
2. C. R. Tshudy and Barbara Ann Tshudy, *The Pretzl Story* (Lititz: Sturgis Pretzl Co., n.d.), p. 5.
3. Simon and Howe, *Dictionary of Gastronomy*, pp. 310–13.
4. Tshudy and Tshudy, *The Pretzl Story*, p. 15.

Here Let Us Feast

1. *American Heritage Cookbook and Illustrated History of American Eating and Drinking* (New York: Simon and Schuster, 1964), pp. 346, 360.
2. James W. Parkinson, *American Dishes at the Centennial* (Philadelphia: King and Baird, 1874).
3. Ibid.
4. *American Heritage Cookbook*, p. 361.

The Cup That Cheers

1. Stevenson Whitcomb Fletcher, *Pennsylvania Agriculture and Country Life,* Vol. I (Harrisburg, Pa.: Pennsylvania Historical and Museum Commission, 1950), 211.
2. Ibid., p. 411.
3. Ibid., p. 410.
4. *Inns and Ale Houses of Old Philadelphia* (Philadelphia: Robert Smith Ale Brewing Co., 1909).

5. Fletcher, *Pennsylvania Agriculture and Country Life,* pp. 212, 411–12.

6. Ibid., pp. 120–21.

7. Solon J. Buck and Elizabeth Hawthorn Buck, *The Planting of Civilization in Western Pennsylvania* (Pittsburgh: University of Pittsburgh Press, 1939), pp. 466–67.

8. Ibid.

9. Fletcher, *Pennsylvania Agriculture and Country Life,* p. 213.

10. Ibid., p. 451.

11. Ibid., p. 452.

12. Brewers' Industrial Exhibition, *Essays on the Malt Liquor* (New York: Francis Hart and Co., 1876).

An Herbal Tea Party

1. Marcus Woodward, ed., *Leaves from Gerard's Herbal* (New York: Dover Publications, Inc., 1968), p. 261.

2. Ibid., p. 163.

3. Ibid., p. 233.

4. Marian Harland, *Common Sense in the Household* (New York: Scribner, Armstrong and Co., 1875), p. 521.

5. Woodward, *Leaves from Gerard's Herbal,* p. 135.

Glorious Gadgets

1. *Godey's Lady's Book,* 70 (June 1865), 554.

2. *Ladies' Home Journal,* 17 (October 1900), 46.

3. Ibid., p. 47.

Kitchens: Restored and Reconstructed

1. Christine C. Ritter, "Father Rapp and the Harmony Society," *Early American Life,* April 1978, p. 43.

2. Daniel B. Reibel, *A Guide to Old Economy* (Harrisburg, Pa.: Pennsylvania Historical and Museum Commission, 1972), pp. 12–13.

3. Una Pope-Hennessy, ed., *The Aristocratic Journey* (New York: G. P. Putnam's Sons, 1931), p. 288.

4. Mrs. Sarah Yeates's manuscript cookbook is in the collection of the Pennsylvania Farm Museum of Landis Valley, Lancaster. It is described on pages 17–18 above.

There's No Place Like Homestead

1. Margaret Byington, *Homestead: The Households of a Mill Town* (1910; rpt. Pittsburgh: University Center for International Studies, 1974), p. vii.

2. Ibid., pp. 40–45; see also chap. 5, pp. 63–80 and chap. 10, pp. 138–44.

3. Ibid., p. 75.

4. Ibid., p. 65.

Subject Index

Acrelius, Israel, 164–65
Akron, Pa., 199
Alberts, Robert, 138
Allegheny Portage Railroad, 149
Ambridge, Pa., 242
American cooking, 183–88
Anderson Bakery, 199–200
Apples, 115–20; dried, 116; history of, 115–18; varieties of, 116–17, 118
Appleseed, Johnny, 117
Armstrong County, Pa., 77
Arthur, T. S., 218

Bachman's pretzels, 199
Bake ovens, 33, 133, 234, 236, 244–45
Baloney, 85
Banquets, 203–11
Bashaar, Charles, 246
Baum's bologna, 87–88
Beachey's Cider Mill, 93
Beaverton, Pa., 194
Beer, 213; spruce, 96
Beissel, Johann Conrad, 162, 166–67

Berry-picking, 189–93
Biography of Distinguished Women, 71
Bird-in-hand, Pa., 7
Bishops Mill Historical Institute, 247
Bloomfield-Lawrenceville, 177
Blueberries, 190–93
Boggs, Mrs., manuscript cookbook of, 13–15
Bologna, 85–90
Box Huckleberry Natural Area, 190
Brewers Industrial Exhibition (1876 Centennial Exposition), 218–19
Brininger, Mrs., 134
Buccher, Frederick, 58
Bucks County, Pa., 115
Bully Hill Winery, 124
Burpee, David, 108–10
Burpee, Jonathan, 108, 110
Burpee, W. Atlee, 108–09; company, 107–12; experimental farms, 107–08
Burroughs, John, 26
Butler County, Pa., 77, 81, 242
Butter making, 235–36
Byington, Margaret, 253

279

Subject Index

Canals, Pennsylvania, 149–50
Cantor, Jerry, 110–12
Carnegie, Andrew, 204
Carnegie Library banquet, 205
Casselman Chronicle, 95
Casselman Hotel, 148
Catalogues, seed, 107, 109
Catnip, 229
Centennial Exposition of 1876, 218
Center County, Pa., 180
Center for Science in the Public Interest, 170–71
Century Inn, 148–49
Chapman, John (Johnny Appleseed), 117
Chester Country, Pa., 79
Chocolate, 39–46
Chocolate World, 41–43
Churns, butter, 235
Cider, 116, 120, 212–13
City Tavern, Philadelphia, 213
Cobbett, William, 217
Colonial Pennsylvania Plantation, 247–49
Coltsfoot, 231
Common Sense in the Household, 230
Community College of Allegheny County, 141–42
Cookbooks, 12–18; *Directions for Cookery,* 69–70; *Domestic French Cookery,* 68; *Housekeeping in Old Virginia,* 85–86; *Ladies' New Book of Cookery,* 63–65; in manuscripts, 12–19, 250; *Miss Leslie's New Cook Book,* 71; *More-With-Less Cookbook,* 57; *Mrs. Hale's New Cook Book,* 62–63, 75; *New Cook Book,* 65–66, 73; *Penn Family Recipes,* 30–31, 34, 35–38; *Sausage Book, The,* 86–87; *Seventy-five Receipts for Pastry, Cakes and Sweetmeats,* 68
Cubelic, Charles, 263
Culinary Institute of America, 51, 141

Darby Association for Discouraging the Unnecessary Use of Spiritous Liquors, 217
Delaware County, Pa., 217
Dickens, Charles, 149–50
Dictionary of Gastronomy, 198
Dining cars, 100–02
Directions for Cookery, 69–70
DiShetler, John, 141
Distilleries, 213–17
Dollhouses, 221–25
Domestic French Cookery, 68
Dore, Andrew, 122
Doylestown, Pa., 108
Dreiser, Theodore, 102

Eichelberger, Thomas, 122
Elizabethtown, Pa., 87–88
Endicott, John (governor), 115
Ephrata Cloister, 162–69
Erie County, Pa., 121–26
Expanded Nutrition Education Program, 175–77
Exposition, 1876 Centennial, 218

Fairs: Ambridge, 261; Greek, 157–58; Kutztown, 129–34; McKeesport, 261; Middle Eastern, 155–57; Pittsburgh, 261–68; Springs, 91–97

Subject Index

Festivals: Kutztown Folk Festival, 129–34; Maple Syrup Festival, 23, 25–26; Pittsburgh Folk Festival, 261–68; Polish, 261; Slovak, 261; Springs Folk Festival, 91–98; wine, 125
Fireplace cooking, 234, 236, 244
Folk, Lura, 92–98
Food distributors' exhibit, 172–73
Fordhook Farm, 107, 109
Fracatelli, Charles, 204
Franklin, Benjamin, 117, 118

Gann, Margery, 178
Gehmann, Richard, 86
Gibbons, Euell, 194, 229
Godey's Lady's Book, 62–64, 68, 237
Goodfellow, Elizabeth, 68
Good Provider, The, 138
Grand Concourse, 99–100
Grantsville, Md., 8, 24, 93, 148
Grapes, wine, 121–26
Groff, Abe, 52
Groff, Betty, 51–53
Groff's Farm, 50–53
Groff's Meat Market, 88

Haag's Hotel, 49–50
Hale, Sarah Josepha, 63–65, 71–72, 237
Hall, Mrs. Basil, 150, 246–47
Hanover, Pa., 199
Harder, Jules, 207
Harmonist Society, 243–47
Harmony, Ind., 242
Harrison, James, 29

Harvey, Fred, 101
Heinz, Henry J., 137–39
Heinz Company, H. J., 137–42
Henrici, Jacob, 247
Herbal, Gerard's, 229–31
Herbs, 228–32
Hershey, Milton, 40, 41
Hershey, Pa., 40
Hershey bar, 40, 41, 43
Hershey Hotel, 40, 41
Homestead, Pa., 253–58
Housekeeping in Old Virginia, 85–86
Huckleberries, 190

Ilyas, Roujina, 155

Janvier, Jane, manuscript cookbook of, 251–52
Jordan, Philip, 148
Jordanoff, Nicholas, 263

Kekua, Lake, 123
Kennett Square, Pa., 79
Kieffer, Marie, 174–75
Kitchens, 233–38, 241–49
Kitchen utensils, 234–36
Klingenberg, Helen, 178
Kresge, Dorothy, 132
Kutztown Folk Festival, 129–34
Kuzma, Margaret, 245–58

Ladies' Home Journal, 67, 237–38
Ladies' New Book of Cookery, 63–65
Lancaster, Pa., 4–7, 47, 49, 50, 200, 241

281

Subject Index

Lancaster County, Pa., 121–22
Landis, George and Henry, 241
Landis Valley, Pa., 241
Lawrenceville, Pa., 177
Lebanon, Pa., 85
Lebanon bologna, 85–90
Leeks, wild, 193–94, 196
Legaux, Peter, 122
Leslie, Eliza, 68–72
Lighton, Shirley, 248–49
Limited Winery Act, 125
Liquor, 212–20
Lititz, Pa., 198
Longacre, Doris, 57–58
Losh Run, Pa., 190
Love feasts: Ephrata Cloister, 165–66; Old Economy, 245
Lutheran Service Society of Western Pennsylvania, 177

Malovich, Mary, 178–79
Mann, Jean Maust, 24
Manuscript cookbooks, 12–19, 250
Maple sugar, 21–28; festival, 23, 25–26
Markets, 3–9
Martin's pretzels, 199
Maust, Cora, 24
Maust, Rhoda Miller, 95
Mazza Vineyards, 124, 125
Meals on Wheels, 177–80
Mennonite Central Committee, 56, 57; relief sale, 56
Merritt, Mary Lesher, 221
Merritt Doll Museum, 221–25

Metz, Ferdinand, 139–42
Meyersdale, Pa., 21; festival, 23, 25–26
Michter's distillery, 216–17
Middle Eastern food, 153–61
Miller, Joel B., 24
Milton Hershey School, 40, 41
Mint, 230
Miss Leslie's New Cook Book, 68, 71
Moonlight Mushroom Farm, 77–82
More-With-Less Cookbook, 57
Moses, Elaine, 156
Mount Joy, Pa., 50
Mount Washington Tavern, 148
Mrs. Hale's New Cook Book, 64
Mrs. Rorer's Philadelphia Cook Book, 67
Muer, Chuck, 100
Museum of the City of New York, 221
Mushrooms, 77–84

Nalbandian, Mrs., 154–55
National pike, 146–49
National Road, The, 148
New Bloomfield, Pa., 190
New Cook Book, 65, 66, 67, 73
New Wilmington, Pa., 8
Nutrition, 56–61, 170–82

Oakland, Pa., 54, 155, 157
Old Economy, 242–47
Olive, Justine, 176–77

Parkinson, James W., 183–85, 205
Penn, Gulielma, 30, 31, 33, 34, 35, 36
Penn, Hannah, 31, 32

Subject Index

Penn, Thomas, 32
Penn, William, 29–34, 115, 122, 213, 242
Penn, William, Jr., 30, 31
Penn Alps, 95
Pennell, Elizabeth, 81–82
Penn Family Recipes, 30–31, 34, 35–38
Pennsbury, 29–34
Penn Shore Winery, 123, 125–26
Pennsylvania Dutch: doll house furnishings, 222–23; food, 4–9, 47–57, 59, 85–89, 91–98, 130–36; herbs, 229; pretzels, 198
Pennsylvania Farm Museum, 241–42
Pennsylvania Liquor Control Board, 125
Pennsylvania Main Line Canal, 149
Pennsylvania State University, 121; cooperative extension service, 173–77
Pequea Valley Winery, 121–24
Perry Company, 190
Peter, Daniel, 40
Philadelphia, 62–72, 176; City Tavern, 213; 1876 Centennial Exposition, 218; Penny Pot Tavern, 213; Thousand Dollar Dinner, 206–07
Philadelphia and Lancaster Turnpike, 146
Philadelphia Ledger, 183–85
Pickles, 137–42
Pittsburgh and Lake Erie Railroad, 99
Pittsburgh Chamber of Commerce banquet, 204
Pittsburgh Gazette, 237
Pittsburgh History and Landmarks Foundation, 99
Plumstead, Mary, manuscript cookbook of, 16–17
Presque Isle Wine Cellars, 124

Pretzels, 197–202
Processed foods, 171–73
Proud, Robert, 212

Railroad museum, 102
Ramps, 193–94, 196
Rapp, Father George, 242
Reading, Pa., 199, 221
Reclay, Mary, 133
Reibel, Daniel, 245
Reibel, Pat, 243–44
Ridley Creek Park, 247–49
Robert Morris College, 263
Root, Waverly, 78
Rorer, Sarah Tyson, 65–78
Rosemary, 231

Saffron, 48–49
Sage, 229–30
Saint Francis Church, 177
Saint George's Orthodox Church, 155–57
Saint Nicholas Orthodox Church, 157–58
Sandwich (Mass.) Glass Museum, 221
Sausage Book, The, 86, 87
Sceiford, George, 125–26
Scenery Hill, Pa., 148–49
Schnitzen, 116
Schoepf, Johann David, 146
Schpruce beer, 96
Schrock, Dr. Alta, 92–97
Sechler, Daisy, 134
Seeds, vegetable, 107–12
Seely, Sallie, manuscript cookbook of, 15–16
Seltzer's sausage, 86

283

Subject Index

Seventy-five Receipts for Pastry, Cakes and Sweetmeats, 68
Shartlesville, Pa., 49
Shenk, John, 216
Sky Brothers, Inc., 172
Slovak cooking, 253–58, 261
Smith, Captain John, 212
Smith, Robert, 213
Snitzel Creek, 216–17
Somerset, Pa., 8
Somerset County, Pa., 26, 174
Spoza, 25
Springs, Pa., 8, 24, 91–98; folk festival, 91–98; historical society, 92, 95; museum, 92–93
Spruce beer, 96
Stagecoaches, 146, 147, 149
Stanton, Josie, 193
Steven, Fitzgerald, 213
Stoves, 236–38
Strasburg, Pa., 102; railroad, 102–03
Sturgis, Julius, 197
Sturgis Pretzel Bakery, 199, 200

Taft, William Howard, 205
Taylor, Walter, 124
Taylor Wine Company, 123
Tea, herbal, 228–32
Temperance movement, 217–18
Thousand Dollar Dinner, the, 183, 207
Thyme, 231
Tours: Chocolate World, 41–43; Ephrata Cloister, 162–67; Merritt Doll Museum, 221–25; Michter's distillery, 216–17; Old Economy, 242–47; Pennsbury, 29–34; pretzel factories, 197–201; wineries, 121–26
Townsend, Richard, 115–16
Trains, 99–106
Travel: by canal boat, 148–50; early American, 145–50; by stagecoach, 145–49; by train, 99–106
Trollope, Mrs. Frances, 147–48
Tuscarora State Forest, 190

Valentine, R. B., 205–06
Vegetable gardening, 107–12

Waible, Jane, 134
Warminster, Pa., 107
Waterford, N.Y., manuscript cookbook from, 18
Weaver's bologna, 86
Wege Pretzel Company, 199
Weigley, Emma S., 67
Whiskey, 213–20; rebellion, 214–15
Wild food, 189–96
Wood, Alice, 121–22
Wood, Peter, 121
Worthington, Pa., 77

Yeates, Mrs. Sarah, manuscript cookbook of, 17–18, 250
Yoder brothers, 81
Yoder's Country Store and Meat Packing Plant, 8–9, 93
York, Pa., 7, 122

Zerbe, Ellen, 133
Zimmerman's store, 8
Zinsser, Helen, 178–79

Recipe Index

Apple: charlotte, 75; charlotte, modern, 75; pancakes, 120; tart, 119
Apples, maple baked, 27
Aunt Stella's kolacky, 266

Batter bread, cheese, 210
Best biscuit mix, 152
Biscuit mix, best, 152
Blueberry freezer jam, 195
Bourbon balls, 280
Bran bread, 182
Bread: biscuit mix, 152; bran, 182; cheese batter, 210; cranberry nut, 186–87; Gulielma's loaf, 36; mother's, 239; Mrs. Rorer's corn meal loaf, 73; nut-filled coffee cake, 267–68; Pennsylvania pita, 160–61; pumpernickel, 168; soft pretzels, 202; too make a buttered lofe, 35; updated corn meal loaf, 74
Brownies, 46
Buckwheat pancakes, 151
Buttered lofe, too make a, 35

Cake: diet bread cake, 250–51; nut-filled coffee cake, 267–68; pound, 227; Schwenkfelder, with topping, 135

Cheese batter bread, 210
Chicken: and dumplings, Gulielma's, 38; too make a fregasy of, 37; with white wine, 128
Chocolate: brownies, 46; pie, 44
Chowchow, 54
Charlotte, apple, 75
Chowder, fish, 105
Cider sauce, 120
Cocoanut jumbles, 20
Coconut jumbles, 20
Cookies: Aunt Stella's kolacky, 266; bourbon balls, 220; cocoanut jumbles, 20; coconut jumbles, 20; filbert shortbread, 226; gingersnaps, 98; healthy cookies, 61; Jane Janvier's Scotch cakes, 252; Scotch freezer cookies, 252
Corn meal loaf, Mrs. Rorer's, 73
Corn meal loaf, updated, 74
Cracker pudding, 136
Cranberry nut bread, 186–87

Desserts: apple charlotte, 75; cracker pudding, 136; double chocolate pie, 44; elegant apple tart, 117; fruit cup with champagne, 211; Indian hasty pudding, 71; maple baked apples,

Recipe Index

27; maple sugar flan, 28; my soft gingerbread, 240; peaches in orange juice, 10; rice pudding, 19; sherry rice pudding, 19
Diet bread cake: à la Bartlett, 251; to make, 250
Dilled green tomatoes, 143
Double chocolate pie, 44
Dutch fries, 98

Elegant apple tart, 119

Filbert shortbread, 226
Fish: seafood scallop, 106; chowder, 105
Fish chowder, 105
Flan, maple sugar, 28
Frittata, zucchini mushroom, 84
Fruit cup with champagne, 211

Gingerbread, my soft, 240
Gingersnaps, 98
Granola, 181
Gulielma's chicken and dumplings, 38
Gulielma's loaf, 36

Hearty veal stew, 259
Healthy cookies, 61
Herbal tea, 232

Indian hasty pudding, 71

Jam, blueberry freezer, 195
Jane Janvier's Scotch cakes, 252
Jumbles, cocoanut, 20
Jumbles, coconut, 20

Kolacky, Aunt Stella's, 266

Layered pork chops, 260
Leftovers, soup from, 60

Maple baked apples, 27
Maple sugar flan, 28
Meat and poultry: chicken with white wine, 128; Gulielma's chicken with dumplings, 37; hearty veal stew, 259; sherried pork, 127; stuffed roast pork, 38; too make a fregasy of chicken, 37
Modern apple charlotte, 75
Mother's bread, 239
Mrs. Rorer's corn meal loaf, 73
Mushrooms and pasta, 83
Mushroom zucchini frittata, 84
Mustard, my, 90
My soft gingerbread, 240

Nut-filled coffee cake, 267–68

Orange juice, peaches in, 10
Oyster-stuffed cocktail tomatoes, 208

Pancakes: apple, 120; buckwheat, 151; pumpkin, 188; rye, 169
Pasta, with mushrooms, 83
Peaches in orange juice, 10
Peas, Polish, 11
Pennsylvania pita, 160–61
Pesto, 113
Pickles: chow chow, 54; dilled green tomatoes, 143; red pepper relish, 144

Recipe Index

Pie, double chocolate, 44
Pilaf, 159
Pita, Pennsylvania, 160
Polish peas, 11
Pork: chops, layered, 260; sherried, 127; stuffed roast, 210
Pound cake, 227
Pudding: cracker, 136; Indian hasty, 71; rice, 19; sherry rice, 19
Potato filling, 55
Potatoes: Dutch fries, 98; filling, 55
Pretzels, soft, 202
Pumpernickel bread, 168
Pumpkin pancakes, 188

Ramp soup, 196
Red pepper relish, 144
Relish, red pepper, 144
Rice pudding, 19
Rye pancakes, 169

Sauces: whiskey, 220; cider, 120
Schwenkfelder cake, 135
Scotch freezer cookies, 252
Seafood scallop, 106
Sherried pork, 127
Sherry rice pudding, 19
Shortbread, filbert, 226
Soft pretzels, 202

Soup: cream of walnut, 209; fish chowder, 105; from leftovers, 60; ramp, 196
Squash, summer, casserole, 114
Stew, hearty veal, 259
Stuffed roast pork, 210
Summer squash casserole, 114

Tart, elegant apple, 119
Tea, herbal, 232
To make diet bread cake, 250
Tomatoes: oyster-stuffed cocktail, 208; dilled green, 143
Too make a buttered lofe, 35
Too make a fregasy of chicken, 37

Updated corn meal loaf, 74

Veal stew, 259
Vegetables: Dutch fries, 98; mushrooms and pasta, 83; mushroom zucchini frittata, 84; oyster-stuffed cocktail tomatoes, 208; Polish peas, 11; potato filling, 55; summer squash casserole, 114

Whiskey sauce, 220
Wine, chicken with, 128
World's best brownies, 46

Zucchini, mushroom frittata, 84